Crooked sixpences among the chalk

Seventy-five years of schooling

by

Hilda Pickles

Leading Edge™
press and publishing

**Dedicated with affection to teachers and pupils with whom I worked
on Tyneside so long ago and in Cumbria since then**

Published by Leading Edge Press & Publishing Ltd, The Old Chapel,
Burtersett, Hawes, North Yorkshire, DL8 3PB. ☎ (0969) 667566

**A CIP Catalogue record for this book is available from the British
Library.**

ISBN 0 948135 49 2

The names of some of the characters and schools in this book have been changed to protect the identity of
individuals.

Edited by Barbara Allen
Line drawings pages 20, 146, 174 by Anne Robinson. All others by
Ruth Abbott
Design and type by Leading Edge Press & Publishing Ltd
Printed and bound in Great Britain by Bath Press, Avon

*Cover features the 1940s schoolroom at Dewsbury Museum, courtesy of
Kirklees Cultural Services.*
Cover design by Ruth Abbott; photography by Nick Bagguley.

CONTENTS

There was a croooked man
Who walked a crooked mile
And found a crooked sixpence
Beside a crooked stile...

INTRODUCTION

Hammer it in

My father was organist and choirmaster of a large parish church in Newcastle, my mother a pianist. Times were hard on Tyneside all through the 1920s, so she continued to give private lessons at home throughout our childhood. Her pupils were carefully taught and some did well, though none were brilliant.

One day when I was five-ish, a large unknown lady appeared at the door, a young girl beside her.

'This is Evelyn Mounsey,' she said, pointing to her. 'She is nine, and her father wants her to learn the piano. Will you teach her?'

They came in and talked with Mother, while I continued to hover near, liking the look of Evelyn, hoping she would stay. But to my disappointment, I heard 'Evelyn is hardly ready for piano lessons yet.....'

Before Mother could go further, the strange lady, red in the face, burst in aghast.

'I went all that way to Shields Road for that piano and it cost a lot — a whole year's savings — it has a lovely polish. Her father will go mad if she doesn't get to play it now. Can't you just hammer it in?'

The scene is vivid to me still, perhaps because the outrage in Mrs Mounsey's voice frightened me. Those threatening words — 'hammer it in' — which I had never heard until then, are in fact a familiar Tyneside saying but I thought it was a threat. To my surprise, however, Mother was chatting happily on — she wanted Evelyn to come to our house, perhaps for six months, just for pleasure, to the little music club which she held on Fridays after school. I called it 'musical Brownies', it was such fun. After listening, we joined in the tunes Mother played, with combs, recorders, castanets and drums. We sang rounds, two or three to a part, and gave each other ear tests. As Evelyn had had no enjoyment in music, either in school or home, Mother hoped this would appeal to her, and give the necessary stimulus to begin 'lessons'.

So the issue was happily resolved. 'Hammer it in' became a family joke. But when, later, I found that Shakespeare himself had used the phrase, figuratively, ('to put into shape with much intellectual effort'), it struck me that almost everything I knew had been hammered in by parents, teachers, friends or — because a radio had crept into our home in adolescent years — by the BBC. Needless to say, no stick was used, but when a tap drips continuously over a dozen years, an impression is made, even in a stone. We all read greatly in the Twenties and early Thirties, but still a large part of formal education was taken in through the ears. Today this is less so. Most people are viewers now. Talk and 'musak' are available continuously, so, even among children, only a small minority ever truly listen.

In our home we were actually taught to listen. In hard times, in those years of depression and unemployment, music immeasurably enriched our lives. I want to leave a little record for my grandchildren so that they may glimpse something of the flavour of life in an age already half-forgotten, when we lived and loved without benefit of television — and counted ourselves rich.

The following pages describe a journey — a journey of seventy-five years. No deserts have been crossed, nor frozen miles of Arctic or Antarctic waste. One or two outstanding personalities have been met, but in the main it is a record of ordinary, long-suffering men and women, showing a normal complement of virtue and vice.

I have always been impressed by the wealth of heroic history available to us all to read and brood upon: Cabot, Columbus, Hakluyt, Hawkins and many, many others, continuing to the great heroic travellers of our own time. What puzzles me is why no one — so far as I know — has seen fit to record the whole great, and continuous, adventure of the changes in British education throughout the past three-quarters of a century.

From 1926, the year of publication of Sir William Hadow's most famous report, *The Education of the Adolescent*, great changes for the good were envisaged for our Public System of Education. Of course, 'economic stringency' delayed their implementation in many areas for ten, or more, years. They were only trickling down to Newcastle when I started teaching.

Nevertheless, from then until the early Seventies, I was aware of spectacular changes, many of them for the better.

Of the past twelve years I find it hard to speak temperately, since teachers have been whirled about by a succession of new circus directors from Whitehall, who required them to box the compass, often while simultaneously standing on their heads.

So this is not the 'Extraordinary History of Education, 1918-1993' which lucky survivors may ultimately live to see from some magisterial, objective hand. Perhaps a seeker for a 'further degree' is already busy with that 'official record' writing quietly in a newly-upgraded 'university' library? This is simply an attempt to show how pupils and teachers tried to make the best of their (mainly) war-time life together in schools of great variety, from Newcastle to Workington, from Tynemouth to Carlisle.

From 1948 onwards, no longer on Tyneside, but in Cumbria, I was connected with education in some capacity until 1991. Regrettably I have done little on the practical side; only part-time cook or stop-gap nurse, often at camps for schoolchildren or Guides.

Bred to the chalk, there I have stood by my corner, though chalk has been dusty and disheartening beyond normal in recent times of upheaval and recrimination. Nonetheless, what a heap of unguarded treasure has lain there to be picked up from the scarred fields over seventy-five years.

I have loved schools all my life, and have written these little stories as encouragement to those who feel new and nervous as teachers — though spies tell me no one now is as green and silly as I was.

Hilda Pickles
Armathwaite
Cumbria
1993

CHAPTER ONE

Listening

The Tyne and parish: families and schools

The only sounds I heard in childhood came from voices of people, musical instruments, or animals, or from mechanical objects in houses, factories, streets, mills or shipyards. I did not live in any house with a TV set till I was over fifty. I mention this only lest some young scholar of the Nineties assumes that the Dark Ages lasted until seventy years ago. Listening was a major part of living, and thought of as an art. We were brought up 'by, with and from' it, and tried always to improve. Nowhere that I taught ever had a TV set, but how we delighted in the BBC's schools' radio broadcasts, rejoicing also in their *Pupils' History Pamphlets*, so rich in contemporary pictures that we could never have obtained locally.

It is the province of knowledge to speak and it is the privilege of wisdom to listen

was a framed text hanging in my auntie's bedroom, so I begin this tale by trying to give some idea of listening in those far-off days before TV...

The River Tyne ran through our childhood like a skein of beauty, vigour and romance. The Tyne rises near the summit of Peel Fell, in that stretch of the Cheviots known as The Middle Marches — a land of moss-hags and bent-grass, the Battable* land of the old days of Border warfare

---

* The sparse population of the lawless Middle Marches on the English-Scottish border lived by raiding — hence the 'Battable' land.

where high fells are drained by a hundred streams, of which Tarset, Tarret and Kielder are three of the more famous in Northumbrian history.

When I first walked there with others of our family we heard only the far cry of sheep and larks in the clear air, but 500 years ago this corner of the Border had a war-cry of its own

Tarret and Tarset head
Hard and heather bred
Yet-Yet-Yet

'All your ancestors came from these parts,' said my mother, as we walked among the tomb stones in Bellingham churchyard.

From Bellingham, where, the parish history says, 'even honest men did a little shifting (stealing) for their living', the Tyne flows on to join the South Tyne at Hexham. For ten miles beyond that, the river banks are green and wooded, but thereafter, in my childhood, the water turned muddy, and brick and rope yards appeared with engineering and armament works and marshalling yards.

Over the years, with one or other of my family, I walked almost every step of the Tyne, from Hartshorn Pike in the Cheviots, to Armstrong Whitworth's works at Scotswood. We belonged to both town and country, for we had been brought up to the sounds of the river, and its folk songs — *Bonnie Fisher Lad*, *Sair Fyeld Hinnie*, *The Hexhamshire Lass* and many others.

We lived with cat, dog, music and a variety of musical instruments, in Heaton, an east end suburb of Newcastle which stretched southwards, beyond our church through a maze of dispirited terraces to Shields Road, Byker and the shipyards of the Tyne. Yet within easy walking distance of our home were fields, country lanes and a beech avenue.

Sometimes, on a Saturday, my mother would take my brothers and me to the Quayside in the centre of Newcastle where, 'doon the lang stairs' were ships' chandlers, stevedores, soap works, and across the water a vast palace called Baltic Flour Mills. We heard the hooting of ships' sirens before the Swing Bridge; the jingle of harness as dray horses waited, pawing, for their loads; cheery Tyneside jokes and laughter.

From journeys to the Quayside we went home by jangling tramcar over the bridge across the Ouseburn tip. In backyards far below the bridge were barefoot children skipping, or playing with box carts. Among the cinder waste, surrounded by tumbling pigeon crees with rotting roofs, boys played football and thin whippets yapped. Cullercoats fish-wives called in the steep back lanes 'Caller-Herrin! Caller-Herrin!'

There is a poem* by Tony Connor which vividly evokes the games played in this kind of decaying limbo

Routes of my childhood fixed the shape

---

* *The Poet's District* OUP

**of thought; I cannot now escape
shadowy entries, streets that wind,
alleys that are often blind.**

There were early evenings of total contrast to these river outings: each child in turn would be taken by Father to organ practice. I remember the excitement of being allowed to play, legs dangling from the high and slippery organ stool, and hearing the tiny click of the keys beneath nervous fingers, while the tune itself echoed back from the distant forest of silver pipes.

My two brothers were in the choir, so on Sundays I would crane my neck to see father come through the vestry door which, for the past five minutes, had been half open. The Voluntary began, the door was flung wide, and choirboys and men marched in — my brothers among them — strangely virtuous and aloof. Like Chaucer's pilgrims 'Then passed they forth Boystly goggling with their heads...'

Life itself was a pilgrimage to my parents. They lived, no matter what their economic troubles, with a welcome to the unexpected, always busy, but at the same time quiet; their lives turned, I think, on a spindle of inner certainty.

In the dining room the electric light shone full upon my father as we sat at table. He was grave and reflective, six feet three inches tall, with fine head and massive eyebrows. He walked quickly, wrote faster than anyone I knew, and added columns of figures like a calculating machine. Speed and energy were characteristic, yet perhaps one remembers most vividly his unique silences. He did not talk to find out what he wanted to say. He thought first. So great was his own concentration, that the preliminary pause seemed a telling addition to the final comment.

He was beloved, my father, in the parish, and for twenty years our family life was bound up with church and parish in a way perhaps known only to children of vicars or organists.

Sitting on the hearth rug in our night clothes while sidesmen or church wardens smoked a pipe with father, my brother Denis and I were enchanted auditors of parish affairs. To postpone bedtime, we spun out our supper, toasting it on pencils at the gas fire, and many a fascinatingly obscure sentence was overheard, while the bread curled at the corners and the butter dripped palely in the hearth.

Nothing I have ever read brought back so strongly the recollection of adult conversations overheard as Henry James' novel, *The Awkward Age*. Not that my parents, or any of their friends, talked in Jamesian phrase: such literary style would have been affectation to them. It is the enigmatical conversation that is at once familiar, the unexpected questions followed by apparently irrelevant replies. I had a mania for mathematics from a very early age, and invented a kind of psychological algebra

Given: fragment of story involving someone's guilt.
Required: to deduce what and why, done by whom?

Frequently, I concluded, how justly it is too late now to know, that the anonymous culprit was the vicar, an awesome but naturally enthralling thought.

Our vicar, Canon Trotter, loomed through our childhood with wild eye and vibrant voice like some latter-day Cuhullain. I personally remember him with affection. But that he could dictate and storm and bully, many other parishioners would testify. Perhaps he never wholly conquered the savage Irish temper of his youth, for some trivial blunder by his church officials might bring on a sudden rage at any time.

He seemed to me essentially humble and sincere, but he was also an eccentric, in the grand tradition, taking no thought for food or raiment, still less for the conventional dignity of clergymen. When in a hurry, he held up his cassock and ran — for the parish, already large, was growing steadily. He bought a bicycle and went off one November afternoon to learn to ride, returning at dusk to inform the scandalized verger, awaiting his appearance to ring the bell for Evensong

'There isn't a hedge or ditch this side of Benton* I haven't been in.'

He was forgetful too, and his sudden darts from choir stall to vestry in the middle of a service for notes or books needed for his sermon were as familiar to regular churchgoers as they were alarming to visitors.

All those hundreds of sermons — mile upon mile of words — the scolding tone of his preaching voice remains, but as to Christianity, or how we were to apply its tenets in our life, I remember nothing.

Only one complete sentence struck home. He had a habit, after service, of hurrying down the aisle to speak with people in the porch. In this sortie one morning, he nearly knocked me down. Snatching me upright again, he stared silently into my face.

'My dear,' he said, 'you're turning very like your mother,' and was gone.

Until then it had hardly occurred to me that Mother had a face and a life of her own. If I was like her, who was she? The person who washed and scolded, who took us to the museum on wet days and planned outings on fine; in short, a comfortable extension of the picnic basket, part of the family belongings.

I have a faded snapshot of her, sitting in a little wood beside the Tyne, just a homely, smiling body: not tall, not smart, not noticeable in any way. But for five years continuously, and intermittently for years after that, hers was the voice I listened to, for she was a great reader-aloud. She read

*Benton — a north eastern suburb of Newcastle

to us, not just children's classics of infancy, but extracts from whatever she happened to be in the middle of herself — prose or poetry.

To a large extent, children make up their mother, putting her together rather as they make 'Yule Do's' from scraps of pastry. 'Mother' is simply the walking embodiment of everything familiar, and mine was a conglomeration of meals, music, people in books, and all the friends to whom I heard her talking — for people came and went about the house like starlings.

Many children were among our home visitors for mother gave piano lessons. She had taught at the Conservatoire in Newcastle before marriage, and her help was often sought.

At Easter and the patronal festival, the house was given over to musicians. A small orchestra, strings and drums, played with the organ, and three friends of Father's came difficult cross-country journeys of more that thirty miles, to a parish church in the east end of Newcastle to make music for the glory of God.

After morning service, mother hurried home with me, to dish up the roast left to cook itself in the oven. In the afternoon we washed up, then listened while the men sang. After tea we all went back to church for Evensong. The pattern never changed, yet those Sundays were festive in the truest sense — gay, mirthful and looked-forward-to from one year to the next.

It became the custom for festal Evensong to end with Holst's festival motet *Turn back, O man, Forswear Thy Foolish Ways*. In those bleak years between the wars, every person we knew on Tyneside, and in Durham, suffered. In such hard times, people cling most stoutly to their vision of Utopia. We sang the last verse of Holst's anthem like the *Te Deum*

Earth shall be fair, and all her people one:
Not till that hour shall God's whole will be done,
Now, even now, once more from earth to sky
Peals forth in joy men's old undaunted cry —
Earth shall be fair, and all her folk be one.

Our world was not, however, limited to music, parish, the Tyne and the Cheviot hills. Mother had two older, unmarried sisters, Mamie and Lucy, who visited us often and for whom our visitors, our parish activities, high and holy days, disappointments, hopes and squalls, were a source of never-failing interest and comment.

'Oh where is All Sinners if this is All Saints?' I heard Aunt Lucy murmur, when she arrived one afternoon in the middle of some childish internecine dispute.

We saw those loved aunts often, for they kept a private school in

Tynemouth only ten miles away. Their house, Ravensworth, was older, larger and more romantic than our own, sunny at the front, but dark and mysterious behind. To this happy house our whole family, including cat and dog, migrated every Christmas, with lesser visits of one, two or all three children, whenever we were recovering from illness or 'needing a change'. A house forever associated with the family Christmas ritual is itself beloved, but Ravensworth gave also my first glimpse of a world dearer than any fairyland, a world made up entirely of the noise of children at work and play.

There were about sixty day pupils and four boarders. Mamie, eighteen years older than my mother, was the Headmistress, Lucy the housekeeper. In her quiet voice Lucy uttered mischievous remarks of the sort that make children hold their breath and wait for the sky to fall, for she did not treat education, the monarchy, or the established Church with the reverence her elder sister showed. She actually derided certain clergymen, and laughed at Queen Mary's hats.

Aunt Lucy was a walking Mrs Beeton. Her dark cupboards were lined with neatly labelled jam; on the fender a pan of dough rose twice each week, and on Fridays the air was scented by newly baked soda loaf.

Somehow the things we did with Aunt Lucy always led to food. On summer holidays, she never set out for 'a good walk', like Mother. She strolled happily to the nearest grassy bank and sat there making dolls' parasols from thistle heads. She knew what would make jam or chutney or pies. But Mamie was a true naturalist and taught us not only the names of birds and flowers and trees, but gave us our first understanding of how living things are grouped in families.

Mamie had cupboards too, even more beguiling ones than Lucy's, for hers were full of books, pencils, little notebooks, jigsaw puzzles and children's games. From about three years old she took me into the babyroom in her school, and soon I was allowed to stay there, sewing with a crewel needle on coloured cards, threading beads, or doing 'sums'.

Mamie, pivot of the house, believed in higher education for women. Extremely able, both intellectually and administratively, she was swift and decisive in speech, perhaps a little austere to outsiders, but endlessly kind and understanding to her family and in school.

Towards Aunt Mamie, many, I think, felt respect rather than affection, standing in some awe of her ability, but I loved her more than any other aunt or uncle, and spent much time trailing in her wake.

Neither in temperament nor interests were these two sisters in any way alike. Yet they lived together the best part of sixty years, providing for well-over half that time a house where feeding of mind and body was made equally attractive.

This private school which I loved so well had no playing fields. It was cramped by modern standards, and had few facilities for science or craft. But the teachers were good, well-qualified academically, and good in the moral sense, with an integrity that children respect. Work was of a high standard, and there was grace and dignity everywhere.

The school where I was myself a pupil was very different, one of the Girls Public Day School Trust schools, which had, and has, a high reputation. I went into the kindergarten there just after the age of four with my older brother. We moved from home to school, hardly aware of which world we were in, painting, talking, classifying and counting things. We read certainly, though where we learnt, or how, I do not recall. From home we explored the Northumbrian hills and streams; from school, our whole form, when we were nearly seven, followed the Ouseburn, a tributary of the Tyne, from source to mouth. At home we were caught-up in a world of music; at school, we danced, sang — however tunelessly — and played in the percussion band.

Then, in an instant, we were told we had to leave the junior house and move up to the 'big school' across the way. We were given a panegyric on the joys to be found therein: French and singing; gym in a gymnasium, art in a studio, science in a lab.

From the rapturous description, I imagined something like the last act of *Mother Goose*. But alas, my expectations, as always, were fantastically rosy. That year of turning eight was the quintessence of tedium.

Oh, those dreary hours and days of being mildly silly and learning nothing much, from a bored and boring teacher. Miss Parsons (who clearly did not care about learning herself), sat at her high desk like a wilting lily, endlessly talking, her voice high-pitched and querulous. And we had to repeat things: repeat, repeat, repeat —parts of the body, parts of the room — la main, la tête, le plancher, le mur, la fenêtre.

Our faculties were never fully occupied, so ear and eye sought movement, any movement, indoor or out, to lighten the dead weight of repetition within: wasp on window, thrush on wall, the call of the fish wife. All these had freedom while we sat sulkily apathetic and confined. And these names she taught us had such ugly sounds — la main, le plancher. Why didn't she teach us a French song? I tried to make up one, only to be rebuked for wool-gathering. My mother could have knitted several jerseys with the wool I gathered in that year alone.

Yet in history, with a different teacher, everything was changed. Miss Chew was the oddest and most uncommanding figure any schoolgirl could invent: little, fat, pale-faced, with a heavy fringe of black hair. She taught us facts and dates, my word, yes. We were to say ten dates each morning, while pulling on our stockings. But we learnt much more than 'Columbus

1492'. We were given a moving picture of the vision and endurance that made possible the great voyages of the late fifteenth century. And later on, I remember, and will always remember, the last words of Thomas More to his friend

Quiet yourself, good Mr Pope, and be not discomforted. I trust that we shall once again in heaven see each other full merrily.

History lessons, alas, came only twice a week, and indeed the more vividly they brought to life a world of sound and colour, love and hate, a world of invention, learning and discovery, the more stultifying became the inertia within our green-painted classroom walls. Our room all that year was on the sunless side of school. Children, like lambs, do better with a share of sun.

Perhaps my parents guessed about the paralysing boredom in Form II, because they began taking me with them to some of our city concerts, especially to the lectures and recitals of the British Music Society, in King's Hall at Newcastle University. The recital of Hebridean songs given by Marjorie and Patuffa Kennedy-Frazer to the accompaniment of a Gaelic harp was a landmark, not only because the songs were so hauntingly memorable, but because — by happy chance — I sat next to a girl wearing our own school uniform, June Manson, whom at that time I knew only by sight as we were not then in the same form. We must have recognised a comfortable homeliness in one another because, as a result of this first meeting, thereafter June came to our house to tea before the concert, or I went to hers. In each other's homes we became life-long friends, something very different from casual school acquaintanceship.

June lived in Park Road off Westgate Hill, a longish journey by rackety tram, downhill to the old St John's Church, and then in another tram far up Westgate Hill. I remember still my first sight of the Tyne from that hill in the west end. Spread before me, far below, I could see the winding river, and on the distant bank the great panorama of Dunston, Swalwell, Blaydon, Gateshead — to any real Tynesider, an awe-inspiring view of a great city.

But the Park Road door bell must be rung, and that first step into alien territory be taken. June had two sisters — an older and a younger one. They amazed and humbled me on that first visit — they were so neat, so deft and thorough in every household task. I felt gauche and clumsy.

June's father, different from my own in almost every way except in quiet kindness, sat reading in his armchair surrounded by the largest collection of books I had ever seen outside a public library. He was small, stoutish, with smiling face and snow-white hair, giving me — even at nine years old — the impression of meeting the Saint Nicholas known to all Dutch children.

Over many years on each visit to Park Road, I thought of what the high school lacked through not having June's father as a teacher; his mellow voice, patience, smile of welcome to our hesitant suggestions, and above all, his own love of knowledge — these seemed the very qualities that young people would put foremost in 'requirements for teachers'.

I liked the evenings best when June and I were on our own, to talk with — or mainly 'listen to' — Mr Manson. Like my own father, he had left school at thirteen to help support a widowed mother, educating himself thereafter through night-classes and books. Grocer by trade, socialist by conviction, historian through personal study, philosopher from his experience of life and people, he helped to expand our narrow minds. His talk was not 'better' than the talk we heard at home, but different. We could question, and he showed us books from which we could get answers. It is doubtful if we actually read many of the works he offered, but we learnt to know the feel of original sources: step one for budding students.

On each visit, I came to know the family collectively a little better. The two sisters, bright-eyed and quick-witted, were born to stand out in any crowd. It seemed to me — the silent observer/listener — that they often snubbed June, though to me she had much the nicest nature and the most good sense. One would have expected her modesty and thoughtfulness to commend her favourably to our high-minded schoolteachers. But no, she suffered from such anxiety not to appear stupid and slow, that, blushing furiously, often she never got her answers out at all. This silence seemed to arouse a kind of petulant annoyance in certain teachers, disturbing to listen to, as it was all too obvious that help, not scorn, was needed. It is hard for any pupil, we know, to be the excessively shy one between two sparkling sisters, but pupils expect teachers to be able to tell when one of their number is suffering, and give help.

After we had both left school June told me that the deafness for which she was later treated had been with her always, but no one had realised it then.

June was the reverse of stupid. She had (and still has) a gift for delineating character in a telling sentence. But that gift, so marked in letters and in conversation, she never used in formal essays, and she was everlastingly in trouble in school about her 'written work'.

As we grew older, there were often matches or other school commitments on Saturdays, so June and I went to each other's houses on Mondays, from school. After tea we did the family ironing in the kitchen, away from adult or sisterly ears, so we could talk more easily. But I sill loved to go to Park Road on a free Saturday. There, we sat round the fire, the older sister a model of female accomplishment doing her embroidery. It was like a scene from Jane Austen. I admired the family exceedingly — but had no wish to emulate.

As we moved up the school, the pressure to conform to the standards of high school success increased: to be in the first hockey eleven, the first tennis six; to win the high jump; to hold the opinions of everyone else, and be popular. June derided this openly. I — a born Fabian — suggested that we wrote a play, a skit on the school stories of Angela Brazil — at that time still most amazingly popular with girls even as old as fifteen. We did write our play, in the Christmas holidays when we were in the sixth form — *Life at St Monica's* by Angelica Walnut. This project grew, and finally it was decided to give a public performance towards the end of the spring term.

Before the date fixed, June had left to take up nursing at the Babies' Hospital in Newcastle. I missed her very much, but was working hard, one of my four A-level subjects being mathematics, for which I had fifteen periods alone each week. This side-lined me a little from the rest of the form, any girl actually caring greatly for mathematics still being thought eccentric if not decidedly 'queer'.

In all those years since I was myself a sixth-former, I do hope that the chaotic absurdity of sixth-form life has at least been modified. There were cloakroom duties, stair duties, bells to ring, junior school games practices to supervise, House meetings to conduct in break or dinner time — and much else that is now blessedly forgotten. We had this terrifying anxiety to be thought 'reliable'. I used to wake up from nightmares in which I had arrived late to unlock the cloakroom doors.

And then, in the midst of all additional end-of-term frenzy, two weeks before the 'very last day' my younger brother developed measles. He has done a lot for me all through life, but never had I thanked him so sincerely for anything before! Although I had had the illness in childhood, regulations were such that I had to be in quarantine for three weeks, and this meant missing the play, the House singing competition, various hockey and netball matches, and the House dance. To my surprise, I found that any initial disappointment was far outweighed by profound relief. For the first time for eleven weeks I could go to bed and sleep without a care. Someone else could stand up in front of the school and conduct a choir that did not want to sing. Of course I was sorry not to see the play that we had written, but delighted not to have to act in it. As for the netball matches, old Uncle Tom Cobbleigh could take all the silver cups with my most fervent blessing.

It was spring-cleaning time at home, and I asked Mother if she would play the piano to me every afternoon if I worked hard all morning at the cleaning. She refused. Measles at home and depression at large, and rain, and arthritis, and no practising done — 'she could not'. But she did of course, in the end, and we had a wonderful week together, with Beethoven's D minor Sonata, opus 31 no 2, one of her favourites. She had been a very good pianist, teaching with Edgar Bainton in the Conservatoire in Newcastle. If, after years of domesticity, there were faults in her playing, which indeed there were, it had a control, structure and forward drive that enabled Beethoven to speak. Can there not be an ear, as well as an eye, of love? This special ear hears what the spirit intended to be there. And, after all, Mother was playing for our joint delight — not for public performance.

There is always a moment when music, like poetry, pictures or people, speaks to us for the first time. The astonishment of those who first heard this stupendous sonata in 1802 can hardly have been greater than mine when I first attended fully to each movement; just the two of us working together, going back to try and understand development, enjoying the freedom, — and also the space and freshness of the newly spring-cleaned room, with no one to interfere.

The patient, not seriously ill, was not neglected. He had books, radio and the dog beside him. So, in the end, that extended Easter holiday became as thrilling to me as a modern school journey abroad — and quite as memorable.

Indeed what I had been ruminating on while washing paint-work, or ironing floor-length curtains, had been whether there would, in fact, be a journey ahead for me at all.

My secret longing was to continue learning, to go to university. How or where I could not tell, for the time was 1930, yet one more year of that ongoing great Depression on Tyneside, and elsewhere.

I could not ask my hard-pressed family for three years residence in Oxford or Cambridge, the only universities our Headmistress recognised. What to do? It was already April, the school year almost over. For weeks I had agonized. In despair, I sought out an older acquaintance, Dorothy, a former pupil of our school, who had been for the past year an undergraduate in King's College in Newcastle — at that time still a constituent college of the University of Durham. How had she found her place?

By chance, she told me, through advice of another friend, pupil of a local authority grammar school. Through promising to become a teacher, she had been accepted into the Education Department of King's College, Newcastle, her fees to be paid as a kind of scholarship. March was the time for application, but I could send in my modest application although two weeks late.

I rushed home. To continue living at home would cost nothing like so much as residence elsewhere — and I would be a help to my family — or so I fondly thought.

My parents, though wisely advising caution, were excited too, so I wrote off that night. Within two weeks I was interviewed and accepted. We were stunned and delighted. At the interview I was given new advice which seemed good: to take Intermediate BA at university instead of staying another whole year at school to take A-levels. In that way, the choice of whether to read for Honours in mathematics or in history could be left open until a whole year later.

My Headmistress had known nothing of all this until, following my application, the Registrar had written to school for a reference. So, when I went to tell her of acceptance, she was decidedly cool ... without advice, without consultation, I had signed my future away for the sake of four years at a provincial university! I had planned my future without guidance, and could embark upon it without blessing.

In justice to Headmistresses, these may not have been the words she uttered. As a result of all those years of training in listening, I do, as a rule, remember words exactly. But in times of great stress and apprehension, we remember a tone of voice, an impression of anger, condemnation, even scorn. Old childhood fears revive and the faint path of communication between Head and pupil disappears. If I seemed headstrong and impetuous to my Headmistress, she, to me, seemed about as approachable and understanding as the Albert Hall. Her frowns, her tones, her eyebrows, shrivelled up provincial universities, teacher training departments and my own shallow nature in one haughty shrug. Too late I realised that my behaviour would seem rude, and felt very badly about it, although it was entirely due to ignorance of procedure (we had been told nothing at school) and the necessary haste to get an application in before it was too late.

Until this year in the Sixth, I must have accepted school and its rules and customs without consciously criticising them. I had thought, moreover, of our Headmistress as one of the Old Testament prophets. Now it dawned upon me that she was trying to make us accept all her social conventions; not just as if they were matters of etiquette, in which it might be courteous to conform, but as if they were moral principles. The phrase 'things that are just not done' was constantly on her lips. What did she mean by it? If she meant something like lying, that was morally wrong, even I knew that in business, in politics, in social life, it was constantly done. And if she meant going into town without hat and gloves, why should such things not be done?

I had been with my father to shipyard towns, to Jarrow, Hebburn and Shields, to mining villages in Durham, and had seen men standing idle and defeated at street corners; shops boarded up, derelict; grey-faced women watching listlessly from their doors. There was a life of which we heard nothing at school, that had never once been mentioned. Why? If there were absolute standards of right and wrong, what was right in the tranquil well-kept terraces up which I cycled to school was equally right in Jarrow. I had been reading a history of the Northumberland and Durham miners, and had been deeply stirred by the dignity and restraint of that pitiful story. It had awakened also indignation against the 'history' lessons we were given at school. Living as we did in the heart of a mining and engineering district, studying as we were supposed to have done in the previous two years, the eighteenth and nineteenth centuries, the struggle of the miners and other industrial workers to win decent conditions and a civilised life had been totally ignored. As far as school was concerned, we might be dwelling in a world composed entirely of respectable terraces, where clockwork dolls would clean brasses and scrub steps for the rest of eternity.

I suppose it began to dawn on me, dimly, that the teachings of a school could be separable; that one need neither accept nor reject everything belonging to the past ten years; the standards of scholarship could be accepted, but the stifling snobbery in which they were embedded need not.

But a feeling of disloyalty returned as the summer term drew to an end. Everyone else expressed such pathos at leaving. Tender farewells were taken; tears flowed. All this seemed, and still seems to me, silly and affected. I was seventeen and wanted to be in the real world. Before leaving, I wanted to make one comment that really was my own. But what could I say that wouldn't seem rude?

Alone among all school-leavers I refrained from joining the Old-Girls' Guild. Hardly a telling gesture of defiance! But even this faint flush of independence brought little joy. I had returned home nonchalant and dry-eyed, carrying my very last school report. When my mother opened it, there in prominent blue ink, written in the 'Literature' space, with our Headmistress's confident, expansive flourish, was her final comment

English Language and Literature: Her work in this subject is immature. She seems to be afraid of saying anything that means anything, which leads to a lack of sincerity, in essays a fundamental defect.

Such ferocious criticism fell on my listening ears like a passing bell.

I could hardly bear the thought of my parents reading it. After sacrificing so much to give me 'a good education', now to suffer the news that their daughter was almost a moron.

My mother said 'She does not seem to know her Pope very well,' and when I asked why, quoted

Whoever thinks a faultless line to see
Thinks what ne'er was, nor is, nor e'er shall be.

Nothing more was ever said about it to me. Our Headmistress's remarks were, in fact, quite penetratingly true in part: we had written these fortnightly essays only to find that she had a horrible habit of reading out bits from one's effort in class, adding devastating comments, in public, of her own. Consequently, at least one of her victims thought it fair to behave like Charles I, who (I had been taught) concealed his own thoughts in a confusion of platitudes.

After a week or more I forced myself to try to be like Beethoven who, when criticised adversely said, 'I think with Voltaire that mere fly stings will not hold back a runaway horse.'

That night, in bed, I essayed a little Dunciad of my own

Matilda, who was very cowed
Disliked her essays read out loud
Her friends were never shown her stuff
Because she wrapped it up in guff
Her Pedagogue was ever ready
To say 'Your style is too unsteady...'

It was easy, and quite rehabilitating to one's ego, to run on and on like this. All that was lacking was the linguistic fluency of an Ogden Nash — of whom, alas, in those days I had not heard.

Late in August, my father announced that he had arranged to take a brief holiday, so that my mother, my younger brother, he and I, could have a little visit to the Scottish Border abbeys and Abbotsford. We had five unforgettable days, in perfect weather, in that old war-torn country, now a place of dream-like beauty .

It was the last holiday we had together.

CHAPTER TWO

Loving and liking
The university and hard times

In the first week of October 1930, I became a student of King's College, Newcastle, then a constituent part of Durham University, and fell in love with the place first, then the people. In the vast university library, at first so impressive and silent, all knowledge seemed available for the asking. It seemed as if the years at school had all been a preparation for living in this library, and there I did live, a large part of my student life — though many would frown upon that today. I only came truly alive at the university, which may be the right and natural course of development. But if so, what of the army of boys and girls who do not have this opportunity which university life provides for silent study, reflection and discovery?

We were much less sophisticated, less confident, in nearly every way more naive than students are today. There was still a huge preponderance of men: fifty men to three women in our first year in mathematics, and I don't think I learned the names of more than five. The men I saw most frequently — those in the history school — appeared particularly alienated from normal conversational life. I can see now that we were all shy and bewildered, all from single-sex schools, unused to making contact with strangers. The men were taciturn, moving stiffly, like the clay figures at which we shied wooden balls for 3d at the Hoppings, our Newcastle Fair. Many of their faces were spotty and their hair had a glued-on look. It is only fair to say that my companion, Madeline, and I (the only two women in our History Honours year) scarcely out-did them in fascination. She was thin, white, knowing and anxious, looking 'Whist and shrivelled, like nothing going nowhere and less coming back,' as my mother said. I was the opposite — rosy, buxom, immature, like an amiable young St Bernard.

Madeline gave up before her first year exams, so then, of women, there was only one in our history year.

It was all so different from school. We were free to browse; to ponder; to write and re-write essays instead of offering them raw. And for the first time we were taught by men, with deeper and less nagging voices; voices which sounded enthusiastic, and more challenging than those we had known at school, conveying a greater liking for the subject and for us. We thawed and blossomed, like backward plants in the sun. Young people want to be liked, not endured with pious resignation.

I associated the new-found friendliness of tutors with the greater freedom and naturalness of a mixed community of men and women. Yet it was years before I sought to apply this awareness in my own teaching life. I never sought a mixed school, simply took the first Newcastle job that I was offered which was in an all-girls school. Not for seven years did I make any positive effort in what seemed the right direction.

This was typical of my general slowness of development. No rapid reading course would have been any use to me. I liked to dig back to sources, to pore over old diaries, letters, and memoirs, and plod through columns of parliamentary reports. I read slowly, listening to the voice: Bede, Piers Plowman, Thomas More, Erasmus, Burke and many others are alive for me today because their voices are unforgettable. I could feel sympathy for Newcastle Corporation when, as late as 1653, it had to pray for deferment of a case at court 'by reason they were not ready, the Scots having tumbled their records'. My own records were equally often 'tumbled' but I could never blame the Scots!

And, strangely, nothing was forfeited to pay for all this new-found pleasure — or so it seemed at first. Our musical life at home continued. If I had gone away to university I would have gone to concerts, but would have lost all the music-making in our own home, as well as the Philharmonic concerts and chamber music recitals in the lovely old Assembly Rooms near Newcastle's Quayside, built in 1774.

Throughout those years of working for a history degree, we were never allowed to forget that we belonged to the Education Department and were destined for schools. We did two hours of physical education every

Saturday morning, and attended — or gave — a demonstration lesson every Monday afternoon. Even in vacation our teaching fate was dangled over us. We were urged to spend a few weeks on the staff of the Lord Mayor's Holiday Camp for Poor Children run throughout August in those years of depression on Tyneside. 'Good experience' our education lecturers called it, though I much doubt if any one of them had actually worked through that experience.

It was a horrible warning of everything a camp should never be, in conditions of mass manipulation that no teacher should allow. Each Friday night 400 girls, twelve or thirteen years old, arrived for a week in the dreary, flat campfield at Amble on the north-east coast, with the cemetery on one side and Hauxley pit on the other.

Somehow the little exiles had to be got to bed in this 'Valley of Dry Bones', each group of forty into three bell tents. There were tears and temper every first night. They would push and argue, and suddenly a pair would be found tearing one another's hair.

'Shurrup, wor Maggie! Aa'll bray the lights oot o' yeh when aa's get hyem.'

'Shurrup yersel! Aa'll gi' yeh yor hammers if ye dinna ger off me bag.'

This would go on long into the night, for they had neither enough room nor enough bedding to keep them warm. A chamber pot was left by each tent pole, and door flaps were supposed to be fastened, as the fiercer and less cowed children often tried to run away. Dorothy and I never fastened our children in because the smell, even with the doors open, was indescribably foul. Meals at long trestle tables, in a marquee from which the smell of stale food never cleared, came straight from Dotheboys Hall — thin porridge, dry bread and one sausage with suet roll.

Once, working among old manuscripts in the library of the Society of Antiquaries in the Black Gate in Newcastle, I found a *History of Newcastle* by E Mackenzie, which gave a bleak description of St Nicholas Poor House, founded in 1803. Reading this brought back the very smell of those holiday camps

The unfortunate paupers are doomed continually to witness the sufferings of humanity. Many contrive to exist upon a miserable pittance rather than go into the House, which certainly possesses few attractions, even for those steeped in poverty and acquainted with misfortune.

By 1930, the Poor House was gone. Its humiliations remained, extended to many hundreds more.

The first day of each holiday week had a nightmarish quality. The girls seemed apathetic, suspicious, withdrawn. We would try to start games, to be met with frozen passivity, even with tears from the most homesick. Only slowly did they begin to warm and chatter. Nearly all were from large families, not one used to having adult attention for long. They could never master the rules, or enjoy games that demanded initiative and enterprise. They liked best jingles that I had learned in childhood, and we marched along the country lanes, ten or twelve abreast, arms linked, chanting

The Maid was tall and slim and fair
And her hair Was a delicate colour of ginger, ginger

(steps backward on ginger, ginger and start off again).
We varied this with

Left! Left! I left my wife and three fat babies

(hitch feet)

Right! Right! Right in the middle of the kitchen floor

(hitch feet again)
Of these two singing games they never tired.

We did no real teaching; only a visit each week to the brickworks at Amble, on return from which a lesson had to be given (with diagrams, on blackboards) on the making of a brick.

I went four years running to that camp and out of it all came a fused, unforgettable experience, of how one can hate and love at the same time. Each year, ladling porridge to child refugees from a 'distressed area', marooned in that dead grass between pit and graveyard, I vowed never to return. Yet gradually hatred for the process lessened as affection for the children grew. Good things in the camp did show: kindness and trust between staff and children; and the capability of the camp commandant, who greeted each weekly horde with a motherly smile, and met each crisis with sensitivity, firmness and calm. And the fact is, the children did go home looking brighter, happier, rosier, even if their only tonic had been a week of adult affection laced with good sea air.

Was it better than nothing? I have never been able to decide, for there was nothing we could do to change their long-term environment, and on the seventh day they returned to it. We offered love that could not be sustained, and does this not serve only to tantalize?

A few months before Finals my father died. His death was unforeseen, to his children at least. It had never entered our minds that his inexhaustible energy and determination could be extinguished. At the annual choir dinner he had said, in his brief speech of thanks, that he imagined this life as a probation, for choirmen and musicians in particular. Next day, he played the services to the accompaniment of strings and drums, and Evensong closed with his own orchestral variations on *Praise the Lord, Ye*

Heavens Adore Him. His own probation was at an end.

In order that I might complete my training and my younger brother finish his medical course, it was necessary for Mother to sell the house and much of her furniture. She did so with stoicism. At the time, I fear we gave her little comfort, for to us the spiritual loss was all, and we did not realise how she could derive comfort from at least a few of her material possessions — objects she had cherished all her married life.

My elder brother, now in his first year of work, was away from home, so Denis, my younger brother, Mother and I moved to Tynemouth. There, for six months, we lodged in my aunt's house, Ravensworth, no longer a school. All through childhood those sunny rooms at Ravensworth, colourful as Dutch interiors, had been my second home: the sitting room with rich red table cloth where Aunt Mamie sat writing letters below an old map of Warwickshire; music room with blue walls and windows open to the sea; Delft ware and pewter dishes in the kitchen where Aunt Lucy was forever busy, in white cuffs and apron. But upon the death of Mamie, the eldest sister, the school had been closed, and when we moved there, that leafless February, the house seemed alien and melancholy. There were no children now, only Lucy, many years older than my mother, and very frail; my cousin Joyce, who gave piano lessons at a school in Shields, and Miss Maria Baldock, who, having taught at Ravensworth for forty years, had thrown in her lot with Lucy rather than return to her relations in Nottingham.

So we lived, the six of us, like the strangely assorted characters in a Chekhov play: only Miss Baldock genuinely happy, the rest of us each seeking something we had lost.

From childhood I had hoped, if I ever became a teacher, to emulate Miss Baldock. To teach singing, maths and history in some modest schoolroom was the height of my ambition.

One's own school teachers never fully live. They die daily at four o'clock to be mysteriously resurrected at eight forty-five. But Miss Baldock was of the family. Often that spring and summer, we walked together on a Saturday morning, over the firm sand to Cullercoats from Tynemouth Point. She loved to talk, and I loved to listen. Her reminiscences of school and pupils scarcely faltered, even with the north wind in our teeth. Yet somewhere, vaguely in my mind, was apprehension. Would a lifetime of teaching, of putting up with the humours and foibles of others, leave me so cheerful and kind? I knew, even at that early age, that it would not. Miss Baldock was happy with my aunt and mother, but she was their shadow. It was never her home. She had fewer actual possessions than anyone I ever knew. Was this self-abnegation essential to a teacher? I could not really see myself accepting her ideal of luxury: a 'nice' book on Sunday afternoon — Flora Klickman's *Trail of the Ragged Robin* or *The Flower Patch Among the*

Hills — with a peppermint or two.

Knowing how much my parents had sacrificed to allow me to go to university, I hoped to get a first class degree. When I did do so, my father was no longer there to know. What a lesson in the emptiness of so-called 'honours'.

After Finals there was another year in the Education Department to obtain a diploma in 'Theory and Practice of Teaching'. As this meant daily attendance in Newcastle and the expense of travelling to and from the coast, Mother, Denis and I returned to a small flat in Newcastle.

'Practice' began with two weeks in an elementary school in Byker*, during which half of the time was spent observing one of the most curt, soured and bad-tempered teachers I have ever met. She had the top class of fifty girls, every one of whom presented a front — docile, polite, attentive and superlatively neat. It was as if they had been coached for two years to be parlour maids in a Noel Coward play.

'I'm a woman of few words' this teacher snapped, and for two weeks we lived on commands: 'Atlases!' 'Rulers!' 'Hands on heads'. This last was a way of ensuring that no one fidgets, and so exhausting, it must also ensure that no one thinks. After two days 'observing' I had to teach — arithmetic, spelling, grammar, and geography, plus, as she grudgingly conceded, two half hours of history 'since that's your line'.

I hated every minute of that fortnight, and left to the invigorating few words, 'When you've been at it as long as I have, you'll not be so soft.'

Our second school practice was ten weeks in a grammar school for the whole of the spring term. The teachers were courteous and kind; and it was a good school in a narrow conventional sense. Public examinations were important: girls wanted jobs and were complaisant so long as teachers served them information which enabled them to pass exams. They toyed with their academic mince and mash, daily, and the thought that there might be other ingredients, other dishes, on the learning menu did not trouble them. Even my adviser, Miss Richardson, the senior history mistress, universally respected, gave lessons like college lectures. She dictated, girls wrote down what they could, of all she said. There was perfect order, no whispers, laughs, shuffles, and yet the room felt oppressive and dead. The dictating voice droned on, carried away with Rockingham and The Stamp Act. Where the pupils' minds were flitting who can tell?

My mind on this second day of 'observation' was with my friend June. We had corresponded regularly in the four years since our parting, mainly about her new work. Knowing how little true enjoyment she ever had in school, I deliberately avoided any reference to our academic work. I had written to her for Christmas commiserating on her stultifying toil in The

---

* East end suburb of Newcastle, adjoining Walker

Babies' Hospital and telling her of our changed life back in our little flat in Heaton. Her reply, received that morning, had shattered me.

Don't you be sorry for me

she wrote.

The boot is on the other foot. For me it may be wash, wring and hang out half the day, perhaps for ever and ever. But I don't mind. I was unhappy at school every day of my life; always in trouble, frightened, lonely, and loaded down with inferiority. I loathed and hated the whole set up. The only thing I shall never understand is why you can be working so hard to become another of that batch of terrifying women?

It was as if my 'best friend' — the one I thought I knew, had suddenly stood up in a crowded hall and screamed. Of course I knew she 'didn't much like school' but clearly I had never imagined the extent of her misery. How could it be that I knew her deepest feelings so little, though we had shared so many pleasures, artistic and 'open air', as well as work — guide camps, picnics, music, each other's families? If it had been any other friend writing so, I would have thought 'Oh, she's letting off steam after a miserable day,' and laughed it off with her. But June was not like that, she was blunt and decisive, and when she spoke it was what she had been thinking for some time.

I remembered Boswell's comment in his account of a discussion with friends

I enlarged upon the anxiety and suffering which are endured at school

and it seemed as if June felt much as Boswell did. Why should schools, brought into existence to be a help to young people, appear so often to alienate them instead? Moreover, June wrote of teachers as 'terrifying people', as if I intended to leave the world of ordinary workers to join some extreme barbaric sect.

Our respective parents had strained themselves grievously, in harsh times, to send us to the high school believing that its traditions, for 'good scholarship' mattered to us all. I did not 'hate' school as June did — indeed I liked many of the teachers, especially in mathematics and Greek. But many of them did snub June in lessons, to a point which I could never understand, and which made me very angry.

Years ago I read, in a book called *Lay My Burden Down,* how an old Negro, when asked if he remembered slavery, replied slowly

There is no way for me to disremember it unless I die.

I have thought about this often since, for it is, I think, the way many people — certainly among women, feel about school. Most of us, surely, experience some happy companionship there, but all too often, in addition, there comes fear, frustration, alienation and, for a few, even despair.

My complaint about school was that the whole atmosphere was stifling and confined. We kept alive the school's 'traditions' — singing Harrow school songs — *Heroes* and *Forty Years On* — at the end-of-term ceremony three times every year. The emphasis was all on 'leadership', whereas many of us, without being in the least sanctimonious, were much more concerned to do useful work in a wholly inconspicuous fashion.

Our school was never part of the society in which we had all been born — that Tyneside which had suffered the devastation of all its heavy industries — mining and civil engineering, ship building, and bridge building. Craft and art skills, through the work of the Beilbys and Thomas Bewick, were held in high regard too, and we had had a good reputation for musical education in the city from the time of Dr Avison. None of this was ever mentioned (or certainly not in my hearing!) in school. Our Headmistress encouraged the singing of one or two north country songs for each prize-giving, and we sang them (as I thought we sang everything else) rather daintily and mincingly. We never pulled off anything with the verve and enthusiasm that I heard West Walker boys give to *The Daniel Jazz*.

What I felt most conscious of in the last two years of school, and the years of teacher-training was the vast amount of wasted talent. In every school I met, starting from our own high school, a huge amount of time and care was given to the Oxbridge aspirants who were going to stay three whole years in the sixth form.

But there were many who left earlier to become primary school teachers — good ones too, who would have benefited greatly from good inspiring sixth form teaching in all general subjects.

There are now, thankfully, books of such kind available, head of which I would put Bronowski's *The Ascent of Man* and Kenneth Clark's *Civilisaton*.

Certainly there is a place for lectures, if short, to provoke and arouse students' interest in a topic, and to sketch a background that makes possible the pupil's own study and research. Yet I can never believe that continuous lecturing to older students, as in the classes taken by my dear Miss Richardson in the Western (Girls) High School, are a true answer to 'advanced study' for those pupils, many of whom hope to go on to become teachers themselves in their turn.

Is it not a good illustration of the truth of this argument that I could abandon Miss Richardson so unceremoniously two pages ago, in the midst of her lecture on Rockingham, forgetting her altogether for so long?

Though *intending* to listen to her the task was made difficult by the weight of detail she included, which had no bearing on anything in the lives of those Tyneside girls, nor hope of benefiting them in any future job which they might, if lucky, obtain. The only purpose of all their feverish writing seemed to be the prospect of reproducing it in some exam to come! Yet pupils can get excited over political history when they see that it has any meaning for their own lives or thoughts. When I had to make history syllabuses for schools in my turn, I always included Tom Paine in the late eighteenth century. Showing how his ideas in *The Rights of Man* travelled between Britain, France and America and, later, much further, is absorbing to them — often a revelation.

It certainly would have been a revelation to my own school companion, June, for if ever there was a case of a pupil whose abilities were wasted, June was one. We were both at 'a good school' as schools go. June was, and is, wise, sensible and artistic. Yet her own young life seemed, at least to herself, to be unenriched by anything school offered.

The waste of talent was, of course, greater by compound interest in the girls's senior school in Byker where my first school practice had been done. Senior schools in Cumbria with which I am still very happily familiar give all their pupils so much more than teachers could hope to give sixty years ago, that I can never look with the jaundiced eyes of some publicists and politicians, upon the educational scene today.

But this chapter set out to try to show how a student of fairly well-marked interests and outlook was hammered into the teacher she became. Once when prowling in our university library round those history and literature shelves which I so much loved, I found a 'Conversation' by Henry James on George Eliot's novel *Daniel Deronda*. I was immediately arrested by these words (spoken of Gwendolen)

A perfect picture of youthfulness — its eagerness, its presumption, its preoccupation with itself, its vanity and silliness, its sense of its own absoluteness.

This seemed — and seems — a telling description of ourselves all too often when young! I try to remember it when watching today's undergraduates.

We next had to apply for posts. I was determined to teach in what was then known, in spite of the Hadow Report, as 'an elementary school'.

Everyone in authority in the university Education Department tried to dissuade me from what I planned to do. Our professor warned of classes of over fifty, strict discipline, short holidays, the cane. I was offered posts in grammar schools which I declined. With a kind of mad mulishness I persisted in the determination to know the worst. I wanted to know 'the system' from the bottom up.

But how, knowing neither school, staff nor children, could I ever teach anything that first day? So far as history was concerned, I did what I could: the uninterrupted labours of those weeks before my first real teaching term began saw an assembly of notes on every topic that a school history syllabus could possibly contain: constitutional law; economics; political philosophy, ancient, modern; Special Periods — Dark Ages, Medieval, Europe, Renaissance, Reformation, eighteenth century, French Revolution and Napoleonic era, nineteenth century, Europe, Russia, USA ...

It was an aspiring teacher's votive offering. Everything I had ever learnt that could be included under the generic title 'history' was dragged in, noted, tabulated and arranged. While busy with it, I imagined it all set to music — *A Symphony of History* in the manner of Stravinsky's *Symphony of Psalms.* And I sang — if not like a nightingale, perhaps like a Kookaburra.

In various lumber-rooms there lay for years those mouldering unopened files and pictures, a monument to the most futile and misguided holiday labour of my life. Yet there must be ways for a young teacher to prepare for the classroom. Perhaps knowing what to expect would increase the chances of finding a good way? I would try to keep a record.

No sooner had I made that momentous decision than word came from the Office that I had been appointed to Washington Road Senior School in Walker, to begin on the first day of term. Great was my mother's relief. But did she remember, as I did, the wedding of a friend of mine, attended by an elderly lugubrious solicitor?

'Very nice wedding m'dear,' he said to the bride on leaving, 'but I prefer a good funeral myself. With a funeral you know where you are. A wedding opens the door to all sorts of trouble.'

I opened the door to trouble when I walked into Washington Road Senior School. But we got a pay cheque of fifteen pounds at the end of every month which kept us precariously afloat for the next three years.

CHAPTER THREE

The Songs of Sion

Walker in the Depression

That route to Washington Road School in Walker was a symphony in grey. Daily we trudged along it, my friend Dorothy and I. We left our sunny suburb at eight each morning to go south and east, in the opposite direction from our walks to university. On this journey there were no neat gardens with lilac, daffodils and dahlias in their season. There were shabby houses fronting the street, bill boardings and grimy shops, where faded blinds were never fully raised, and the windows advertised OOK B DS or ADB COA*. Once out of the street where we lived, not a single tree grew anywhere on the road from there to school. Instead, the stench and smoke of the city Destructor** greeted us as we passed each morning from Heaton into Byker where my friend taught. To reach Walker, I went on another half-mile towards the river and the shipyards, through an ever more depressed and depressing world of dingy curtains and derelict roofs.

Washington Road School stood grimly at right angles to the main road, fronted by a concrete yard and a blackened patch of wasteland, fringed by nettles, referred to by our Headmistress as 'the playing field' — whether in unquenchable vision or black cynicism I never knew.

Our old Board school had been designed in 1890 so that not an inch

* Brook Bonds or Cadburys Cocoa
** Incinerator which burned rubbish

of accommodation should be wasted, nor a halfpenny extra spent on maintenance in the ensuing years. It had two identical floors, each with a wide central corridor from which classrooms opened, on either side. Cloakrooms and stone stairs squared off the ends of each corridor like pewter candlesticks on a mantel-piece. When I entered school that first morning, the dead load of grey symmetry hit me like a gong.

To this forbidding fortress some genie of Education had allotted upwards of 600 pupils, eighteen teachers and a Headmistress, Miss Sarah Ivinson: tall, grey haired, already stooping in weariness, though surely not yet fifty. She came to greet me as I entered the stone corridor, and pointed to a book laid open on the window sill.

'The time book. Sign here morning and afternoon. Exact time of arrival, please. You are to have class VA.'

Classes were still named after the old elementary school 'standards' — V, VI or VII for ages eleven, twelve, and thirteen. Girls left standard VII after their fourteenth birthday. My standard VA had already had their first term of senior life although the brightest were still only ten, having been pushed forward by their junior schools to give them a full year in the seniors before the scholarship examination.

Miss Ivinson led me into the green-tiled room which looked like a station lavatory, where two fair haired girls were silently laying out Bibles and arithmetic books on the old-fashioned double desks. She showed me the register and record book. It seemed I was to take my own class for arithmetic, English, needlework, physical training, as it was then called, dancing and games, and all the 'A' classes in the school for history.

'I have been told you are keen on athletics,' Miss Ivinson said, 'So you are to take class VIB for physical training in addition to your own. Miss Pringle is our gym specialist but she cannot take the whole school. Your class will take the Scholarship exam next March. You mustn't let the standard of work down. Never waste time.'

She pointed to the blackboard where ten words were already printed in a firm, straight hand.

'Put up ten words from the reading book each morning and the girls can copy them into spelling books while you mark the register. Take ten minutes later in the day to test the words you gave the day before.'

Whenever she paused, I said 'Yes' or 'No'.

'I'll come back after scripture and show you how to take arithmetic. On Mondays, scripture is always memory work — you'll find it in the record book there, — Psalm 137. Tell them to learn that. The monitors have put the Bibles out. On Tuesdays ... ' but a whistle blew outside, and Miss Ivinson hastened to the door at the end of the corridor, with me at her heels.

The children marched in twos through cloakrooms at either end of the corridor and halted there; marched to classroom doors and halted; marched into their rooms and sat two at each desk. The register was called, milk halfpennies gathered.

'A double line at the door,' snapped Miss Ivinson, and on the command 'Forward' the girls marched back into the corridor.

Three classes were tightly packed at each end, facing the centre, where, raised on a foot high stool, Miss Ivinson stood in command.

'Fair Waved the Golden Corn,' she announced, and the hymn was sung with little joy.

'I hope you've all had a nice holiday, and that you've come back ready to work. Hands together, eyes closed. Get your chins up. Let us pray.'

The smell of stale dust and warm human bodies swept over me. I gazed at the pale, cramped children obediently standing with eyes closed and hands clasped and heard 'Make us obedient and respectful to our parents, teachers and elders, kind towards our suffering fellow creatures, and earnest and sincere in doing our duty towards Thee...'

A steady tramping could be heard overhead as the six classes who had been praying in the corridor above marched back to their rooms. The younger children, in the bottom corridor, began the Lord's Prayer to a wandering, shapeless chant. I listened in a horrified trance. For the first time I felt as if in a prison.

'About turn! Forward.'

The children turned like well-drilled infantry and marched back to their rooms. I followed, and found the class standing politely until told to sit. Their faces were eager and expectant; and hair ribbons, red, pink and yellow brightened the dreary room.

I said 'Open your Bibles at Psalm 137,' and opened my own. It had not occurred to me to take a Bible into the corridor for a peep at Psalm 137 during prayers, so I had no more inkling than the children of what was to come.

By the waters of Babylon we sat down and wept...

Two weeks later I might have dared to catch someone's eye and laugh. As it was, I was stunned. How could I say 'Learn that' without a word of explanation? The mental paralysis, dreaded for the past six weeks, had struck. Who had enslaved the Jews — Persians, Egyptians, or Assyrians? Where were the Jews anyway? Would I dare to draw a sketch map on the board? But if I turned my back, the expectant hush would surely end. I would have to say something quickly, one girl was already dipping pencils in her ink. But what? How long did the Captivity last? I could not even remember in which century it had occurred. For a horrible moment, if I could have escaped from that classroom to become a poultry girl I would have gone. Then I remembered the anthem that I had heard my father's

choir sing: Coleridge-Taylor's setting of *The Waters of Babylon*.
I plunged into talk. Captivity, homesickness, the songs of exile of
Irish, Negroes and Jews, and the story of the young Coleridge-Taylor. It
was incoherent scripture talk, but the girls listened. What was more, they
looked entranced. They answered questions which showed that at least
they understood the drift of what I said. It *was* possible to teach a strange
class after all. The twenty minutes that had loomed ahead so terrifyingly
at 9.10 slipped away, and we applied ourselves to the business of learning
only just in time. On the stroke of 9.30, when Miss Ivinson reappeared
outside the glass door, the children sat, earnest and absorbed, chanting the
verses antiphonally.

Months later, I discovered that no established teacher ever 'taught' in
that Monday morning memory period. The children sat, muttering their
verses, while the teacher attended to the milk and dinner money, attendance slips and other Monday morning chores. The attention accorded my
impromptu lesson was due to relief from the boredom of tradition. I still had
everything to learn, the hard way, but momentarily life seemed fair enough.
I had a class of my own. I had taken a lesson, without preparation, and it
had gone well. Perhaps, subconsciously, I half expected Miss Ivinson to
walk in and say, 'You've made a splendid start,' as our college lecturers had
been wont to do.

But Miss Ivinson was the right Head to put a sharp end to daydreams.
She strode to the desk.

'Fold — your — ARMS!'

She stared at the girls, counting them, as I learned later, but I thought
it a form of disciplinary hypnotism at the time. She took a pen, entered the
number of children present — fifty-four — and closed the register. It was
a solemn rite. Registers, as I was to learn through much tribulation, were
the most important documents in state schools. The children watched. How
well they understood each other, the Headmistress and my new tribe. Like
well-bred dogs they gazed into each other's eyes, alert but silent. They had
a private code, too, for in a moment signals passed between them which
meant nothing to me.

'Hands on heads. Books FRONT.'

With a convulsive movement every child turned back, forward, back,
forward, back, forward — and fifty-four Bibles lay in nine, neat piles on the
front desks.

'Monitors,' said Miss Ivinson, and the two serious, silent, girls put the
Bibles into the cupboard and went back to their desks. Scripture was over.

'Multiplication of decimals,' said Miss Ivinson. 'Eyes FRONT.'

After working several examples on the blackboard, the class was set
to work on an exercise, and handed over to me. From then on, throughout

the time I taught in elementary schools, I 'taught' maths, and that was all the instruction as a teacher of mathematics I ever had, other than what I read in books.

The first day, as I went round marking, I was impressed most by the neatness and carefulness of the work. When, after break, the top class came to my room for a history lesson of eighty-five minutes, the impression was reinforced. I deduced only that the girls, like myself, were weighing up form.

Amid all the hours I had spent wondering how to manage those first days in a strange classroom, I had not spent two seconds thinking of, or preparing for, my first venture in among the staff. The only advice we ever had from our education tutors was 'Be sure not to take the best armchair in the staff-room.' They need not have worried. Armchairs were then unheard of in senior secondary schools.

At Washington Road two dingy, low-ceilinged cloakrooms, at turnings on the stairs, were officially designated staffrooms. They were little more than outsize cupboards, each with a small window high in the wall, each furnished with one kitchen table and five wooden chairs. Yet ten teachers with hats, bags, coats and umbrellas plus their entire school accoutrements were housed in each room. In both rooms, the door opened immediately upon the fireplace, making it impossible to gather round the tiny fire, while in the lower room, where I found myself, there was a gas cooker to add to the clutter. Ten of us stayed at school for dinner, five upstairs and five down, and all the frying was done downstairs, so that by 12.30 the atmosphere was unbearable with tea, stale bacon fumes, and cigarette smoke. The old hands seemed in no way put out by this and sat on after lunch, knitting and chatting, keeping up appearances, in truly English style.

At one o'clock there was a stampede. The kettle was put on for washing-up (there was no hot water). Piles of arithmetic books appeared on the table among hastily stacked plates, and the mirror beside the cooker was in great demand. We jostled one another at every turn and, in the minute table space left for washing-up, progress was so slow that even scalding water became cold and greasy before the pans were done. Suddenly the door opened to admit three more teachers, all large, to whom introductions were made through the haze. The first, stout and important, was Miss Olroyd, second mistress. Panting from the ascent of the stairs, she sat down before taking off her toque, black coat and button boots.

Between her and the door were squeezed Miss Harrison, who looked sad and sallow, in heavy, horn-rimmed glasses, and Miss Charlesworth, of whom all we could see was a rosy face peeping out of an enormous fur coat.

Miss Harrison said: 'Afternoon ladies. Nice weather for the time of year,' and sat down, with a cigarette, almost on top of the fire. Miss Charlesworth's friends dived upon the fur coat with squeals of admiration, and Miss Olroyd unrolled her paper and began to give me the headlines. She seemed chatty and friendly and I wondered why the rest took no notice of her. They told me afterwards it was because she was 'a wicked gossip,' but her tongue hardly seemed appreciably more bitter than the rest. Like other Scottish teachers who have taught south of the Border for many years, she tried her companion's patience by constant reference to the superiority of the Scot. In education, road construction, local government and administration of the law, England still had everything to learn. These things apart, however, Miss Olroyd thought the British (with the exception of most of the children of our school and all their parents) good, and everyone else bad. Spaniards were lazy, French frivolous, Italians shifty and Russians — well, after all, what could you expect of them? How or why Miss Olroyd taught geography, I never understood.

It took a while to get the rest of the staff of twenty placed, as we never met in one room. There were two other newcomers besides myself, but they never seemed in doubt or confusion as I persistently did. They were from the same training college, bound together by their reminiscences of college lecturers and their interest in each other's young men, mutually congratu-latory and supportive. Miss Ivinson trusted that they had been taught how to teach: she had no such hopes or illusions about myself. It was not, as I discovered later, that she disliked graduates as such. She had four others on her staff and obviously trusted them. But they had had five years of her guidance and that made all the difference. I had none.

I was raw in every sense. Not only had I made the error of arriving at Washington Road with no practical experience, I had not even been a pupil in the kind of school in which I now aspired to teach. I was so over-anxious to fit into this community that I was on edge all day. Accustomed as I had been all my life to attentive listening, I heard every shade and inflection in every voice in the staffroom and imagined criticism where, I think now, there was none but the experienced teacher 'voice'. I simply did not understand this 'status' tone. I liked my fifty-four children, and thought they were good, lively and intelligent. But no 'real teacher' referred to pupils except in a derogatory way, '*that* Alice Mather,' '*that* Mavis of yours'.

The more self confident the teacher, the more she liked to show her disdain of the dross with which she had to work. Miss Pringle, for example, who took my class for science while I took hers for citizenship, was never tired of telling me what she thought of my 'brats'. To my over-strained ears, it was entirely due to my incompetence that they were 'brats'.

Then there was the shade of Bertha, the teacher whom I had replaced.

Evidence of Bertha's talents sprang up on every side. Her discipline, speed of marking and general efficiency were enlarged upon by her former colleagues every dinner time. I sat, dumb and disheartened, jealous for the first time in my life — and of someone I had never met: she obsessed and haunted me for months.

So I made heavy weather of staff-room conversation, always looking for inner meanings and symbolism, as if listening to a very modern play.

'Pass that pan Nancy, I may as well scramble this egg. I can't face a fry after the hour I've spent with those pestilential VA kids.'

'Say, are you seeing George tonight, Nellie?'

'No, I've promised Ken. The Roxy, half-eight. You seeing Fred?'

There was a charmed circle from which I was irrevocably excluded because I had no boyfriend. It turned out, as so often in education, that I was only a late developer. But it seemed a barrier at the time.

Of course one is appointed to a school to teach, not to sit talking in the staffroom. But in the early days, a teacher may spend six and a half hours a day actually in her room, isolated from other adults. And so great is the need, at all ages, for contact with one's contemporaries that it may not be uncommon to be, as I was, as powerfully affected by new colleagues as by the pupils, who seemed, in comparison, docile, affectionate and blessedly easy to live with.

Miss Pringle, as official gym mistress, had a bossy manner and in the staffroom alternated between spells of radiant garrulity and sulks so profound that everyone present was plunged in gloom. She was one of those common products of girls' grammar schools of the Thirties — athletes who reached their mid-twenties still unable to decide to which sex they belonged. In her role of gym and science mistress, Miss Pringle saw herself as the man of the staff: efficient; thorough; brusque. She dressed in appropriate costume, very short, and trained her big girls to watch every item of games equipment like retriever dogs. Even small balls, hoops and bean bags were kept in Miss Pringle's private cupboard, and if physical education stock was returned short by as much as one team band, Miss Pringle's monitors stood over the delinquent class and teacher like storm-troopers till the missing object was found. It was an unnerving experience.

The task of forming a school netball team was handed to me by Miss Ivinson in my first week. The ball, however, was still kept under lock and key in Miss Pringle's room. When I kept girls back for practice after school, the ball had to be put temporarily into my cupboard at the end of play, as the games cupboards were all locked.

At 8.55 the next morning, the time of the gathering of milk halfpennies, Annie, the fiercest storm-trooper, would stride into my room, push her way through my pygmies,who were lining up at the door for prayers, and announce hectoringly to me 'Miss Pringle wants her netball.'

'Well, suppose you say 'please', ' I would counter, wondering how to cultivate a Colonel-in-Chief voice myself.

As I was almost equally terrified of Annie and her mistress, there was no question of not handing over the ball. Still, after a few days, Annie substituted 'Miss Pringle says please may she have the netball,' and I felt that if I was routed, at least I had waved my flag. Annie was, in reality, a brawny but harmless girl. I had let myself be intimidated by her flash hair-slides, loud voice and fancy blouse. Young teachers are often ridiculously sensitive to the opinions of the older girls, making for themselves ordeals that exist only in their own imagination. I imagined Annie's silly giggle was laughter at the way I conducted class business, but probably it was only the expression of her own gaucherie. After a year or two's teaching, it is hard to remember just how frightened we all were, at first, not only of the big girls, but of the experienced staff.

I was terrified also by the prominence given to needlework which was treated as if it were the Holy Communion of the school.

Each class had two long afternoon lessons a week, and extra time was often taken towards the end of term. Garments were made to be worn: knickers and petticoats in standard V, dresses in standards VI and VII. In the making of all these, crossway strips had to be put on, and my introduction to needlework was a demonstration lesson on this process, given on my first afternoon in school by Miss Ivinson, ostensibly to my children but in reality to me.

Miss Ivinson could rarely have had so unpromising a learner-teacher. I knew needlework solely from recollection of high school lessons: half torture, half mockery; a time for chat, badinage and idling while the teacher was taken up with others; pricked fingers and tedious fidgeting with ugly, bulging seams, on the rare occasions when she bothered with my work. Neither I nor any of my friends had ever produced at school a garment that could be worn. What we made was the cause of laughter among ourselves and inward shame when taken home. But at Washington Road, needlework had to be efficiently and deftly done, with results that could be displayed with pride. So, Miss Ivinson's instructions to my class were curt and clear. She moved up and down the narrow gangways, checking and encouraging, and her results were a revelation to me.

Years of training in junior schools had accustomed these pupils to work to command. Their deft fingers, their concentration, their neat small stitches were such as, in twenty years, I had never aspired to, much less attained. This quiet, this working to instruction, this corporate discipline were all foreign to the idea of teaching I had gleaned from my reading about progressive schools. I had heard scarcely a good word for 'class instruction' yet here it was successfully in operation. Personally I never found some of the things I was made to teach wholly necessary to salvation — run and fell seams done by hand, for example. There are short-cuts that should be taught. But there is a craftsman's attitude of mind, a longing to do things well and competently, that brings lasting satisfaction. The 'play way' in needlework, as I knew it myself in high school, led to nothing but boredom, while the opposite, rigorous attention to every bar of work as at Washington Road led to a high degree of capable and confident performance. Mentally, one of the disturbing aspects of my first term of teaching was the discovery that, contrary to all we had been taught, some degree of old-fashioned practice turned out to be useful, not despicable and what is more, a sound foundation for the ideals of individual development in which I had myself been nurtured.

This I discovered over the months. In that first term my lessons fell far short of the standard set by Miss Ivinson. I wanted that absorbed and busy hush, and somehow I was going to get it. It was the very atmosphere of the university library that I loved so much. But could I keep 108 hands busy once the garments were begun? Answer, I could not. I stayed in school after 4.00 every night for three weeks till we had cut out the last knicker leg and every child had work. But even so, I could never arrange that thirty of the fifty might not need help and guidance at once. Chatter and scrimmage reigned.

Children can live on a diet of needles. At the end of every lesson fifty-four were placed carefully in fifty-four bits of work, stowed away in work bags, which were then packed in the needlework basket. Ceremoniously, at the end of each lesson, the basket was locked before my eyes. Invariably, at the start of the next , ten girls would be without a needle! Of all forms of 'sacred stock', needles came top.

We could only go to Miss Ivinson for stock on a Monday morning and even if needles were put on the list, I have known her issue only two. The contortions to which we were put over this problem defy description. The smallest and most appealing child would be sent out begging from class to class. 'Miss X says can she borrow a needle?' and much wit and cynicism went into the replies. Why it never occurred to me to buy ten dozen packets of needles, I shall never know.

Outsiders thinking, as I am sure they do occasionally think, of school, look upon the subjects of the curriculum as a grocery list — tea, sugar, pepper, cheese: modest things scarcely noticed till one goes to the cupboard to find it bare. But school is not a cupboard. No subject is part of a grocery list. Each has its music, colour, moods and style. I have never seen a teaching book that does anything like justice to the flavour of different subjects or to the emotions aroused by each when imaginatively taught.

When I heard on my first day at Washington Road that I had to teach needlework, I sighed, never guessing how closely teacher and pupils come to know each other in those hours. The giving of lessons on a subject we ourselves found tedious, at which we certainly never shone, is a salutary change. We can learn a great deal from our pupils. In hard times I always found it encouraging to hear a child say confidingly 'Look, Miss, this is how I do it to make it neat'.

Smiles all round, and a lasting strengthening of the pupil-teacher bond.

On the surface, all the work done in that school was authoritarian — though, as I was to learn, the best work went on underground; individual and unremarked. Every arithmetic lesson had to be preceded by ten minutes' mental drill. Questions were rapped out in a sergeant's voice and a forest of hands had to wave, instantly, to show a really well-taught class. I am not sure that I ever mastered all the quick methods and do not wonder that the slower children constantly got the various dodges mixed: call the pence pounds and subtract fifteen: add three nothings and divide by eight: multiply by seven and convert to bushels and pecks, whichever inspiration of the moment might suggest.

Determined to encourage reasoning rather than memory work, I set my untried pupils to problems from my second day. After two weeks, the result was a set of books with a tapestry of crossings out, erasions and blots so horrifying to see, after the neat work that had gone before, that I resorted to tearing pages out. Needless to say, I was caught in the act. No thief can be more embarrassed by the concealment of his booty than an inexperienced teacher trying to cover the tracks of incompetence.

Though formal methods were universal in arithmetic there was great variety of method among the different teachers in other subjects. Miss Olroyd, geography, taught lists of capital towns, rivers and chief commodities. These were copied from the board and learnt. Miss Harriman, who had attended courses on The New Art, applied the modern methods very quaintly, sitting immobile at her desk and howling abuse at the terrified juvenile creators. Mrs Frazer, who had returned to teaching after eighteen years of hectic married life during which she had produced six children, took several forms for literature putting the zeal of a proselyte and the practical sense of her copious motherhood into every word she spoke.

Sometimes I overtook this Mrs Frazer on the way home. Her husband had died unexpectedly, leaving her with her six sons, the youngest a baby of thirteen months and the eldest still at the grammar school. She was stout, grey haired and often struggling to keep the family clothed and fed, yet she laughed and joked and spoke with such loving sympathy of her backward VIIC girls, that one would have thought she had no cares. Unfortunately I never saw her *in* school as her classroom was on the top corridor and she used the upstairs staffroom for lunch.

To get away from the horrible smell of frying in our staffroom I occasionally took a quick walk down to the river, to catch the Walker ferry or the children at play on Fisher Hill. It haunted and fascinated me, that part of the river, with all the life of the shipyards of which I really knew so little.

In childhood, it was the Tyne of folk song and old prints that had played so large a part in our lives. It was the pastoral stretches of the river that we had visited at weekends, and the sources of Tyne, Rede and Coquet in the wild Cheviot hills, that we had sought on holiday. Neither at home nor at school had we ever learned how coal, iron, steel and shipbuilding had made the river what it was. I knew that if the history I taught at Washington Road was to have strong local roots, it should start from, and account for, this industrial life that the children knew, not ignore it as my high school history had done. Yet the syllabus I had to work on, drawn up by my predecessor, was a scheme so unimaginative that it was hardly possible to believe a history graduate had written it at all. Each year's work was divided into three chunks, each chunk into fifteen or twenty disconnected parts. Any pupil who worked through three full years would have three sets of historical Meccano, but no notion of how any of the pieces fitted together to make our own society.

As we walked, Dorothy and I talked about this problem. The history we were supposed to teach was irrelevant to the children's lives. We let off much more than indignation about history syllabuses, particularly on the road home. We were two angry young women in those days. We had cause to be. We were seeing daily social conditions as bad as that described in parts of Rowntree's study of housing in York, written forty years before.*

Disheartened by what seemed a total lack of progress in school, I fell into a mood of despondency unlike any brief gloom known before. I could not laugh spontaneously; could not loose a nagging tone of voice. After exhausting days, it was beyond endurance to sit at night preparing lessons, but if I did not prepare, the result would be abysmal. The syllabuses were archaic, the text books a bore; the pictures with which I had gaily brightened the classroom in my first days now looked garish and infantile. Worse, it seemed I was a constant irritation to my Headmistress, something she strove daily to put right.

In this despairing mood, I set off one night to explore a part of the

---

* *Poverty* (1897-8) 28 per cent of the population fell below a minimum income

riverside beyond school where I had never been before. For nearly three hours I walked, through mile after mile of smoke-blackened houses, with old tin cans and broken fences and here and there a shapeless heap of rubble: weary women still in curlers; bare-legged children playing with a shovel or scratching the derelict heaps for coal; bedraggled cats, broken window panes, a lorry piled with carcasses coming from the slaughter house. Neptune Road, Buddle Road; ales, wines and spirits, mild and bitter.

Turning a corner by an empty, boarded up shop, I came suddenly upon the first new building I had seen that day. The stone was clean and light, the paint shining. In green capitals a foot high were the words 'Urban District Council Mortuary.'

Beside the river I watched the gulls wheeling in the leaden sky, and lingered beside a dreary stretch of grass. Most of the children were indoors. A scream came from a window close at hand, a slap, a wail, and then a woman's rasping voice 'Get yer hand oot o' thi dish and stop yer bloody clart. What's the marrer wi' ye ?' rising to a screech 'What is the marrer wi' ye. Aa say?'

I got into a bus and went home.

The next day was Wednesday of my fourth week. By this time my head was almost permanently sideways on my neck through apprehensive watching for Miss Ivinson's approach. She looked in every day, often several times, and no matter what the lesson, or how still the class, there was always *something* that should have been done some other way. On this Wednesday, the girls were writing their weekly compositions, models of industry and concentration, when Miss Ivinson appeared. For once, I thought, there can be nothing wrong, and she smiled, wearily but unmistakably as she came across the room. She began her customary walk round the class, looking at the children's work.

'What's that?' she said to one girl, pointing at her book, 'And what's that, may I enquire?'

The girls fidgeted and turned red but said nothing. Miss Ivinson looked at the two girls behind, gave a snort of disgust and came back to me. The children, copying a habit of mine, were writing '&' in their composition books — a lazy, slipshod practice that threatened the moral fibre of the school!

The day turned cold and blustery. For the last period of Wednesday afternoon, my class and I were due to turn outside for games. I took balls and team bands, instinctively pronouncing the first law of motion, 'A Double Line at the Door'.

'The gym's empty, Miss Dunn,' said Sadie, my busybody, a sandy ferret-faced child, first cousin to Squirrel Nutkin.

Any normal day, I would have been sufficiently wary of Sadie to reflect that since there were fourteen classes, each with two periods of physical education and one dancing a week, at no time could the gym be officially unoccupied. But I dreaded this half hour in the school yard, on the public highway, more than any other lesson in the week, and when a cloud of gritty dust swirled I snatched at Sadie's straw and called 'Lead on — to the gym'.

The gym was in the domestic science and woodwork block, separate from the main school. Not one piece of apparatus of any sort, fixed or portable, spoilt the purity of its line; but those green colour- washed walls, with windows six clear feet above eye level, formed a paradise of privacy.

I flattered myself I had got my fifty-four busy with a minimum of fuss, and was jumping about among them at their four separate ball games, coaching and encouraging, when an awed silence fell. The child to whom I had thrown a ball, dropped it, looking apprehensively beyond me, and I turned. Miss Pringle stood there, glowering, with her double line at the door.

'MY period' she said, icily. 'The gym is never free for games.'

My class got back into their jerseys and outdoor shoes without a word, and we trailed out, ignominiously. For the next week, I was invisible to Miss Pringle.

The same could not, unfortunately, be said of our Headmistress. Miss Ivinson watched over me day by day and appeared in nightmares by night. She corrected and admonished me, took in the children's books when I had marked them and supervised every garment that my children cut out. She was determined that a raw girl should not waste one of her best classes, and equally determined that the raw girl should become a competent teacher if mortal vigilance could make her so. Unfortunately, I did not understand this then. I concluded that she looked in at me so often because I was so bad. I made mistakes with the milk money, lost my keys, and almost brought about the resignation of the caretaker by asking if he had put out my autumn leaves. I did not make the children use their thimbles, left spelling mistakes uncorrected, but worst, by far, I forgot to close the register.

In the morning it was done at 9.30, at the end of scripture, and before arithmetic, so that it was relatively easy to remember. However, in the afternoon it had to be done at 1.45, in the middle of a lesson, and I constantly forgot. Shortly before 4.00, Miss Ivinson would come in and discover my lapse. Banging on the desk she would scream 'You'll lose your certificate! You'll lose your certificate'. Night after night I dreamt of registers in a state of irreparable confusion and raging inspectors striking me off the roll.

It was a hard probation. I grew thin and harassed, but I learned. I had got by very comfortably for twelve years with bad spelling and forgetful ways because of various other attributes, but I learned under Miss Ivinson, that bad ways can be changed — at least partially — at any age.

We owed more to Miss Ivinson than we realised at the time. Like good teachers in whatever art, she wanted perfection, and put her students through a drilling that tested every muscle and every faculty of mind. Teaching was not, for her, a profession that one drifted into because of 'liking children'. It had its rules, strict and numerous as the classical rules of harmony. It was useless saying to Miss Ivinson 'I forgot'. She simply said 'Then don't forget'.

When I think about that first term now, I recall a story told by John Ireland of his training when a boy. During a lesson at the Royal Academy of Music he made one mistake in a Beethoven Sonata several times.

'Go home, practise that passage for three hours, and then come back to me,' thundered his master.

That was the spirit of Miss Ivinson's teacher-training, too. But nobody, in my young days, ever drew for teachers the parallel with training in other arts. I had realised, naturally, as a student, that there was 'a lot to learn' but had imagined it all lay somewhere ahead of me. I had not bargained for having to go back to kindergarten days, to re-think each step of my own learning if I wanted to understand children's difficulties. Miss Ivinson did not put her lessons in this form. Her psychology was not learnt from books. Her knowledge was all clinical. Before she could trust me as a teacher I had to learn to spell, to write on the blackboard, to cure forgetfulness, to do quarterly returns. And, since it was easier to get these right the first time than to spend three days finding the mistake, I had to learn to keep the register correctly day by day. I went back to the infant school.

And the children? Fifty-four of them. Mary Algar, Mary Atkinson, Joan Bell, Winifred Bolton, Marjorie Bosomworth, Eileen Bramwell... The odd thing was that my forgetfulness seemed to put them on my side. It was as if, having recognised a fellow erring mortal, they had all silently agreed to hide my worst sins. Monitors gave out the right books for lessons, knew where to get atlases, song books, netballs. The first monitors were a legacy from the past, quiet conscientious girls who had held office perhaps all through junior school. They forgot nothing, dropped nothing, spilled no ink, trod on no chalk. They were always clean, always in time, and, like sober, middle-aged matrons, they tried to keep the strange new housewife to the accepted ways.

Three more weeks passed, and many a prayer of thanks I breathed for the unobtrusive efficiency of these permanent civil servants. I was marking books one afternoon long after four when I noticed that they were still whispering together by the board.

'Please can we have these?' one said, indicating the discarded ends of coloured chalk.

'Whatever for?'

'Just to play 'hitchie' with.'

They were neither as old nor as stately as I had supposed. I handed over the spoil, and they went off gloating.

After that I changed monitors every two weeks. It was perhaps the biggest effort of that term, for when, to my incompetence, was added the slow, fussy, fiddling or talkative ways of each new pair of monitors, confusion was added to the ever-present anxiety. But it was perhaps one of the few good things I did in my first year, all the same. Monitors in elementary schools had real responsibility. They had much to remember, and a good deal, under supervision, to prepare. When every girl is given a turn, it is soon clear that there are few, if any, who cannot be coaxed into displaying dependability and leadership, often supposed to be the prerogative of a privileged few. To watch a flighty, untidy girl take herself in hand because she is a monitor is one of the more restful and entertaining aspects of teaching.

As the weeks passed my hatred for our building, and the system which condemned children to such buildings, grew. I began to feel like Johnson's Dear Bathurst, a very good hater. I hated the smell, the walls, the desks. I hated the barren uniformity upstairs and down; the dingy stone corridors and wilting aspidistras; the stench from the lavatories; the iron railings round the school yard. Most of all I hated the teacher's room and the disgusting washing-up water. In fact I hated everything connected with school except the people in it. The loyalty of fifty-four children to me, and mine to them, had grown faster than any hate. In a strange way, which I could not explain to myself, I could no longer be objective about the 'system': I was part of it. I began to see something that underlay the pushing, slapping, shouting and nagging, and that was an extraordinary depth of affection.

While waiting outside the Headmistress's door one lunchtime, for needlework material, I heard her talking to a tall, awkward girl of mine, who, perhaps because of her ungainly development, always appeared sullen and usually slow. That very morning, Miss Ivinson, had been shouting in exasperation at this child.

'Get yourself awake girl. Seven nines I say? Are you going to sit dozing all day?'

Yet there was Patsy, not two hours later, talking to her Headmistress as to an elder sister, and, what was more, talking without hesitation, as she had never done to me.

I went as usual to the staffroom for lunch. Only Miss Lawson was there. The others had gone to town to celebrate pay day. Apart from odd moments in the corridor, it was the first time I had spoken to Miss Lawson alone. She was an English graduate, small, quiet, very reserved. Perhaps she sensed my gloom.

'It's paradise here to the school I started in,' she said consolingly. 'In that place we had no staffroom at all. We used the Headmaster's room and it was smaller than this, and had no water. There were two classes in each room. I shared with a man the Headmaster politely called 'an inebriate': ex-officer, ex-scholar, too, I suppose. He was certainly a well-read man, particularly edifying when drunk.'

We talked in a desultory way, nevertheless it was memorable. It was the first time I had had a part in staffroom conversation. For half-an-hour I was of the Inner Circle, and the rest of the day went by on wings.

My good spirits lasted forty-eight hours. Next day, when Miss Ivinson took her customary walk round the classroom during arithmetic, I felt proud of my fifty-four. Every head was bent in studious attention to simple interest. When even Audrey Graham, who was erratic and myopic, was commended for the careful start in her new book, I felt that good fortune had again taken us all under her wing.

'A spelling book, please,' said Miss Ivinson. 'I shall give them a spelling examination tomorrow.'

I was undisturbed: I had put eight or ten words on the blackboard every morning, and, as I had been careful not to cheat by putting up the same word twice, the children must have had something like 500 words during the term. I had tested the words, as instructed, allowing the children always to mark their own work and a good part of the ten minutes had been spent each day in making sure that they knew the meaning of the words. My conscience was easy.

The test was given: forty words, and from what I could see of the papers from the front, the writing at least looked creditably neat.

The next day Miss Ivinson greeted me with a frozen 'Good morning' as I signed the time book. Immediately scripture was over, before we could start our arithmetic, she strode into the room, the sheaf of examination papers in her hand.

'Every girl — desk clear. Hands behind backs. Sit straight. Attend.'

There was a deathly stillness. Very slowly, weighing every word, Miss Ivinson began her diatribe.

Never, NEVER, in the whole course of her teaching career had she witnessed such a disgraceful set of papers: the average mistake was nine out of forty. Nine. NINE. NINE. It was incredible. Unthinkable. Unbelievable. It was worse than anything ever done in any junior school. Not one girl would pass her Scholarship Exam. Not one was worth bothering with. The onslaught lasted until break at 10.45. Long before then, half the children were in tears. The strap had been sent for — though not actually used. I might have been in tears myself but for my own unshakeable belief that nine mistakes out of forty words chosen at random from over 500, was not bad. It seemed to me an honest and reasonable result. However, it was clear that something different was expected.

Miss Ivinson's parting shot as she left the room was 'You're not a speller yourself, are you?'

I started my reform campaign that day, a late convert, but a zealous one. In time, I learnt that experienced teachers only put up new words two or three times a week, and revised on the other days; that when exam time drew near, they held several minor inquisitions before Miss Ivinson conducted her own; and that they wasted no time on teaching the meaning of the words. We improved a little on that system. I paired them off, a good speller with a bad one, and they taught each other, very efficiently, which made them and me wiser and more responsible.

After that exam, our average class mistake never rose above one-and-a-half out of forty words, a result which seems to me obviously faked by preparation. But it kept the peace. To have even a degree of freedom in history, English language and literature was ample compensation for driving myself and fifty others to spell.

But my graduation as Bachelor of spelling was in the distant future. The day of wrath was not yet over, and humiliations never come singly. On needlework afternoons, monitors came early to unlock the basket and give out the work. On this day of disaster, my keys could not be found. Upstairs, downstairs, in class and cloakrooms we searched in mounting frenzy. Nothing. 1.20 had come and gone. At 1.29 precisely, Miss Ivinson would look through corridor windows and expect to see 329 children intent upon their tasks or she would know the reason why. She knew the timetable too. With one empty bobbin, three pearl buttons, a card of knicker elastic and 108 neatly-folded hands, could I hope to give the impression of a well-run sewing room?

'Send to the Woodwork, Miss' was the advice of my irrepressible Sadie, 'Mr Naylor will open it.' It seemed the only chance.

At 1.27, an elderly, grey haired man strolled down the corridor with an infuriating calm, slow, step. He took one glance at the basket, then turned and gave me a withering stare.

'More ways of killing a cat than drowning it in cream' he said, making two swift cuts with his pen knife.

The basket lid had no hinges and was tied on with a piece of string. For twelve weeks we had mounted guard over that basket, locking and unlocking it as if it contained the Lindisfarne Gospels. Not one of us had noticed that a marauder could have undone the string at any time.

I tell this foolish little story because it is typical of my first year of teaching. Shocked initially by the atmosphere of incarceration within the building, I had set out, above all else, to make learning freely available for all my class. My happy, if bemused, children must have thought they had stepped 'through the looking glass'. Day after day they were confronted with my 'inventions' and an endless succession of new ways of learning old things. This was enjoyable for us all, but it was not 'structured'. At least they began to see, however, that real learning continually led us on.

Not that this helped me in my Headmistress's eyes. In the teaching profession, esteem is given to the teacher who is 'sound', 'has good discipline', 'keeps her feet on the ground'. Every novice senses this, and I despaired. I really wanted my Headmistress to be pleased. Yet how could she ever be placated when what she had been allotted, instead of a 'sound teacher', was a female curiously resembling Lewis Carroll's White Knight. I felt that there was a connection between us, but at that time was too low in spirit to find it, or to see what hope might grow therefrom.

So I left school that wet December night in disgrace and disappointment. The following ten days of the Christmas holiday were the most despondent of my life. At night, sleepless, I saw with loathing every stick and stone in the school building and pictured years of incompetence and crabbed old age within its walls.

CHAPTER FOUR

Uphill all the way
'The craft so long to lerne'

That gloomy end to my first teaching term must have dashed Mother's high hope. True, we were back in Heaton, and the terraced flat was cheap; but it was awkwardly shaped and sunless, and try as we would to show Christmas spirit, despondency and bad colds hung over us all three.

From that profound depression we were extricated, on the last night of the holiday, by Beethoven's B flat major quartet, opus 130.

We had gone to spend the evening with friends, string players, who had often joined in chamber music in our old home. They had been given records of the first five movements of this great Beethoven quartet for Christmas, and wanted to share them with us. We sat round the fire and listened, playing the records again and again.

I had read so much of the profundity of these late quartets that I had imagined them all far beyond my understanding. It was a revelation, therefore, to find that the first four movements were in a language immediately recognisable. I was caught up, at least to the fringe of Beethoven's world, through years of devoted playing of English country dance tunes. And I do not think Beethoven, with his love of humour, would despise this juvenile approach.

When Beethoven wrote this quartet he was in fact ill, morose, and distraught with anxiety about his nephew. Yet regardless of sorrow he created music suffused with joy. What a poor broken-winded creature it must be in contrast who allowed herself to be crushed by four months' adversity in school.

Hardly had this thought registered before the music stopped abruptly, almost in the middle of a phrase and we were plunged into the *Cavatina*, the most profoundly tragic music I had ever heard. It seemed as if the experiences of a lifetime were concentrated in the music we listened to.

In bed that night themes from the several movements ran through my mind while conscious thoughts plodded round the same weary treadmill: what to do with my fifty-four children that would give *them* scope for freedom and initiative and yet satisfy the school standards of effort and control? And suddenly an answer came: we could dance. So next morning, at the start of the new term, I made record time to school to commit class and self to the experiment before there could be any retreat. Could I enter a team in the country dancing class for ten to twelve year olds in the North of England Musical Festival? Miss Ivinson was taken aback, but agreed — doubtfully.

'Well — as long as you're not bottom ... I suppose I don't mind.'

We had 'practices' as the children called them every day in the gym after four o'clock. Anyone who liked could come, and more than half my own class did, together with friends, all shapes and sizes. At first it was a kind of music and movement: a simple way of getting them to move with natural spontaneity to such music as we had for the gramophone. But after a few weeks Miss Lawson offered herself as pianist which gave much more scope: all those lovely tunes — *Jack's Maggot, Dick's Maggot, My Lady Cullen, Cheerily and Merrily, The Queen's Jig, Up with Aily, Love Neglected, Orleans Baffled, My Lady Foster's Delight* — these and many more they learned to love. Of course they did not learn the figures for all these dances, some of which are too difficult for their age. They learnt to *listen* to the music and move to it. About a month before the competition they learnt the set dances, and a team was chosen, but any one who wanted could still come, to join in or to watch.

When competition day came, Miss Ivinson saw us off with a frosty smile, for there was a teacher absent which meant she would have her class to deal with as well as mine. As we were going out of the door, however, her heart softened.

'I suppose it's a morning out for you, anyway,' she said, managing one of her rare but rewarding smiles.

The class began at ten o'clock and there were nearly forty entries, with ourselves well down the list, so it was nearly one o'clock before our turn. To my surprise, the months of training triumphed over the tedious wait, and they danced as children should, with lightness and gaiety. At least they had justified their presence.

When all schools had performed, our team and one other were asked to dance their 'own choice' again. Our girls had chosen *Piper's Fancy*, and to general applause they were pronounced first. The adjudicator, friend and collaborator of Cecil Sharp, Miss Maud Karpeles, spoke generously about them and presented not only the individual medals but a silver cup, given to the winner of the highest marks in their class and the one above.

The girls were stunned. Reporters took photographs and by 2.15pm we got away. When we reached Walker, I sent the girls home for dinner and went apprehensively and alone into school, carrying the cup in a heavy wooden case. I had prepared all the morning's work for my class, but had never dreamt of missing half the afternoon. The first lesson was sewing. Probably twenty children would have been discovered without thimbles; another dozen would have lost their needles, and the horrible hemming of the 'bottom section' of the class (which I had eventually allowed to pass, in despair of ever getting the garments finished) would have been revealed.

Through the corridor windows I could see my class sitting with straight backs, every head bent dutifully over a seam. Miss Ivinson sat in splendid isolation at the teacher's desk. I opened the door and felt immediately the frozen hush which denotes a recent storm. All my carefully rehearsed speeches evaporated. I could think only of hunger. I pushed the wooden box on to the desk, and Miss Ivinson snorted at it as if it were a bomb. I gave her the key and she opened the box. It was like a scene from a Chinese play, intense emotion conveyed without words by almost imperceptible movements of hands and eyes. The children gave a stifled 'O-o-oh' of delight when the cup was displayed. I think Miss Ivinson was pleased, since for the first and only time in my teaching career, horrible hemming was allowed to pass without comment. I was dispatched to the staffroom to make myself tea.

Dancing of this kind was a very partial answer to the problem of giving all children creative opportunities. They had free movement in the early months, but ultimately they had to dance the figures of the dance — and those I had to teach. Yet it gave to all a grace and freedom they had never had before. If Plato and Wordsworth are to be believed, our girls must have gained in equability and good-humour from the music we listened to — I know I did. Folk tunes are prophylactic with their beguiling freshness and amiability. Young and old, we *need* good-humour in life. I enjoy and admire modern dance movement and would love to have taken this in school. Nevertheless, with its emphasis on release for violence and aggression, I cannot but wonder if it satisfies children's needs for order and reasonableness as our old folk dances with their very lovely music did.

I watched the children who had been in the successful team closely for a good many weeks, and none seemed unduly cocky. They had all improved in oral self-expression, in co-operation with others in the classroom and above all in dependability. There was no doubt about the effect of their success on their self-confidence.

The biggest problem of a teaching life may well be the creation of conditions in which every pupil may achieve some modest personal success. A child's intellectual development is by no means the teacher's only concern, nor indeed her primary one. Loneliness and withdrawal is a more crippling condition than inability to spell.

The worst case of withdrawal I had was Edna, a stunted child, eleven years old but only three feet high. She had a big head with a heavy Hapsburg jaw, and pale, straight, dirty hair. When the class marched out, two by two, to sing or dance, she shuffled mournfully along alone, dragging her feet in big slippers. At playtime, she stood alone, clutching her books in a newspaper parcel. She rarely spoke voluntarily, replying if goaded into it, in husky monosyllables. She would sit quite silent throughout lessons, looking as wise as an old city counsellor, but comprehending little. Once, after a lesson on the Pilgrim Fathers, in which she appeared absorbed, I asked her what she had learnt, and in her husky whisper came the answer 'Drake'. But she adored writing and her books were a joy to see. She copied notes with the loving care of a monk transcribing Holy Writ. Every morning, no matter what the weather, she brought a bunch of flowers.

It was January, and lists were prepared for the Poor Children's Holiday Camp, and inquiries into home circumstances made.

'How many children under fourteen, Edna?'

'Nine.'

'Is your father working?'

'Yes, Miss Dunn.'

Most of the fathers in that school were caulkers and riveters, in the shipyards.

'What is he, Edna?'

'A grave-digger, Miss.'

Edna embroidered a tray cloth with infinite care. To her amazement and my delight, this was shown at a needlework exhibition at the local art gallery. Edna heard her patience and industry praised, first by the Headmistress, then by an HMI. Yet she still sat unmoved, and in the playground continued to stand alone. The other children seemed ready to make overtures of friendliness if only Edna would come half way. But she could not, or would not, and the tray cloth was not an object that appealed to schoolgirls sufficiently to break the barrier of reserve.

Edna became almost a favourite child. I racked my brains to think of ways to encourage her, to make her smile spontaneously.

Summer came and we were making dresses. Edna was so small that her length of material provided twice as much for her skirt as for anyone else. I decided to pleat it on all round, and lifted her up on my chair to try it, and get some idea of the effect. I was so busy with my mouth full of pins that I did not notice the stir and bustle, but looked up suddenly to find half the class surrounding us, gazing with rapturous envy at what they called 'Edna's Shirley Temple dress'. I looked at Edna's face and knew for the first time what Milton meant by 'wreathed smiles'. After that, though always quiet, Edna never returned to her total isolation and gloom.

Still convinced of the value of historical study, but sceptical of the value of traditional syllabuses and methods, I had been trying, tentatively, to find out about the teaching of history in other schools in Newcastle and Northumberland. Somehow, in my own college days, I had acquired a copy of *The New Era Teaching of History* produced in 1930 and dedicated to the League of Nations. For years it had been a source of encouragement. What others were doing to make history live in Brussels, Chicago and Connecticut, someone could do on Tyneside. But I could discover no schools within visiting distance where teachers were even working on progressive lines. At last, greatly daring, I wrote to our Director of Education to ask if any investigation had been made into the methods of history teaching in local schools, and if not, whether I would be allowed to ask other teachers for information about textbooks, and the use made of them.

I received no written reply, but shortly after was visited by the local HMI, Mr Gardiner, a fussy, small man, who had published a spelling book.

'Now Miss Dunn — yes, just set the girls some reading and let's have a little talk. What is it you really want to know? What is it you want of us? You've written a letter, quite a long letter. I have it here. I won't say I haven't read it, because that wouldn't be true. I have read it. But if you could just *tell* me what you want to know...'

I repeated the list of questions I had drawn up with such care — and as I had imagined, with precision.

'Well, Miss Dunn, nothing has ever been done that I'm aware of, nothing. Frankly, there has been very little interest in the subject. But how are you proposing to *make* these enquiries, Miss Dunn? I *hope* you're not going to ask us to let you go into our schools. I simply do not see how it could be arranged. Head teachers are so busy with this school feeding and one thing and another. Conditions are so far from normal. Frankly, Miss Dunn, you've chosen a *very* inconvenient time to do this research, a *very* inconvenient time — not that we wish you ill because of that. Of course if you care to ask *me* any questions, naturally I know all about what is done. Not that I'm an historian of course, but I have my own ideas on these subjects. Yes, I certainly have my own ideas ...'

I knew Mr Gardiner had never seen any one of the four history graduates at that time working in the Newcastle senior schools, so I felt some doubt as to his universal knowledge, but asked which textbooks were most used and if history teachers were satisfied with them.

'Well, really Miss Dunn! There is hardly a school in which the book is poor. Firth's books are a great help, especially the teacher's book. There is a need, you know, for a commentary — just as great a need as in scripture. There is a tendency for teachers to give nebulous opinions, 'history cum philosophy' some teachers call it. But I believe in facts, the more facts the better. Don't go trying to put ideas in people's heads. Now Miss Dunn, you're a good historian. How many houses were destroyed in the Great Fire? Ah ha! that's caught you. Where was Nelson born? You see you don't know. And you must remember, Miss Dunn, that ninety per cent of our teachers are not students of history at all. Many teachers have to hand on a very imperfect knowledge themselves ...'

I tried to get in that that was one of the main reasons why I wanted to see better books provided for their use in the classroom but Mr Gardiner swept on 'And do you know what the allowance for senior school apparatus is? Six shillings a *year* per child. Yes, with three and six in junior schools, and two and nine for infants. That does not allow much to be squandered on history books. No, Miss Dunn, I can't see you making any headway with your ideas — not that I want to discourage you. Don't think that for one moment. It is splendid to find young teachers taking an interest in their work. But perspective, Miss Dunn! Keep things in perspective You must face that, Miss Dunn, and after all, who hands history on?

'Dear me, can that be twelve o'clock already? How time flies! Well I'm glad to have heard all your ideas, Miss Dunn. Go on as you are doing. Yes, I'm sure everything will turn out very well.'

So I went on, like so many teachers, preparing lessons in the evenings, making large coloured pictures for the walls, cyclostyling parts of contemporary documents for the children to use; reading, marking, and filling spare seconds with O or A level coaching in latin and maths. This is the dreariest form of teaching known to man, only to be undertaken when a teacher's finances are tottering, as ours always were throughout those years.

A woman graduate, first class honours, was paid £180 annually (less than £3.50 a week) and this had to keep my mother, self and my young brother, in mid-career on his medical course at the university.

Already, two-and-a-half terms of my first teaching year had passed. In a desultory way I still talked with my friend about history on our journeys to school, but we raged less, and read scarcely at all. The pitfalls of needlework teaching were more obvious than the trials of history. By fair means or foul, fifty-four pairs of knickers had to be finished and paid for and fifty-four petticoats and dresses begun in the first week of the summer term. All through each play time and lunch hour, relays of children made petticoats and dress patterns and cut them out. I had barely adjusted myself to this life in which scripture and arithmetic alternated with brown paper patterns, huge, stiff torturing scissors, and mile upon mile of flowered print, and blue, pink and yellow cotton material called Sparva Spun, when my Headmistress asked me casually to draw up a new history syllabus for the school. I was faced with the intractable problem of choosing from the history of mankind, topics suitable for children who would have no formal 'history' after the age of fourteen.

For years I had distrusted the grammar school type of history, with its politically orientated textbooks and taking of notes. Political history is but a fraction of what the syllabus must contain if school-leavers are to get a hint of forms of power in the modern world. For children who will have no further education of a cultural kind, industrial development, big business, the application of science to agriculture, racial discrimination and the conquest of space are more important than the Wars of the Roses or even Charles I and his Parliaments. Yet vast, vague concepts are useless tools. How does one deal with these vital topics in a way at once homely and concrete, without simplifying to a point where they seem no more than latter-day witchcraft and fairy tales?

I spent hours in the university library and ransacked the teaching of history shelves. I pored over the 'new methods' and sampled other peoples' syllabuses by the gross. And still I was unsatisfied. While I went a long way with the progressive teachers, their schemes gave a view of the world that was demonstrably false. To make room for the new (social) history, they rightly left out much dull detail from the old. Of 'political history' the barest skeleton remained — and it consisted entirely of 'great' ages and 'great' men. The parts left out were the times of drift and muddle; the men ignored were the mediocre. Yet, is it not often in the time of those men who shift responsibility and prevaricate that the seeds of change, perhaps of disaster, are sown?

I spent several months, including most of the summer holiday, working on a four-year scheme of my own, and, though far from satisfied, looked forward to taking a class right through it. I had revised the one-year course of 'Citizenship', for the top two classes at the same time and having, by good fortune, secured the co-operation of the literature specialist, we were able to make considerable cross-reference between these three subjects. We hoped the fourteen year olds at least might catch a glimpse of knowledge as 'a seamless garment', and I began my second year in good heart.

But before three days were over, there was a new disturbance. I was in the gym one morning, with a third year class, working very rightly and properly through my 'table' as we did in those unenlightened days, when the door opened behind me and Miss Ivinson came in. It was a C class of lumpy, but docile and affectionate, maidens. I had taught them for the past year and liked them. They put such effort into their ponderous movements. Carried away by Miss Ivinson's presence, they finished the table with unprecedented rhythm and grace

'Very nice, girls,' she said with her rare smile, so that the girls simpered with delight.

There was an air of mutual compliment in their glances.

Miss Ivinson handed me a note.

It was a curt order from the Director of Education to report at the Western Grammar School the following day, to replace the senior history mistress who was ill.

'But I don't want to go,' I said like a fractious child. I was for telephoning the Office to ask if history was more truly history because it was to be taught at a grammar, instead of a secondary modern school. But that kind of sarcasm had no meaning for Miss Ivinson. She saw an opportunity for one of her teachers and she put that before abstract questions like the value of history teaching in different types of school. Perhaps too, she put compliance with the Office higher than I did. It was for my good. I would go. And I went, greatly enjoying it once there.

In its prime, the school building set, like Glasgow University, on a hill, had been a focal point among fine trees and houses, with a wide view over the rooftops of Scotswood to the blue haze of the river valley beyond. Through the years, Ryehill declined, and the school, hemmed in by shabby tenements, was taken over by the local authority to be the girls' grammar school for the western end of town. Though shabby and greatly over-crowded at the time when I was there, it had an air of faded magnificence still, compared with the barrack-like uniformity of our own old-time Board school. It was the school where I had done my 'long school practice' as a student, and so a return to good friends.

At first, the work was mentally a change and physically a rest, but after a while I began to feel slightly, very slightly, bored. The return to a grammar school teaching diet of unrelieved English and history was dull. Provided a teacher knows and loves the work he is trying to teach (and I did)

there seemed, at that time, little that could go wrong in a grammar school. (This would be quite untrue now.)

The junior forms were a joy to teach. I wrote a play about Raleigh for them, taking the words, so far as possible, from genuine 'sources of history' — from the State trials, Raleigh's letters to his wife, and other contemporary writings. It would have been far better for us to write the play together, but those rare old books could not be taken from the library and the work had to be done there alone, at night. Nevertheless the girls themselves did some honest research into early seventeenth century manners, dress, music and politics before they could produce the play. Knowing nothing, any of us, at that time about play production, we had our work cut out to make the play move. Most of the girls stood, stock still, centre stage and delivered their lines as if reeling off their mother's grocery order to a deaf assistant. The struggle to get them to move and speak unselfconsciously was unremitting, and hardly a spectacular success in the end. We all know, now, how absurd it was to bulldoze into 'acting' this way. If that time could come again! Despite only two periods a week of history to work in, we still might have come at it all more freely and spontaneously if we had started from the Elizabethan masques. To have devised some simple pageant, and acted it in masks themselves, might have helped these very inhibited girls to some measure of spontaneity. But alas, Elizabethan theatre 'was not in the syllabus'; Raleigh was, and in those days I still did as I was told.

At least we tried to make our given period seem real. In performance, two girls did give the play validity. The one who played Raleigh was quiet, sallow-skinned, with close cropped dark hair, big glasses and a superb voice. Glasses apart, she was a Paul Robeson in miniature, with a consuming passion for the study of the past that I had not met before in a child. Yet she was in the C stream of that school and her work in other subjects uninspired.

She read and re-read the articles and books about Raleigh that I brought to school until, instinctively, as it seemed, she put into her performance something of the strength of mind and restraint that she had perceived in his character. The other girl had an enthusiasm for acting so great that she was prepared to be, not merely to mouth the phrases of, that fierce and arrogant bully, Sir Edward Coke. Pointing at Raleigh, she declared with hissing venom

'It was he I say, that viper with the fertile brain, who made the plot to seize His Majesty. Thou viper, thou traitor. Thou has a Spanish heart and thou thyself art a spider of hell.'

And slowly, with a control and dignity very moving to watch, Raleigh answered

'It becometh not a man of quality and virtue to call me so, but I take comfort in it, it is all you can do.'

To a degree that is rare in school productions, these two girls portrayed character, not merely a succession of incidents.

Apart from the initial class reading, the play was produced in out-of-school hours, but no one could question the benefit of these informal activities for both teacher and taught. The formal class lesson, teacher's talk, questioning and summing up made by dictating notes, can never bring out the patience, resourcefulness and good sense that children show when they work on their own or in groups.

But the older forms had examinations to pass. It was the necessity for so much formal teaching with the older forms that disheartened me in grammar school work. I believe with my whole heart in activity methods. No power on earth can force a child to learn if the initial impulse is not there.

Whanne the disciple wole not here
It is but veyn on him to swinke
That on his lerning wol not thinke ... *

And for adolescents, the incentive to learning does not come through lecturing.

With grammar school classes of thirty instead of fifty, it should have been easier to have all sharing actively in lessons, yet it was not so. With these older girls, I was constrained to talk and give notes far too much, because that was what they were accustomed to. A high proportion of the abler girls took up teaching, and the results of public examinations were of supreme importance to them. As a substitute teacher, I could not switch them to a term of unorthodox methods without clear authority to do so — and it was useless to seek that for a matter of months. I remembered many of the girls from School Practice days, and, save for two or three in VC, they not only wanted to memorise but could and did. They were polite, docile, and in the main, attentive. What more could any teacher expect or want?

I suppose I wanted the mutual understanding and confidence that existed at Washington Road. There, not only could I find out something of each child's general background, her illnesses, home life and father's work, but I was free to use, in my history teaching, the methods that seemed natural to me, and right psychologically.

At the grammar school, I knew the big girls only as dolls, and from the neck up: rows of decorous faces, stuck on to rows of navy bodies and white arms.

Yet something goes on in those dolls' heads, bent dutifully over the yawning pages of notebooks. I did not, I do not, believe that thirty young minds are ticking over the points of the Peoples' Charter or estimating the worth of Marlborough's campaigns to the exclusion of all else.

Romaunt of the Rose, Geoffrey Chaucer

The dolls look up, awaiting the next issue of their mental pap, and their faces and white arms compose a pattern against a dark ground. Behind those impassive features are the intricate patterns we cannot see, dreams and hopes, of food, films, boys and future renown. I cannot be satisfied, as a teacher, with methods that keep us forever outside this heaven of all their wish.

On my long journeys home from Ryehill, I often ran into acquaintances in town.

'I hear you're at the grammar school,' they would say, 'How nice. Why ever don't you apply for a permanent grammar school job?'

Why not indeed? To onlookers, I should have been in my element in this better paid and so much less arduous work. Yet I was not.

To my surprise, I found that sixth form history was no compensation for the loss of arithmetic and elementary needlework. The subjects I missed most were the very ones which I had found hardest in that first trial year. There is a certain pupil-teacher relationship established through united effort that is not attained by any of the easy ways. For three terms at least at Washington Road, needlework lessons had been a bi-weekly nightmare, yet there was, at the end of each term, real reward. A child sent home with a nicely pressed and finished garment is a client satisfied with education, one who sees point in it. Something of that satisfaction is carried over to subjects with less tangible results when the teacher is the same for different tasks. At the secondary modern school I had a knowledge of June, Florrie and Mildred in the round because we had struggled together with buttonholes and areas of triangles, as well as the Napoleonic Wars. Whatever else there may be in a grammar school, that understanding is not there when there is only Tudor England between teacher and taught.

I began to wonder if I had been mistaken in even trying to be a history teacher in schools at all. At any level, school history is only a fraction of the real thing. Because history deals with human nature in all its complexity, as well as with abstractions like economic change and politics, it is a subject that demands experience of life for its understanding. Constantly simplifying, as one must, for children, means constantly falsifying to some extent.

Physical conditions at the grammar school were strikingly better than those in our Washington Road School. The staffroom was huge and actually had a carpet, and wide windows looked out over sloping shrubbery and tennis courts to lanes of chimney-pots made beautiful in the late autumn sun. At one end of the room were bookcases, a table for marking, and flowers. Round the wide hearth were easy chairs and a comfortable settee. At morning break there was time and space for small acts of courtesy like the handing of cups. In Walker on the other hand, daily at 10.45, the stout and querulous second mistress established herself in the wooden armchair between door and fire, so that thereafter it was everyone for herself in the fight to get between damp coats and umbrellas, chair legs, and the feet and knitting of Miss Olroyd to reach the teapot before it was drained. Not that 10.45 tea is one of the things I find necessary to salvation, but since we had no hot water in that school, tepid liquid in a cup provided the only method of thawing hands.

Throughout my two long sojourns at the Western Grammar School — one term as student-teacher and again as a member of staff — I never saw my colleagues other than friendly, helpful and courteous. Subterfuges like kidnapping the only workable sewing machine for three days, or holding the best reading books in fee for one's own class, daily occurrences at Washington Road, would have been unthinkable at the grammar school. I do not suggest that the teachers at the grammar school were thoughtful and kind while those at Washington Road were uniformly the reverse; but I do think it an object lesson in the way human nature flowers when there is enough for everyone and a place at table, if not yet a place in the sun.

When at last I returned to Washington Road for the last three days before the Christmas holiday, I was aware of a change. There was no mistaking the pleasure of the girls who had had a succession of supply teachers, nor their eagerness to produce good work. That, I realised, would be transient. The real relief was in the attitude of Miss Ivinson, who treated me thereafter like a responsible adult. The continuous criticism seemed so much less that a happy thought struck me: perhaps, like children, all young teachers get more sense just by growing old?

On the other hand, perhaps the prediction of that tigress beneath whom I did my first school practice had already begun to be fulfilled —

'When you've been at it as long as I have, you'll not be so soft.'

CHAPTER FIVE

Things done for fun

With things half done and things not done at all

After four terms of chronic anguish as a teacher, my family appreciated the motto culled from my Christmas cracker — words my mother said were Sydney Smith's

Take short views, hope for the best. Trust in God.

How wise, I thought. Live as birds do, trust God, instinct or inspiration.

And occasionally, for one whole hour together this new approach did bring balm.

But old fears die hard and there were bad days in plenty still, days of bad colds and 'flu, when pupils were stolid or the weather depressing, and days of yard duty at playtime when fierce winds lacerated chilblains and ears.

Even bad days now had their lighter moments. One snowy January morning, Miss Pringle's Class VIIB came to my room for history after morning break. I still did not know how to take the knowing looks and laughing whispers of these big girls. They pushed and jostled into seats too small for them, and I was chiding stragglers, when, glancing doorwards, I beheld another of the dilatory tribe still standing behind the blackboard.

My irritation soared in eloquence and sarcasm.

'Don't bother about wasting time; I should just keep on standing there all day if I were you. No hurry at all...' only to be interrupted by a joyous burst of laughter from the class.

I was addressing a large pair of Wellington boots, which their owner had politely taken off when she came inside my room.

Why had I kept on snarling and chiding them? It would never make them, or me, enjoy our history any better, and I had known — none better — all through my own school years that young people like to laugh. Why, when it comes to handing knowledge on in the classroom, do we profit little from all that was so vividly experienced when we ourselves sat in the pupils' desks? Anxiety, boredom and disappointment are often eased with a laugh.

Once visiting a junior school I watched a class of eight and nine year olds with a problem.

'A man gets up at half past seven, takes five minutes to wash, ten minutes to shave and dress, twelve minutes to breakfast and twenty minutes to walk to the station. How much time has he to spare if the train goes at 8.20?'

The short answer given by one anxious pupil was 'Mist it'.

Now this true story exactly describes my own feelings of disappointment at that age, when we moved to the main school building from the junior one.

That first real consciousness of boredom is something I imagined I never would forget. Yet scarcely thirteen years later here I was inflicting comparable disappointment on fifty VIIB girls at an even more crucial stage of their so short school days.

How to bring history and literature to life for them as my parents had done for us? At home, I clearly remembered enjoying the rhythm of the humdrum and familiar. But I had inherited also my mother's passion for the theatre, and somewhere about the age of nine, passed the most thrilling evening of the first half of my life, at a pageant of Northumbrian history, in Newcastle's Theatre Royal. The music, based on Northumbrian tunes, was arranged by Dr Whittaker who had spent much of his life collecting, and arranging, these beautiful melodies.

It was a wonderful mixture, that pageant, of all that makes history truly memorable to the young: the individual and the particular; the gaiety, the tragedy. I lived intensely in every minute and longed to participate in it. We had been brought up to the stories, and knew every step of the ground.

Fourteen years later, we talked about all this, my friend Dorothy and I, as we walked back and forth daily to our east end schools. The two scenes which I longed most to bring to life for our own pupils — because such contrast to the scenes all round in 1936 were the two holidays — Corpus Christi day in Newcastle in the early fifteenth century, and the eighteenth century merry-making on the Quayside on Barge Thursday, Ascension Day. The colours of these scenes, remembered so vividly, were like pages from the Lindisfarne Gospels or the Book of Kells.

Yet no matter how we planned and plotted there seemed no way that we could bring this colour and joy to our pupils in the industrial waste which— in the old Tyneside song — was once called 'Byker hills and Walker shore'.

But that Guardian Angel of Pedagogues, tired perhaps of listening to our star-cross'd projects, decided to end it all by dropping a blunt suggestion into our willing ears 'Why don't you run a summer camp?'

Once the words were out, it was so plainly the answer we had gone round in circles seeking, that we fixed the date that night: Newcastle Race Week, the last full week of June. We would hire a lorry, find a site, and I knew where to borrow tents. We would take seven or eight from each of our classes, of those who had not had a holiday for years — if ever. Before we were both totally rigid in the educational machine we would make one strike for freedom and do something with and for our pupils that was unmistakably for fun.

High in the Tyne valley I found a field where the farmer would have us. We, Dorothy and I, had been taking Guides to camps for years and were well-accustomed to making preparations. We arrived with our fourteen eleven year olds, radiant with hope and with two good friends to help.

The view was magnificent, weather superb. The children grew brown in the hay-field and showed good sense and resourcefulness in cooking, wood gathering and tending fires. They loved the country and, on its tiny scale, the experiment was a huge success.

The following year, Mrs Frazer (our widow teacher, mother of the six boys) begged us, with tears in her eyes, to take two of her little boys along with our girls. We were young, fond of little children, and madly optimistic about all our wild experiments. We agreed to take the seven and four year olds, while Mother took the baby to our own home. Thus Mrs Frazer was to have her first week's rest in sixteen years, and we set off on our lorry with eighteen children of assorted ages, six ridge tents, a 'roof' (no sides) for our wood fire, and no solid shelter of any kind. The British climate did what only it can do: blasted and blew for a week, and rained non-stop from Saturday morning till the following Thursday afternoon.

Many of the children had only thin plimsolls for their feet: none had both an overcoat and a mac. The four-year old coughed all night and dirtied his pants all day. The poor little fellow was completely bewildered and his eyes were seldom without a tear and his nose never without a drop. At night, Dorothy and I kept up a perpetual perambulation of the tents to see where water was leaking in or children rolling out. The kitchen 'shelter' fell down one midnight, and a cow ate our tea cloths off the hedge. Every scrap of wood was soaking, and Dorothy and I were perpetually red-eyed through coaxing wayward fires. For several days we cooked breakfast for the whole eighteen and served it to them in their tents. By Tuesday evening, we were so anxious about the children's health, that I went down to the village to ask the vicar if we might dry out for one day in the church hall.

The vicar, a black and whiskery Mr Murdstone, held his door firmly half-closed against the strange dripping apparition who accosted him from Space.

'Quite, quite impossible ... permission would have to be obtained from the Parochial Church Council ... we can't do things like that ... here and now. Three days' notice of a meeting would be needed...'

Strangely enough, the children loved their 'holiday', and were loathe to leave, even the two little boys. I can still picture them with six girls, tousled and triumphant, gathering wood in the rain.

War, not weather, put a stop to these holidays. They were more enjoyable than the Lord Mayor's Camp, and, (if one must be ever mindful of the teacher) a more useful experience. As teachers, we are very much queen bee within the classroom. 'Yes, Miss' 'No, Miss' enhances our misguided impression that our way is always best, quickest, cleverest. In school, in moments of stress, there is always a temptation to keep children passive, because active children are a threat to our carefully constructed order and routine. A shared holiday is healthily corrective. Pupils have many talents they keep hidden in the classroom, and they are well able to establish routines for sharing both work and fun.

I did things in those far off days, that a young teacher would do today only with a degree, special course or diploma behind her. Plays for instance. There was no drama teacher in our school. If one wanted to produce a play — and I often did, one took a squad of willing pupils and stayed behind at four o'clock to rehearse.

'Let's do a play' is as irresistible to many children as 'Let's make a noise'. Alas, I had literally nothing but enthusiasm to offer. There was rarely any thought-out plan. We never progressed from simple dramatic movement or mime to more complex work. Improvisation, (which we did much of with our Guides) was difficult in a classroom filled with enormous, antiquated double desks. In imagination we tried them as forests, ramparts, dungeons, rows of shops. But they remained a total block to spontaneous movement, and the crowded room greatly hindered freedom in speech. So our drama work was stiff, stilted, scarcely touching the shy, uncommunicative children who needed it most. I knew all this and wanted it changed. But I was so inhibited myself by two years of trying to 'fit the system' that I could no longer make the simple connection: if we want free movement, we'll have to start in a different way, in a bigger space.

It seems absurd now, yet at the time it never entered my head that our huge, bare, school gymnasium was the ideal place to try out the spontaneous drama which had been so successful with our Guides. By my third year as a teacher, I could simply have asked openly for an extra drama period, in the gym, and it would have been granted. 'I did not think' — that pitiful excuse for which some teacher, somewhere, is upbraiding pupils every minute of the year!

Notwithstanding all our known difficulties, when Miss Ivinson looked in on me and said 'Will you produce a play for the 'Boot and Shoe Fund' concert,' I airily agreed. Since in our history lessons we had been in the thirteenth century with St Francis and his friars, we decided to present two of Laurence Housman's *Little Plays of St Francis: Brother Juniper and Sister Gold*. We cast the parts, and made a boldly ignorant start. Miss Pringle, our science and gym teacher, who was a member of the Peoples' Theatre in Newcastle, started to look in on rehearsals, and went out of her way to be helpful, suggesting that her VIIB girls should make the costumes. As she had a natural gift for design and colour, and great ability as a needlewoman, she took charge of the operation. Costumes were suddenly lifted into the professional class, very different from anything I could have rumbled up from old dyed curtains and tablecloths. Our struggling effort became a co-operative enterprise. Other teachers joined in, and, for the first time, I was a part —infinitesimal maybe — but still part of the teachers', as distinct from the pupils', world. This was a step forward at least.

Many — perhaps a majority — of teachers enter upon their career with warm affection for children. In the early years, this valuable quality is seldom balanced with detachment. So the young teacher hovers on the brink — or actually falls into — that flood of smothering possessiveness which other grown-ups find so ludicrous in schoolmistresses. While a teacher is new and raw, without status in the staffroom, perhaps only partially accepted there, she is liable to be over-protective of her pupils and over-identified with them.

I am sure that I was so, and, looking back on that third year at Washington Road, I realise that was the time, after these plays, when I began to see teaching in some perspective. I was no longer perpetually fussed and nervous. I was beginning to be trusted as a teacher and knew it. I knew most of the children, not just in my own class, but right up the school, as individuals, and was beginning to recognise the shy, round-faced editions of older sister, so that in spite of out of school activities almost every night — netball teams, country dancing, 'after-care' visiting of school leavers, life seemed more leisurely. Instead of rushing blindly on from 8.30am till 4.30pm, teaching, talking and shouting, always afraid the children would not 'know enough' by the end of term, I dared to digress, to joke, to experiment with group work.

Miss Ivinson never stood rigidly for streaming. Indeed for her own good reasons, she frequently put a child labelled 'C' by the Junior school into an 'A' form. This made for vigour and variety and the girls helped one another. Each class had its share of behavioural and emotional problems. Minor problems, I discovered, are frequently cured in a group situation when the teacher's efforts have made little change. One such problem was Jennifer, a new girl, pretty, vivacious, an 'only' child. She was like a perpetual bees' wedding: all froth and bubble. Five times in ten minutes she would be out to the teacher's desk, and the rest of the time she was offering advice to her neighbours or wailing for help from me. For days we were patient. She just did not realise there was anything about her that her companions might like changed. Then, one playtime when on yard duty, I found Jennifer the centre of an accusing group of girls.

'It's not fair,' she whimpered. 'Nobody likes me. You're all against me.'

'Well,' said Freda, whom I never suspected of such succinct presence of mind, 'if nobody likes you, Jennifer, at least we're all sorry for you.'

Brutal, but bracing. She took it from them, and improved out of all recognition. But it could never have come from me.

I began to realise I should talk far less and listen far more — in short, return to the role that was native to me.

Then there was put into my class a girl called Mona McHafferty, an amiable child of twelve, with pale face, nose that looked as if it has been flattened against a window, and a bad smell. She wheezed and coughed like a sheep that has been on the turnips, and her attendance slip showed that she had been in school five days only out of the past thirty-five. Unless she could be induced to stay in school, there would be a prosecution, but the Welfare Officer was loathe to go so far as her parents were deaf and dumb. She brought with her her books, which were chaotic, and her sewing, a pair of pink knickers, less than half done but grey with unpicked stitches. Her few compositions were a mixture of wild fancy and incoherence but the child was obviously teachable. She could read too, quite fast, though carelessly.

At playtime, the VC teacher went up to the staffroom with me.

'So you've got Mona now. I wish you joy. She's mad, quite mad. Came in about once a week, but when she did she sent all my bottom section as daft as herself. I've several times prayed for her to stop away. But you can't dislike the kid, there's something open about her. Mr Baring says she has a fearful home.'

A week went by. Mona seemed incurably inquisitive and interfering, but once we had resigned ourselves to this, she was no bother. The girls laughed at her contortions and mutterings for a day or two but soon desisted. Perhaps she was on her best behaviour, pleased at the idea of moving up; perhaps it was just that she got less encouragement to be silly, her new companions being on the whole more studious than her last. She was always pleased, whatever she was asked to do, even if she only stuck at it long enough to break her needle or put a row of blots on her neighbour's book. One afternoon I said 'Could you write something for me at four o'clock?'

She was delighted, stayed behind with much fuss and mystery, fetched clean paper, got a new nib, tried and rejected several desks, finally settling in one to her liking in the very back row.

'What'll I do now, Miss?'

'Could you write a description of yourself?'

I had asked her to stay alone because she was so easily distracted. For once she did not hesitate. She scratched away for five minutes, then came out, pleased as a magpie with a piece of cake. She had written six lines, not a portrait, but a truly poignant sketch.

I think myself I am kind gentil and happy I often think what I will be when I grow up I think I will be a teesher.

Mona was leaning on my desk, turning a piece of white chalk pink in my red ink.

'Do you like it Miss? What'll I do now? I'll do some more if you like.'

I said 'Write down what you think about in sewing.'

She went gaily back to her desk. But the pen moved more slowly and she paused several times. Her small span of concentration was exhausted. In a few minutes she was back.

I think I am a good sewer and wisht I was finisht it and started another one and they were payed for.

We talked a few minutes, then she went home.

In the following weeks, I tried to make her feel that she was accepted in school as the person she believed herself to be. Within the limits of her short span of attention she did try. Every now and then her written work would end in a statement so wildly incongruous and unexpected that it was almost impossible not to laugh when reading it, yet that was the one thing that soured her otherwise happy nature. She could not bear to have her work laughed at, perhaps because it meant so much to her.

One day she worked long and laboriously on the meaning of 'Self-control, courtesy and consideration in school' (an essay set by the Headmistress to the whole school). She put enormous full-stops at the end of every sentence, but no capitals. We had talked about it in class.

> **You must control your self. you should lern to do as you are toled without other people telling you. you should give your seat to an adult when you are in the bus. you should not talk (sic) the hole pavement to walk on in the street. you should always open the door for people when they go out of the room. you must have consideration for others. you must not push your satchels up other peoples noses.**

Poor Mona. She was unreliable, but she had a buoyant spirit. She had kept a cheery, generous nature under home conditions of squalor and buffeting that would have daunted most. Care and love for four or five years could still have made her a useful woman. She stayed a month and never missed a day. Then I was absent. When I came back she had gone; moved with her family, but no one knew where. I never saw her again.

I missed Mona. Perhaps I had sympathised with her in her chronic confusion because it is a state of mind I know so well. When myself a pupil I longed, more ardently than I can describe, to know about electricity, magnetism, turbines and such things. Now and then I would read chapters in my brother's textbooks. 'Thermodynamics' both looked and sounded more appealing than 'De Bello Gallico'. At seventeen, again trailing behind a brother, I was reading books like *The Universe Around Us* and *Science and the Modern World*. All this put me, in my understanding of modern physics, at just about Mona's level in understanding Shakespeare.

In spite of all difficulties, however, while actually reading I experienced something of the exhilaration that comes when listening to great choral works. When Mona was pleased with her work, was she not experiencing also that sense of sharing in something greater than herself? How could she have gone on taking such pleasure in work that she was continually unpicking or writing again unless she derived some inspiration from the constant struggle?

But exhilaration was not the only reaction we had in common.

Through lack of properly graded effort in junior forms, Mona's power of concentration was abysmally short. I could not give her my undivided attention for long enough at a time to clear away all her confusions. She needed infant school work with adolescent appeal.

This too I could understand from experience. In reading about modern science I found my span of attention far less than it was normally, for the distracting reason that every few pages, sometimes every few lines,

I was brought up against elementary concepts imperfectly understood. Of all branches of knowledge, perhaps understanding of modern physics is hardest to gain in adult life. More especially is this the case when feelings of confusion and incompetence have set in in adolescence. No reading about physics at twenty, forty or eighty years of age can take the place of practical explanation and experiment that should begin in the junior school. Heat, light, sound and the flow of water fascinate the young. Surely the time to harness imagination to the study of their properties is before that youthful preoccupation with elemental things has passed? I am sure this happens in good schools now.

But there were few signs at that time of a change of heart in the planning of curricula for girls. Even at the high school there were girls who, from eleven years onward, spent as many hours a week on Greek and Latin as I had done in my high school days, and no time at all on physics at any age. True most girls had science upon their timetables, even in the secondary modern schools, but science usually meant biology. In Washington Road School, Miss Pringle used to send down her monitor every Friday afternoon with her instructions for what I was to put in my class record book for the following week. Week after week, I entered 'Frogs'. Occasionally there would be two weeks of 'Newts'. There must have been other topics in the syllabus, but frogs certainly came first. Our girls with their engineer fathers and brothers were as ignorant of technology and modern engineering principles as I had ever been; as ignorant of all sources of power in the modern world; of modern capitalism and international finance. They had lived through the rise of Hitler, the rape of Ethiopia, the Civil War in Spain, yet they did not know what had happened to democracy in Germany, in Italy, in Spain. And how could they know, at fourteen? But when they left school, who was going to bother? How would they ever learn? Our girls meekly accepted their ignorance as if divinely ordained, exactly as we had done ten years before. When would the pattern ever change?

Often in my classroom when the hush of complete absorption fell, or when the room was filled with the eager whispers of children preparing group work, and I seemed for the moment superfluous, I had time to look at the girls objectively. I could not but notice, with joy, the control, self-reliance and co-operation our children showed. But at times it would come over me with foreboding that we were fitting them for no time like the present, and certainly for no place like Tyneside.

At night, as I tramped home, trying to think, but lulled into stupor by the trolley buses as they whistled by, past and future would merge into a dream, cosy if the day had been pleasant, a nightmare when everything had gone wrong. In this vague projection and reminiscence, I would try to work out new approaches to history or new arithmetical techniques, mindful of what we had been taught in college days.

In my time as student and teacher, one principle dominated the work of every progressive school: study and help the individual child; help him to self-reliance, control and initiative; help him to join with others, not to work only for himself. The teacher's function was to draw out and nourish, not to dictate. It was the theme of lectures; we read books on the play way, the child-centred school, the children we teach; we discussed modern methods in seminars. Oh yes, I believed. It is a standard of professional conduct I have not always achieved, but which I have never, as yet, given up; nor ever will — come who may to the chair of Minister of Education.

During those first years of teaching, however, I began to wonder how this New Education would square itself, first with the world we lived in, and then with the universe, of which we were a minute part. So far as the world was concerned, progressive teachers had staked their all on an ethical system to which neither governments nor business magnates conformed, while the universe, far from sharing in our co-operative ideals, took no cognizance of them, appearing either indifferent or hostile to human life.

These difficulties did not present themselves in two blinding flashes of light. Doubts would loom into consciousness, tower threateningly over me for an instant and pass on like the Byker 'buses, to be lost in the twilight of Washington Road. Then unexpectedly, towards the end of my third year of teaching, I found myself in hospital for a serious operation, and had ten weeks to think over those great question marks: How do we learn? What, and why do we teach? Do we, in the long run, influence our children's minds? What is the teacher's role at present, and what might it be?

CHAPTER SIX

Why do the people imagine a vain thing?

Handel and hospital

On her death, Queen Victoria had 110 albums of photographs, including forty-four full of pictures of her family.

I have always felt sympathy for the Queen in her devotion to this task, and indeed, a humble kinship, for I fear that I am as she was: only marginally creative yet an eager storekeeper of fact. Lying there in the Northern Women's Hospital, instead of wiping out recollections of Washington Road and settling for a refreshing spell of further education, I fretted and fumed, and thought about my pupils, as continuously as Victoria thought about her children, suffering exactly the same temptation to interfere and control from afar. I made up examination papers for the year end, and expected my long-suffering brother to deliver them to school, (which he did not). It is not easy to bear frustration patiently and without fuss. There were two compartments in my mind. In one, were at least 200 mental pictures of pupils; lively, funny, all of them attractive and many of them highly intelligent. In the other compartment were recollections of lessons that had been confused, inadequate, or just plain dull. I wanted to write about this early experience of teaching, but the parts would not come together. I tried writing stories about Walker children. But the truth now seemed a thousand times more worthwhile than invented fantasy.

If I just fixed the mental snapshots in an album, would I find comfort in them there, docile and pleasant for all eternity? Was this the Queen's satisfaction, to see her offspring in pictures, beneath her thumb for ever, when flesh and blood effectively evaded her control?

The idea did not appeal. Snapshots alone add up to nothing. They are just a collection. What can one do with a collection save leave it to a museum on death?

I had been brought in through the night to hospital from a camp we had been running one extremely wet week in the Northumbrian hills. Peritonitis had developed. In those days there was no getting up the day after the operation — it was bed rest indeed. One week became two, and two became four but I had reached no answer to any of my teaching problems. There was some sorrow and much comedy in our small private world. A hospital sojourn is in itself a refresher course in education. The merits of one institution opened my eyes quite remarkably to defects in our own. Nurses, as a class, are patient and kind. They really like their clients to be happy; something not all teachers do. But hospitals and schools share defects. The hospital day is distracting. It reminds me always of the old fashioned wash day which I (just) remember at my aunt's house, before electricity came: 5.00am boiler beneath 'set pot' lit. Piles of sorted clothes on slippery wet flags; the tub and the 'posser'; soap suds and stream. Scrub, wring, shake, and mangle. Ironing till late afternoon.

'The house is that uneasy,' as one little girl said, when writing on 'wash day'.

Five weeks in hospital, washed, possed, mangled, and done over half-hourly with thermometers, clean sheets, treatments, meals or hot drinks, is a powerful incentive to look at our own school day. At Washington Road, we squeezed in eight periods (as well as daily scripture) two of thirty minutes, one of forty, and five of thirty-five! How 'uneasy', to an intelligent and studious child.

The others in the ward were all middle-aged and married. They talked of nothing but husbands, past operations, and food. Hour after hour it went on, endlessly boring to undomesticated ears. I felt worn out trying not to hear, till I was transfixed, like Archimedes in the bath — teaching was my substitute for marriage! For the past three years, I had been wedded to my work, and must have been just as intolerably tedious to others about my pupils as I had now found my bed mates about their cookers and their husbands' fads.

There is a perceptive letter about marriage written by J B Yeats the artist half a century ago.

Marriage means that two people are bringing into the common stock all their weaknesses, and there are two comparisons possible. Marriage is sometimes like two drunken men seeing each other home. Neither can reproach the other or refuse sympathy or help. The other comparison is this: marriage is like two mortal enemies (the sexes are enemies) meeting on the scaffold and reconciled by the imminence of the great enemy of both.

As a picture of my early years in teaching, this could not be bettered. Three years of trial marriage between two hopeful, but often drunken partners, ending on the scaffold at examination time.

But this shaft of revelation, greeted so rapturously when it struck, turned out to be no solution to the problems in hand: how do we learn, why do we teach; how, above all, are the two related in what we vaguely call a good teacher? How does one set about becoming this amorphous thing? Could it be that one just makes a start, as in marriage or bicycling, and acquires, through crashes and misadventure, a modicum of skill?

But in marriage or cycling, we use all our faculties, to acquire whole things: is not this how children would best learn, and how we ought to be striving to teach? Yet it was decidedly not how we were expected to teach in secondary schools. All the emphasis was on repetition and rote-work. 'Use your brains' teachers were heard shouting, a dozen times a day. Pupils were not expected to have feelings of joy or aesthetic pleasure in any subject except perhaps dancing or games. And not always then.

'You don't come to school to enjoy it,' I heard an elderly teacher say crossly to a VIB girl, when I brought her class back from dancing.

The girl, only wanting to share her pleasure with her class teacher, had cried out 'Oh! It was fun.'

It was not only that they were expected to live without feelings — or if they must have feelings, to have them decently and soberly *after*, as pleasure in work done — they were also expected to 'use their brains' continuously on collections of items: spelling for instance, or the learning of grammar. Even songs were learnt, in music lessons, one line at a time: phrase on the piano, repetition three times by the class; next line. Fact upon fact, one brick on another and scarcely a sight of the house being built. How could I get right away from this type of teaching without appearing to 'set myself up'?

I was, and am, convinced that the teacher projects a mental picture of her subject to her pupils. If I was muddled, they were too. When I had the picture in my own mind, whole and comprehended, like a problem in mathematics understood, their picture was whole and vivid, whether of

Chaucer and Piers Plowman, Elizabethan England or the Factory Acts. It is, in teaching, as the farmer said of ploughing: 'You sorter thinks a straight furrer when you starts, and you ploughs one as near as damn it.'

I had got the content of a history syllabus mapped out not too badly. Where I was falling down was in method. I was still doing nearly all the talking. The girls listened with docility, many with interest too. Yet they were not personally involved.

Before I could make any progress with this problem, the summer vacation came, and friends went on holiday, thoughtfully leaving books for the patient. Montaigne's *Essays*, for example, which I ought to have found uplifting, but did not. Opening by chance at the passage where he enunciates his 'principal concern' 'that I may die handsomely, that is patiently and without noise,' Montaigne quickly went to my locker bottom, along with all the unread 'light' novels, cartoons with humorous poetry, or travels in Tibet, with which well meaning visitors imagine that patients will pass their time. For the moment, I had gone off everything but music and Jane Austen.

There were no hospital earphones or portable radios then, but Mother, resourceful as ever, arrived with a life of Handel and her copy of *Messiah*.

If a great work is, like *Hamlet* or *Messiah* 'all quotations', it is easy to be blind to its significance as a whole. I never ceased to be grateful for having those weeks with the whole work to sing and think about in bed, nor to Mr R A Streatfield, whose book* on Handel enlightened me more than any other thing I read in those ten weeks. With book and score before me, I saw the story, as a majestic poem, not just a record of events: saw that the parts had meanings, and were not there simply to give the orchestra a rest.

Curiously enough, in our college days, no historian had ever talked to us about *teaching* history. Professor Morison and Dr Cobban had begun to open our eyes to all that goes to make up history. But neither of them had expressed a view on how we were to convey our knowledge to the young. Could I not try to give history lessons as Handel had given his story in the *Messiah*, not didactically, as something to be got by heart (an inept phrase for things so often got by misery!), but as a song, as a poem, something that would speak to both heart and mind?

History is learning by enquiry and, if pupils are to find out for themselves they must search. The books we had at Washington Road were useless for this purpose. The cramped double desks (which could not be moved) made group work a circus turn, rather than a concerted study. With over fifty in each class, there was no one, simple solution, but first we needed new books: books specially written to enable pupils to find information for themselves, from contemporary documents and pictures, and

---

* *Handel*, R A Streatfield, (London 1910)

work books to go with them in which, putting all our searches together, we could build up a story approaching a whole view.

So a project was on hand for convalescence, and I made a start.

We had moved, in the spring of that year, from the tiny flat to a small bungalow — only a stone's throw in yardage but a world away in sunshine and light. We loved the new home, and to work quietly in the sunny sitting room should have been a pleasure. But there was a menace now which no one could ignore. It was September, 1938. By the end of three months I was at last allowed to return to school. On the 22nd, Chamberlain made his second flight to meet Hitler. War was expected within the week. On the 29th came news of the Munich betrayal, Chamberlain's 'Peace in our time'.

How should we make our protest? I remember going into our church and meeting the vicar*. I poured out my tentative suggestions, fully believing that the whole body of the Church people in Britain would rise up and repudiate what had been done in our name. To my incredulous amazement, the vicar pooh-poohed every suggestion. We must be guided by wiser minds: pray for patience and insight; hope for toleration; trust in God. We must do everything, in short, save stand courageously for the right. We argued in the huge, empty church. When he had gone, I sat alone. I had no idea how to do anything practical. Our vicar was surely meant to be the spokesman for our huge and active Church congregation. How could I initiate a movement of protest which he refused to countenance? Could his complacent acquiescence in the throwing of Czechoslovakia to the wolves, be the policy of the Church at large?

Up and down the country, there must have been individuals of all denominations who spoke out, but at that age, ignorant and provincially minded as I was, I did not know where to look for support. I felt hopelessly ashamed and impotent, as, no doubt, many more young people did. The only thing I was trained for was teaching, and most of the people I knew well were teachers too. Yet of our staff of nineteen, only one, Mrs Frazer, saw the Munich episode as I did, as a shameful disaster. To the rest, it meant relief from the fear of war. And neither Mrs Frazer nor I knew how to organise a protest. She had her family responsibilities. I had filled my 'spare time' with Guides and youth club work, useful enough in a vague way, but lacking plan or coherence. When the testing came, I was lined up with nobody who cared to do anything positive.

From then on, I knew that to take a full share in the responsibilities of a citizen, one must belong to a political party as well as a Church.

To get away from the concerted staffroom adulation of Chamberlain, I took a walk down to the river one lunch time. At the river's edge watching the manoeuvres of a painter slung over a ship's side, was a tall, lean woman wearing a dark beret and shapeless burberry. She turned to me and smiled.

---

*Not Canon Trotter, who had died, but a strange man who laid great stress on the 39 Articles; a stickler for law.

She had fine features and strikingly blue eyes. We fell into talk, and before she had spoken three sentences, I recognised the oracle of our West Walker girls, Miss Riley of Union Road Junior School. Once I had asked in our staffroom 'Who is this Miss Riley the girls are always talking about?'

Miss Olroyd, pillar of the Scottish Kirk, replied 'She's next-door to a communist, very disreputable, I've been told,' adding in a whisper, for which naturally the assembled company strained its ears, 'Don't get mixed up with her, I've heard she's been seen in a public house on the Quayside.'

Beside the river I dallied, fascinated like Red Riding Hood with this notorious profligate. We talked about Hitler, Munich and Chamberlain.

'What makes so many people happy to believe that Hitler has changed his spots?' she asked.

I can only approach questions of this kind obliquely. 'Hasn't it happened all through history?' — and I told her of my recent study of the *Messiah*, and how the phrase, 'Why do the people imagine a vain thing?' ran in my mind.

She was silent so long I thought she had gone into a trance. Then she spoke. 'I used to love music and poetry. But I have turned very prosaic these last few years — in fact since the beginning of the Spanish War. Now I see it's all wrong. There's no virtue in allowing the heart to dry and harden. By sneering at that side of my nature, I have only succeeded in making myself smaller than I was... Let's meet again.'

We met often in the ensuing months. Sometimes she would walk round in the evening and talk with mother, Dorothy and me. Half Irish, half Cumbrian, she was the most witty and dramatic natural story-teller I have ever heard. Mother laughed as she had not done for four years. Janet was well-read too, and a thoughtful Marxist. We talked endlessly about history and economic change. But sometimes she seemed oppressed and sat silent. She took the world's woe to heart more profoundly than most people do.

It was through Janet Riley that I began to reach out to a world that teachers should know, but which our chaste history and philosophy of education had quite ignored; to a world that Dickens knew well, and Dostoevsky even better. Janet mentioned the novels of Graham Greene.

'They are queer, you'll think, but they are alive and evocative. He writes about the lost souls of this age — sometimes race-gangs, sometimes international crooks, but more often the shabbier, less obvious lost, the grey throngs of the lost. Yet there is always life, or its gleam, somewhere. He gets heaps into one sentence. I dreamt in those sentences last night — queer, excitable, nervous sentences, full of shades and light and glimpses near and far. I am fascinated by his books because that world — that sort of underworld has always drawn me, and often I've lived in it — or close in touch with it. Not with the race gangs or international financiers, but with the unrespectable, the outlawed. And often this world has seemed more important to me than the tame world of teachers.'

And I began to understand Miss Olroyd's anxiety about the pub on the Quayside.

A month passed and I was happier at school than before, working hard with the history scheme, and at night, preparing the new work books. In spite of Hitler, cheerfulness kept breaking in.

Then out of the blue came a letter from the Office ordering me, the next day, to take up work at a training college in Newcastle to replace the history lecturer for the next five months. I had not asked, and certainly had never wished, for such a position. I was not old enough, or wise enough. Full of doubts and uncertainty myself, what use could I ever be to students? And did they suppose that I could abandon my own work without a backward glance? Why did the Office imagine this vain thing?

I went to the training college; I had no option. We had no savings whatsoever to live on if I had refused. But it made me very angry that teachers should be treated so like cattle — moved on to new pasture without even 'If you please'.

My main work there was lecturing in history to students doing Ordinary and Advanced courses. At first I prepared lectures at a level equivalent (as I hoped) to the level I had enjoyed most in my own student days. But I found this was no use at all. The standard then at the college was low, and students' general knowledge very limited. They were floored by words like 'Cistercians', had never heard of Garibaldi, and thought Von Moltke was a kind of drink. They were quite unable to take notes from anyone speaking at ordinary conversation speed.

In addition to lectures, I had to give demonstration lessons every week in junior and secondary modern schools. This was exhausting mentally and physically, and a constant source of worry, as I had never watched a *demonstration* lesson in history in my life.

It was not a happy time. With a class, a teacher can count on at least one hearty laugh a day. But my young ladies at the college were so cowed, so inhibited, the most we ever shared was a wan smile. They seemed to have lived entirely on a historical diet of processed cheese and thin cornflour and they felt this suited them best. I showed myself a bad teacher by trying to ram whole steaks into them, when we might have compromised, if I had been wiser, on Heinz strained foods or even mince. The one thing they ever asked for spontaneously was what we might call historical *Alka-Seltzer*, 'a little swot book to cover the period'.

Everything passes. Yes, but we can equally well say 'nothing passes without leaving us changed'. Did these months at the training college make a difference to me as a teacher, or to my understanding of the teacher's role? I think it was then that I began to recognise that teaching is always imperfect; that mistakes are inevitable and that a large part of the teacher's role is learning to bear the frustrations inherent in the job with some semblance of stoicism; learning, like Montaigne, 'to die handsomely' in fact?

I noted down less, and remember less of those months than of any other episode in my teaching, and can only suppose this was because financial worry outdid any pleasure or amusement in recollecting. That time is summed up for me in Mahler's song, *St Anthony's Sermon to the Fishes* from *Lieder aus Des Knaben Wunderhorn*.

According to God's Will
they listen to the sermon
The sermon over
they all turn about.
The pike remain thieves,
the eel stay great lovers.
They liked the sermon
but remain as before.
The crabs go backwards
the cod stay fat
the carp guzzle a good deal
And forget the sermon.

When the two training college terms were over I returned to Washington Road for the few days that remained of the Easter term. I was happy to be back in the barracks that had looked and smelt so horrifying only three and a half years before. When I stood in that Washington Road corridor at the end of my first teaching day, watching the closed eyes and thin folded hands of all those pale children, the strains of

Holy father cheer our way
With Thy love's perpetual ray...*

sounded more tragically nostalgic then any psalm of the Captivity. But we become accustomed to anything. The mind has protective blinds. We pull down the blinds and sit back in a dark tunnel, travelling fast to unspecified destinations. After three years, if the school was hideous, I simply did not see it anymore. I had learnt one lesson. The real captivity was not in school, even in those condemned old schools built last century. It was in the dead-end jobs where our girls landed at the age of fourteen. They were turned loose to earn their living with less surveillance than a farmer gives his battery hens.

They that wasted us required of us mirth...**

By the irony of fate they got mirth and much more besides from the young people who manned forces and factories from 1939 on.

---

* Words R H Robinson (1842-92)
** *The Songs of Sion,* Psalm 137 v3 (variant of)

CHAPTER SEVEN

The old dispensation
Evacuation I and a Teesdale village

Were we led all that way for
Birth or Death? There was a birth certainly
We had evidence and no doubt. I had seen birth and death
But had thought they were different; this Birth was
Hard and bitter agony for us, like Death, our death.
We returned to our places, these Kingdoms
But no longer at ease here, in the old dispensation
With an alien people clutching their gods.
T S Eliot *Journey of the Magi*

Throughout the summer term of 1939, ordinary work was constantly interrupted for the purpose of making lists. Names, dates of birth, addresses and parents' names were written and rewritten, and every list had to be made by hand, in triplicate. Children were divided into categories A, B and C. Index cards were made for each child, in duplicate, and filed. Every two or three days, Miss Ivinson would disappear to hold conference with the Heads of infant and junior schools in the area; every two or three weeks, new official evacuation plans were evolved. Finally a master plan was disclosed by the Office under which each teacher found herself charged with thirty assorted seniors, juniors and infants (mixed) approximately twenty-seven of whom, it was estimated, she would never have seen before.

This masterpiece of documentation had been carried out by infuriated and exhausted Heads and staff, at the cost of whole weekends of continuous list-making. All those children who were to be evacuated from the entire senior school of 600-odd pupils were to be listed alphabetically. But beneath the name of each senior child must be inscribed the names of all brothers and sisters in contributing junior and infant schools. The whole gigantic list was then divided into parcels of thirty.

Not one of my thirty was known to me. Not one of my own class was to be within six miles. There was one week's holiday for teachers throughout August of that year, and even that must be spent near at hand. List-making and rehearsals continued, until the final order came. On September 1st, evacuation would begin. The last red beret was picked up from the cloakroom floors, and I listened to the sound of feet clattering away down the stone corridor for the last time.

Very early on September 1st, children, teachers and helpers were formed into procession, labelled, and carrying gas masks, 'iron rations' of tinned meat, tinned milk and biscuits, we marched through streets lined with parents and friends to a station on the riverside line. The children looked like refugees, each with a kit bag or some other little bundle of clothes or treasures. Many of the watching adults cried uncontrollably. There were children of all sizes, some clean, some dirty and neglected. Some of them tried to sing as they marched. My mother accompanied me as a helper. We had been told to take only a small hand case of spare clothing, but I carried the huge volume of Beethoven sonatas under my arm.

At the station, while we stood in our little group, we could see that several children had nits in their hair. Two looked as if they had scabies, and I wondered what their reception would be in billets. When the train came, we were crowded into carriages, with canvas bags, string bags, kit bags and paper carriers to fill corners. The children watched cranes and ships, and vied with each other in reading advertisements and hoardings 'Currie and Co. Bonded and Duty paid Warehouse Keepers', 'Higginbottom's Baltic Tavern', and 'Salvation Army men's Palace' in gilt letters two feet high.

Over the chimney pots, on the far bank of the river, could be seen the Amsterdam and Dordrecht Wharf, the Hamburg Wharf.

'Oh where are you going to, all you big steamers' one child began to sing.

We watched an old man limping down the Broad Garth Stairs; saw him spit, twist his dirty necktie and turn into a pub; below we saw blackened cinder heaps and rubbish tips, straggling timber sheds, plumbers' yards and derelict trucks. In squalid sunless streets that ran down to the riverside, tattered washing was catching the soot. Haggard women, gazed from their doors. The familiar sights made me look back over my four years of teaching. In spite of all mistakes, the overriding impression was one of enjoyment, a sense of comradeship and loyalty. I thought of struggles to teach games on the blackened wasteland, fringed with nettles, and dignified with the title 'playing field'; of afternoons of quiet sewing and reading; of frantic mornings with 'paths and borders' or decimal fractions of a pound; of country dancing in the yard, mending the gramophone between dances.

But what had been the use of it all? It was all so transient. I myself had already watched, each April and October, eight sets of girls leave school at fourteen. And as one of the two 'after-care' representatives on the staff, had visited these girls in their first and sometimes their second year out of school, and had been appalled at the changes wrought, sometimes by work, sometimes by lack of it. At school, the girls we had known were steady workers, alert and responsible, dependable — so long as they worked with people they could depend on in their turn. But out of school — a few slouched the street with bakers' barrows, others giggled and grew pale in basement kitchens frying chips. Some of the brighter girls from the A classes, were machinists, or errand girls in multiple stores. But many, unwanted altogether, had joined the army of derelicts. Most of them put a brave face on it, and, hiding their insecurity with scent and paint, sauntered from labour bureau to cinema.

The child on my knee wakened from her sleep. One older girl, holding up her little sister at the window, was pointing to birch trees, and heather in flower. The train was running beside the river again, but here the river skipped over white boulders or lingered in dark clear pools. Little streams, fringed with foxgloves and fern, ran to join it, and rabbits and sand-martins inhabited the sand banks.

We ate our sandwiches and played games. The hot, stuffy afternoon wore away at last.

The train grated into a smokey town — the children were herded out, counted, and lined up in fours. A Director of Education, in bowler hat, inspected them. Then the children moved off, and awkwardly under their bundles, descended the station steps. They passed the barrier and came out, blinking into the sunlight, to behold a crowd of spectators. Another tiring trudge through the crowded streets began. But the poignant procession of early morning had now become an ignominious crawl. The crowd stared in antagonism, criticising, condemning. These children had been five hours in the train; their cotton frocks were crumpled, their faces grimy, and their hair awry. They had come from 'the slums' and they looked the part.

The procession moved on to a school yard and was hidden by huge stone walls from the unwinking crowd. I stopped to stare at the stone above the school door. This was the inscription

These Schools
for the Education of the Children of the Poor
in Religious and Useful Knowledge
were erected
from the Bounty of a Kind providence
by Thomas Wilson, 1831.

Several mothers with young babies were in our party. In the bleak school yard, babies cried, mothers swore, till at last, wailing and complaining, they were got into an old and rattling bus and the thirty children and their bundles pushed in behind. For two hours we jolted over rough hill country to our village, Arnistone. There, a reception committee headed by the Billeting Officer, stout and self important, three local school teachers and what looked like quite half of the remaining inhabitants, waited to see what had come. Kind smiles, hand shakes, steam from the tea-urn, tears, tremulous laughter and a thousand questions filled another couple of hours.

At last children and mothers were all sent off to homes and my mother and I were led to our billet in the house of Mr and Mrs Twentyman. They proved to be an elderly couple living with a widowed son and grandsons of thirteen and ten. We were taken into our bedroom, a small room containing an enormous wardrobe, chest of drawers and 'Fear Ye The Lord' in cross stitch above the double bed.

Schools were not open for lessons that first week, and since at Arnistone all three school rooms were full of desks, the Billeting Officer, himself a Methodist, offered the Methodist hall for 'games'. This was to provide, at one and the same time, rest for exhausted hostesses and such useful occupation for the children as teacher devised. But a play centre does not spring to life through the juxtaposition of thirty backward children, several sets of knitting needles, an old harmonium, and 129 Methodist hymn books.

Gathered in that dreary hall the children looked like foundlings in an eighteenth century charity school. Using all my ingenuity, I taught dances and games suitable for such mixed ages; but country dance tunes came out of that harmonium like Revivalist hymns, team games raised a dust like the original plague of darkness of Exodus. As for knitting, only the three youngest infants had anything to learn from me. Luckily, about midday, the weather took up, so from then until school re-opened, we relied on walks for much of our corporate entertainment. In any case, the chief need, as I very well knew, was not for organised games and dancing. It was for prolonged individual help to each child in adjustment to an alien society, and that on the given material, was enough to break any teacher's heart. All the children had dirty heads, and though the Headmaster did his best to minimise other complaints, the Billeting Officer soon made it clear to me that the village was seething with discontent. It was no wonder. If I had tried for a year I could hardly have picked thirty children so unpromising and so untypical of our Washington Road children as a whole.

Freda, for instance, who had gone to the home of Miss Norton, the infant teacher on an outlying hill farm, was twelve, but her mental age might well have been eight. Her face was round and expressionless. In the house, she never spoke unless spoken to, would neither read, paint nor sew. She avoided the men folk, who teased her, and showed no interest in the young grandchildren about the place. Normal girlish emotions seemed to have passed her by. She only lived to eat, and eat she did for the six months she stayed at Arnistone, till she went home looking like an infant Pooh-Bah.

Yet Freda was a femme fatal compared to the two sisters billeted at the next farm, Ash Trees. They were the two oldest of our party, stockily built, both with glum faces and mouse coloured, lank hair. I tried to enlist their help in caring for the little ones, but they resented this.

I think, now, that to some extent these two unhappy girls became the scapegoats for the group. Very complex pressures, which at the time I did not even begin to understand, were at work. Fear, resentment at being 'driven from home', loneliness, exile, were present in us all, and defences were put up to hide all this from strangers and even from ourselves. Yet I anticipated that all thirty would accept me immediately as their friend, as I fondly imagined I accepted them.

We were never warned, in training, that relations between group and teacher are never simple at the best of times. In this unprecedented situation, the group needed to preserve me as a 'good object' — someone who stood between them and total annihilation. But on the other hand, was there not a need (suppressed) to destroy the person who symbolised for them their hated exile? Aggressive feelings, which in our strange situation we dared not show freely to one another, may very well have been projected upon the two who, by their non-co-operation, seemed to invite hostility. Be that as it may, the two sisters tortured us all with their dumb misery for three weeks and went home, unlamented by anyone but me.

North of Ash Trees on the same high, windswept fellside was one more hill farm. Beyond that cultivation ceased for several miles. Bracken, bent-grass and heather were given over to curlews and sheep.

At this distant house were two more of our older girls. Sandy, thin faced, sharp nosed, with freckles, they were like two weasels, and just as distrustful of human kind. They kept apart from the other children and avoided my eyes when I tried to talk to them. I set off to their billet with reluctance for there seemed little hope that they would have shown endearing qualities there.

I walked along a rough cart track and rounding the back of the buildings came suddenly upon the farmyard, ankle-deep in mud. Scattered across the quagmire were boulders, dragged from the nearest wall, to form stepping stones. I leaped and slithered from one precarious foothold to another, watched by a stout woman, perhaps forty, with her hair tied up in a yellow scarf, who stood at the door wiping her hands on a dark apron. I explained my presence, and she led the way into a stone-flagged kitchen that might once have been a midden by the smell. A golden-haired baby was crawling there, trouserless, picking up mud and other treasures from the floor. When he saw me, he retreated beneath the table. He was a fine healthy little boy and I made an admiring comment, but his mother made no reply. She clattered about in her clogs, whisked two cats off a wooden armchair and gave it a slight push towards me. Then she went to the door and shouted across the yard.

'Billy! Bill-ee! Here's t'evacooee teacher.'

A black cauldron was bubbling over the peat fire and emaciated hens ran in and out of the open door. Listlessly the woman shooed them away. She stood near the door, eyeing me yet not speaking. There was something strangely familiar in her attitude. She wore a loose, striped blouse which showed her strong arms and broad figure. I tried to talk but could get nothing from her but 'No' or 'Mebbe'. When I asked directly if she liked having evacuees, she said,

'I don't mind,' adding after a long pause, 'They're not bad bairns.'

Presently a tall, gaunt man shambled to the door. Although young and 'a powerful fine preacher' as I had been told, he appeared to be toothless save for two enormous yellow tusks. He leant nonchalantly on the doorpost and studied me as if I had been a calf in the grading pen. I said I would like to see the girls, but he dismissed that with a laugh, saying they were 'happier ootbye. They'm forking muck. Happy as Larry and fit as lops.' He had no intention of losing his chance to hold the floor.

At first I thought he was just making general conversation, about evacuation and the war. He talked in a slow, rasping voice, on and on like a metronome. His wife did not say a word, just stood there, watching.

I had to find out if the evacuees had suitable underclothes and shoes, so tried to bring the preacher back to facts.

'Could you tell me if...?' I began. But he was engrossed in his argument. It was about gambling and drink.

'Have the two girls got...?'

'So they fling themselves to the worship of Mammon, wives forgotten, children neglected, work thrown away. And before they know where they are, they are unemployed.'

'Unemployment isn't caused by drink.'

'Oh, so *you* know the cause of unemployment, do you? And perhaps you can cure it, young lady? You're a scholar from the town.' The voice was not sarcastic, just self-righteous and amused. He was tormenting me, like a cat with an exhausted mouse.

'I never said I could ...'

'Man *can't* cure employment. But the good Lord can. And how does the Lord cure employment? He sends a mighty snow storm...' He paused.

I believe it was the climax of a sermon he had delivered countless times. The atmosphere in the room was stifling and the pent-up emotion of the past five days seemed to be bursting in my head. His wife had sat down on a wooden chair half turned from him. There was utter resignation on her face. I remembered where I had seen her before, in one of Pissaro's portraits, a peasant woman of Pontoise.

At that moment, the tension in the room dissolved in farce. The cupboard doors below the oak dresser were half open. One particularly repulsive bald hen had found her way inside, and was gobbling her supper from a paper bag. The baby, nigh forgotten beneath the table, squealed and lurched at the hen. The hen, squawking, fled through the door and the child hurled himself after her between his father's legs.

'Willie!' screamed his mother, 'Drat the little bugger,' and almost felled her husband in her leap for the door. But she was too late to avert Willie's plunge into the slime. Attracted by the screams, the two girls came running to the door. They looked like something out of a pantomime, each in two pairs of thick dark socks and enormous clogs. But their faces were rosy and alive.

Already it is over fifty years since that first evacuation, and no doubt all such farm life belongs to the past. It was the most elemental living I have ever seen, yet the evacuees thrived in it. Though little more advanced than the two at Ash Trees as far as book learning went, there was a difference in their response to the new life. How much that was due to their own temperament, how much to the efforts of the strange foster-parents, I do not know. The baby may well have had a share in it.

When I remember that kitchen scene now, and the woman brooding and withdrawn, I am reminded of Lawrence's description of a crucifix in the Bavarian Alps. The Christ, he said

was of middle age, plain, crude, with some of the meanness of the peasant, but also with a kind of dogged nobility that does not yield its soul to the circumstance.

In the course of many visits to that farm, I never saw cleanliness or efficiency. But there *were* other things.

Should the evacuees have been moved from this dirty house? I fancy thoroughly efficient teachers might say 'yes'. But where to? They could only have gone to one of the village cottages and there, problems, though different, were just as acute. Before setting out to distant farms, I had visited the twenty children lodged in the village. Not one billet had water sanitation, and only one a tap. Many of the foster-parents were rheumaticky and getting on in years, and some, as I was soon to discover, were already over-worked or overstrung by their own personal affairs. The prospects for successful acclimatisation there were poor enough, and in the next few weeks, many of the children, while benefiting from good food and air, undoubtedly suffered because their presence was resented, consciously or not.

The prime necessity for evacuees was love. It would have taken a more resolute heart than mine to shift children who had affection to a house less odorous but where the psychological effects of unwantedness could only have been bad. There *were* better-off village homes where there was space, and into which evacuees could have been forced, but could a compulsorily billeted child have had even a dog's life? So, with endless heart-searching, I left the Smithson children where they were, for better or worse.

Often in that first week I took the children long walks over the fell. A few ran ecstatically through bracken shoulder high, to scramble and fall on the rocky bed of a mountain stream. They seemed to be getting the feel of country life. But many still walked morosely, with an air of injury, as if they had trodden on a stair that was not there.

Lottie and Alice, aged eight and ten, seemed among the more adaptable. They were at Overdale, an isolated farm west of the village. Lottie, the younger, had the face and figure of a circus dwarf. She was a little old woman in her habits, with the mind of a child. She kept close to me, holding my hand and talking about her new home. Mr Duncan went every day to the fell on a pony called Topsy to look after his sheep. Mrs Duncan made *all* the bread. She made it in a big basin and put it in front of the fire. Margaret looked after the hens and Frances did the milking. Margaret and Frances, it seemed, were the grown-up daughters of the house. Margaret bathed the children, and had taken them to Chapel.

'Margaret bought 'wer new shoes,' said Lottie in triumph, 'and 'wer vests,' put in Alice, who was walking stolidly along by Lottie's side.

'Frances plays the organ in Chapel,' went on Lottie proudly. 'She has black hair, Miss, coal black. When she's smiling, I never seen a face like hers before.'*

It was with curiosity that I set off to visit Overdale. The grey stone house was visible from our cottage, but it was a long walk round by road, and as I drew near, my heart sank. From the trim front garden to the immaculate stone yard behind, never had I seen a farm with such clean appendages. Dairy and byre were newly swilled, no derelict machines, decaying hen-houses, or rotting turnips lay around. The manure heap was not in sight. Here, if anywhere, I thought despondently, I will get the full recitative of woe: heads, beds, no underclothes and refusal to eat anything but chips. I lingered, morosely, at the back gate. Someone was singing in the kitchen, in a voice young and rich. She was singing 'There's a windswept ocean yonder' from Purcell's Cantata *The Moon*.

When at last I knocked, the door was opened by a girl, perhaps twenty, in a flowered overall and neat cap. She laughed when I thanked her for her song. Lottie had been right. I'd never seen a face like hers before, either. It was not beautiful, taken feature by feature, but she gave an immediate impression of goodness and radiant happiness.

Frances called her sister, and together they talked of their evacuees. They told me to concentrate on the other children for a week or two, as they would see to theirs, heads and clothing included. They spoke as if attending to the children's needs was a pleasure. It was the first time anyone had spoken of our evacuees with genuine warmth.

In the next few days, I constantly found myself bumping into the villagers who had no evacuees. They seemed to stand at their doors solely for the purpose of exchanging stories of wet beds while waiting to way-lay the evacuee teacher. Then they would commiserate at length on the shocking state of affairs. There was a kindly superiority in their attitude, as if their non-intervention entitled them to regular and confidential progress reports. It was impossible to go anywhere without being stopped and put to the question.

'Settling in nicely? Aye, that's right. Good job it's bin sic grand

---

* Many Tyneside children cannot manage the past tense of 'to see'

weather. Chilrun able to get out. I hear there's three mothers 'as gone yam this week? Aye, well, it was a big change for them here: no fish and chips; no picshers. They'll be sharp back very like when bombing starts. Hitler'll have summat up his sleeve yet, aa'm thinkin'... Turrible man that. Aye, bad job altogether. There's some saying those lassies up at Ash Trees isn't settling well?'

I do not doubt that Arnistone was a village fundamentally kind. But raids and invasion did not come. The refugees, tear-stained objects of compassion on September 1st, became, as the days passed, mischievous and self-willed children with hearty appetites, and a few of them, in spite of Mother's unremitting efforts, still with dirty heads. The reactions of most foster-parents were understandable.

'I wouldn't make no complaint, Miss, if it was only her head. There's stuff you can put on dirty heads; though it's the first there's bin in our house. It's the bedding. Sheets every day, and I've four of a family to wash for, and every drop o' water to carry, which you wouldn't credit coming from the town. The mattress not fit to use again. That's as true as I stand here. And she's that sulky, Miss, if I say anything, and out wandering about the place at night. It's not as if I'd let my own girls roam about at night, and I never did believe that tale of how she got those gloves. Not that it's the teacher's fault, of course. I'm not really blaming you, but you do see...'

That was one half of all my conversation in September. I spent hours and days listening to troubles in the hope of promoting better relations and making the difficulties of these uprooted children understood. But not one foster parent who aired her grievances so volubly was healed by that safety valve. Without exception, those evacuees who were resented went home, and within a matter of weeks.

To the teacher, each departing child spelt failure, yet I cannot honestly see anything more that could have been done, from the teacher's side, short of gathering the whole brood together into a hostel or camp school.

An excellent case could have been made for almost every one of our thirty children to be taken into special care. But there were no hostels, at least in our part, in those early months. There was no child psychologist to whom we could hand over our misfits. Indeed we were so isolated that I saw our Headmistress only once from September 1st to January, and never any other members of our staff. The local teachers did what was humanly possible to minimise the criticism felt or expressed towards our evacuees, but we were only too well aware that much bad feeling remained.

In those high and lonely dales all those years ago, families tended to be static, and inbred. While the farmers we met showed splendid qualities of loyalty and endurance, some were narrow in outlook, even censorious. Almost all were thrifty to a degree and expected others to be the same. They were genuinely shocked by this first glimpse of urban hand-to-mouth living that evacuation gave to them.

I was shocked too, but in a different way. It was hard to believe that our evacuees had any connection with the Walker children I had known, in school and out, for four years. There I could count lively and lovable pupils by the score, and had taught girls whom I would have been proud to own as daughters far more often than the other sort. But at Arnistone, all save the three who finally settled with Mother and me, and their two sisters at Overdale, were secretive. These five had anti-social habits of their own, but returned our affection. Not so the rest. It must be rare, I think, for twenty-eight children to live several months in any community and give and receive so little love. Of all those children, only the two at Overdale ever fitted into the new life. With the rest, we had to be prepared for anything at any time. I never felt that I really knew them or had their confidence.

We knew that we had a group of children who had been labelled 'C' stream from their infant school days. What we did not appreciate was the extent to which the children's backwardness was dependent upon their lack of mother love.

We noticed, the village noticed — and did not fail to comment on — the way the children were ignored by their parents. They did nor write, and if they visited, it was only to take the children home. As teachers, we saw good cause for homesickness and disappointment in that neglect, and tried to atone for it by our own affection. Yet we were constantly rebuffed. It was this we could not understand. We both knew, Miss Morton and I, that we could cope with ordinary dullness. We were defeated not by backwardness but by impassivity.

We had the best intentions: we spared no effort, bustling about over their clothes, hair, leisure time occupations and letters home. But all the normal teaching palliatives were useless in the face of that subnormal lethargy. What was needed was not one, or even two 'good teachers', but twenty-eight ordinary scolding, watchful and loving mothers.

It was broadcast talks given nearly ten years later by Dr Winnicott when I was feeding my own first baby that provided this key to our evacuees' unresponsiveness. I heard the doctor speaking of the lamentable long-term results of hasty feeding and care in infancy.

'If you are in a hurry and cannot allow for total experience,' he said, 'the baby will start off in a muddle.'

For the first time it occurred to me that perhaps our evacuees had been sullen because they were confused. Not one of our original thirty children came from a truly happy home. It was more likely that the mothers' negligent attitude, apparent during evacuation, had dated from the children's early years. It may well have been that our evacuees had rarely, if ever, been allowed the satisfaction of complete experience in infancy. Certainly they did not understand start and finish. They could not grasp the idea that evacuation, like all things good or bad, would end, and might, in the meantime, just as well be enjoyed as passively endured. But they were incapable of any such positive attitude. When, to the uncertainty of their family life, exile was added, there was nothing they could trust any more.

By and large, brighter children settled better than ours because they were more adaptable, had more interests, and could keep in touch with home more readily. Perhaps most important, they could grasp the idea that evacuation was an interlude.

If we had ever thought of our girls not just as juniors and seniors who had been uprooted from home, but as little children whose early months had been mismanaged, we might have understood their total confusion better. As it was, nothing that we did or said seemed to make any difference to their outlook. They were content to drift.

In our billet, though not unhappy, Mother and I were the reverse of comfortable. Mrs Twentyman, slight and gentle as she looked, had really a very powerful personality. Though it was she who dominated the family, mentally and morally, at the same time she made herself a slave to her men. If the roof leaked, or the wireless battery had not been charged, or the coal had not come, she meekly took the blame while the men muttered imprecations as if it were her fault. All her retired husband ever did — when not in the Black Bull — was to sit by the fire and criticise. There was unending trouble between him and the elder grandson, and a sense of impending violence hung over the house. Mother looked strained and did not eat. True, she never wished for ease in her own life, but she would have welcomed some privacy.

Every evening was spent, of necessity, in the smoke-filled kitchen, where the men wrangled and the radio was never turned off. But Mrs Twentyman, who was highly-strung and sensitive, looked upon Mother as her special friend. To have told her we wanted to move would have cut her to the heart, and given her yet one more example of human ingratitude on which to brood.

Three weeks passed by. Then, without warning, three of our evacuees

— a girl of twelve and her little brother and sister of six and five — were turned out of their billet. The woman said she needed the room for a married daughter, though no daughter ever came. There was no other billet available, but we had seen a tiny, empty cottage on Hill Top, half a mile out of the village. Mother and I and the three homeless evacuees moved there with our scanty baggage and yet another order of living began.

The cottage was indescribably squalid and, we learnt later, its only use for years had been as a plucking place for hens. There was a dark kitchen, with ancient cooking range, bedroom above almost entirely filled with two double beds, and a loft just big enough for one single bed, above the coal house. All water had to be carried from a tap up the hill. I do not remember what we lived on, or how we cooked in those early days. Of necessity I had to be at school, and to me the cottage was never more than a dirty dream. To Mother it must have been a filthy reality. She spent five or six hours every day cleaning children's heads, and the rest of the time coping with meals for us all and trying to make the cottage into some semblance of home. Sanitation was primitive and revolting.

All through September, the sun shone, day after day, from a cloudless sky, and as I went for water night and morning I watched the colours change over a vast expanse of moor and fell. Listening to the far cry of sheep and the song of the lark, it might have been the country of Moab in the time of Naomi, instead of Britain in a twentieth century war.

The happiest part of the working day was the time in school. Arnistone village school was an ancient building, with no water and shocking sanitation, yet the headmaster was cheery and compassionate; a bit 'easy', but a true friend. There were two women teachers, besides myself. For actual lessons, the thirty evacuees were amalgamated with the fifty village children and shared between the four of us. I had twenty-four, aged eight to ten, mainly flaxen-haired little country boys in clogs, and we shared a room with the teacher of standards I and II. I had never taught juniors before and found them very earnest and confiding. We had nature walks, exploring moorland and ghylls. I taught singing to all these juniors and played morning hymns, but mainly our work was the three R's. On this one thing the Headmaster was firm. Forty-seven boys and girls aged seven, eight, nine and ten in one room, and only a glass partition between us and all the seniors was not conducive to good learning. I felt we were failing them all.

At night, in our cottage, the little ones tucked in bed, we tried to make some home life for the thirteen-year-old. Only a candlestick went with the 'furnishings' of our abode, so we bought an Aladdin lamp. This stood on the deal table, around which we sat on our wooden chairs. The stone floor was bare save for a rag mat before the fire, which burnt fitfully in the sunken range, sometimes filling the low room with smoke. In the darkest corner was a brown chipped sink, but no tap. A minute, unventilated cupboard below the rotting stairs served for larder, crockery and stores. Scrubbing brush, mop and dusters we had to buy, as well as tea towels and new pans.

Everything normally in use in a kitchen had to be bought or improvised — but we had neither 'piece bag' nor tool box to improvise from. It was not the bareness of the cottage that was disheartening, but the dilapidation and filth. Nothing was fit to touch, and every drop of hot water for cleaning had to be first carried a sizable distance and then heated over the ill-natured fire. As a den for children's smuggling games, our kitchen was superb — dank, dim and unfrequented. As a home, I believe, though she never said so, it broke my Mother's heart.

We had no radio, so our break with the civilised world seemed complete. We worked like ants, and talked only of school, our evacuees and the post. Letters, indeed, were our life line, in the first weeks of that evacuated time.

Late in September, Mother and I were invited to supper at Overdale. A neighbour offered to sit with our children, but when the time came, we were both so tired that we struggled almost reluctantly into our least squashed clothes and set out for our first social visit in Arnistone. Had we known that this meeting was to dispel the nightmare of the first weeks of evacuation, giving us both, instead, a strange sense of peace, we would have walked up the hill track to the farm with a gayer step.

A fell pony nuzzled into our pockets as we came through the gate. The door opened and we were drawn inside. Our coats vanished, slippers appeared on our feet, and like travellers rescued from a blizzard, we found ourselves sunk in soft armchairs, gazing for the four weeks at a genuine fire.

Mrs Duncan was tall and stooping, with white hair, Mr Duncan (Harry), short and sturdy. Little tufts of hair stood out of his eyebrows like peewit's crests, and his voice was warm and musical.

Mother admired the pony we had seen at the gate.

'Aye,' said Mr Duncan, 'she's a bonny 'un, but did you see her tail? Yon ginger beggar, Foxy, has bin at her in t' night.'

Foxy, I knew from the evacuees, was the larger horse, that was yoked for working.

'Foxy's a cross-bred 'un,' he explained, 'They're the hardiest, but worst tempered. You can ride him all day, and he's still just same at night, never has a pleasant look. If he had someone wi' him that couldn't ride him, he wouldn't be long o' leavin' him.'

I asked if Foxy had ever thrown him.

'Aye, he has that. Was in maggoting time o' year, one Sunday, a cooly morning. I'd bin to Pier Banks. I thought I'd come back and have a bath while folks were away to chapel. He put me off cleverest I ever were put off in my life. I viewed situation — examined foot marks — but I never could reckon it up.'

I glanced at Mother. There was a look of utter serenity on her face. She might have been listening to the Archbishop of Canterbury preaching on eternal life.

For four weeks in Arnistone we had been watched, catechised and held responsible not only for our own but for thirty others' peculiar ways. Here at last was a family that accepted us as we stood, as friends. We buried 'the evacuee teacher' without honour that night.

Mr Duncan's stories were a treat to us but his wife was afraid we would not be interested in 'old farmer's talk'. Mother was asked to play. We had not been among those who regard it as natural to invite their guests to join in music-making since my Father's death. Mother offered to accompany Frances, the younger daughter, in some of her songs. With no procrastinating affectation, Frances brought out music and sang. It was a voice such as we had not heard for many months: clear, sweet, true. Mother thought Frances should be studying at the Royal College. She had faults of technique, but her ability was unmistakable. Soon Margaret and I were drawn into the music too. We sang duets and trios from *I know a Bank* to *Lift Thine Eyes*. At every pause in the singing, more common interests and pleasures were revealed.

Even during that first evening it was clear that the deepest bond of sympathy between Mr and Mrs Duncan and my mother was their ever-present sense of Christian fellowship. Not that they were dreamers. Over the next few months I saw all three at work, in kitchen and dairy; among the evacuees; on the farm. Mrs Duncan had not a peer at baking or butter making, while Mr Duncan was reckoned a very short neck behind the vet with sick animals. Yet there seemed very little of this world about them. All three had a quality of 'self-last' which is rare and beautiful, and gave a strange lustre to their deep-set eyes.

It was nearly twelve before we left, and dawn came before I slept.

Were we led all that way for Birth or Death?

I do not know. I felt such relief for Mother's sake to know that our coming to Arnistone had not been entirely heartache and drudgery, that I decided to give up worrying about meaning and purpose and simply try to help the children to fit into their new school and homes.

Most of the evacuees were over eleven, and so in the 'big room' with the Headmaster, or under seven and therefore in the infant's room. Only two of our girls were among the eight to ten year olds whom I taught, so I soon found that I knew the country children more intimately than I knew our own. One little eight year old boy, Christopher Henderson, a farmer's son, was one of the most appealing, and the shyest child I have ever taught. He worked painstakingly and inkily in all his books, his head buried on his arm. If by chance, he so far forgot himself as to give an answer to a question, his face turned scarlet, and down went his head upon the desk for the next half hour. He did everything without hope. At prayers one morning the caulkers (metal strips) on his clogs slipped on the wooden floor, and he shot right under the desk, landing at the Headmaster's feet. I thought his face would never recover its normal hue.

Though one of a class less than half the size of a normal town class, it was impossible to predict, at eight years old, what his scholastic future might be. He showed no special ability in any subject, and was slow in all. It was a great pleasure to learn, some years ago, that he had done exceptionally well in the Civil Service.

At the end of October, the three evacuees who had been living in the cottage with us were whisked away by their mother. We had grown fond of them and missed them, but it meant less cooking and washing for Mother, and much less water to carry. Once the October sun had gone, only the hardiest of the evacuees stayed on. By November the countryside was wintry; starved and pinched, bleak and scentless. The hills were powdered with snow and looked chilly and forbidding, while the wind blew continuously, strong and bitter. I was battling up the hill from school one stormy afternoon and met the old road-cleaner.

'Blowy' I said, as I passed. He lifted his sodden hat courteously, surveyed the Heavens, and then, with the pride of the Creator himself, he said 'It's tre-*men*-jous wild.'

Many of the older people had a gift for unusual and poetic turns of speech. I did not notice it in the children. Perhaps it is dying out with standardised schooling. One day I had to go up to Middleton on the little local train, to get vests and other things for our evacuees. I had a talk with the Guard. He thought very little of the way the war was being conducted.

'Gort!' he said in disgust, 'He's nobbut an old goat. Couldn't find his way yam in't dark. It's high time we started to take initiaytive, or we'll be in t' same basket as Chesika-Slavik. Little fellers 'as bin set on all along line to do the barking, biting and scratching. We mun tak initiaytive.'

Early in November we had a Monday holiday. Mother had been invited to the home of the infant teacher, to help her with some songs, so I begged our friends at Overdale to give me a day odd-jobbing.

It had rained heavily in the night, but the clouds were lifting as I walked over the moor road. I went to the back door and joined Mrs Duncan in the wash house where she was scrubbing towels on the stone bench. Through the half open door we could see across the fields to stone buildings, grey and green and purple after the rain, and to bare elms, shining in the dull sky. I began to hang out the clothes, and the wind tossed wet sheets across my face. In the byre nearby, chains rattled and a cow coughed. The sun broke through and a rainbow spread over the hill.

Mr Duncan was in the kitchen having his ten o'clocks, for he had been up on the fell looking round the sheep.

'Gan and catch t' auld Galloway,' he called.

We yoked Topsy and led manure for two hours. At dinner time he left me to unharness the horse while he attended to some pigs. Alone in the stable, Topsy suddenly seemed twice the normal pony size. She kept turning round with a not very nice expression, and pushing me with her nose. Gingerly I unhooked and unlatched her gear, but she gave another shove, her nose drawn back and big teeth showing. I retreated hurriedly, slipping on the damp floor.

'Gan right up tae her,' called a cheery voice from the door, 'She'll nat swaller ower much.'

At last she was fixed in her stall.

'There's no trade for horses now,' said Mr. Duncan sadly. 'Every-one's going for wheels. Horses'll be first to get hammer when t'war's at an end.' The stables were a distance from the house, across a field where there were gimmer lambs. He pointed to two

'Them's sort we don't like, them little snipey snouted ones. They should have a good broad manly nose. Goose-nebbed, we calls 'em. Yon tup now, yon's a good 'un: worth about twelve pound now. I got him for thirty shilling.'

We leaned on the gate before turning into the house, and I admired a little red heifer.

'Nay,' he said, 'She's ower much of a cloggy little feeder. See yon now,' pointing to another, to me in no way distinguishable from the first, 'Yon's a little beauty. I like them cocky in the horn, Got a good head, that y'un, not little crummy close horns.'

After dinner we went hedging.

'That's right, shape him up sides and get him level along top,' he said encouragingly when I looked round for advice. 'Clip 'em off far side too. No, this way — turn t'whole menagerie over. Clippers make tidier job, but t'slasher's quicker.'

The unwieldy tool was anything but quicker in my hands, and I was thankful to be called away when it was time to do up the cows. There was a steamy heat in the byre, and a slowness, that was as much part of the place as the stalls or milking stools. We let out the quiet beasts to water, and suddenly it was like David and his household dancing before the Ark of the Lord. The yard was full of mad things, leaping and bucking and cantering round the buildings with wild eyes. The dog brought them in, we fastened them once more, gave them cake and three turnips apiece, and the slow munching began again.

When we went in to wash, the kitchen was full of the warm yeasty smell of rising teacakes. Mrs Duncan had been delayed by a visitor and was still busy in her white apron, kneading dough in a great earthenware bowl.

The visitor was a cousin, who was to be married at the New Year. When we joined her in the sitting room she burst eagerly into a description of her new house and its decoration and furnishing. Carried away by her own enthusiasm, her voice rose. When at last, she paused, Mr Duncan enquired mildly

'An' ist thou goin' to live in t' house by theyseln? It's bin My house, My bed, My room. I was married thirty year agon and there's been nought 'mine' sin' that day.'

I have often wondered why of all the hundreds of sermons I have sat through (sometimes, at least, really trying to listen) few have left any impression. As I listened to Mr Duncan, it struck me that we teachers, like clergymen, sometimes spend a lifetime rolling round moral points in great waves of exhortation without ever striking the bell. I suppose third rate exposition in any art is easy. In speech, almost anyone who is literate at all can, by making a little effort, be verbose, sentimental and obscure. To be the opposite of these things requires effort. If I had had a tape recorder in those far off days, how children would have enjoyed the casual speech of people like Mr Duncan. To many children the real conversation of men and women at work is of far more interest than the passages of 'imaginative', sometimes pretentious writing, with which some school readers are filled.

In Arnistone, school was the village focus. It was because we belonged to the school that Mother and I were so quickly a part of village life. We were so busy in the present, soon — for me at least — whole days slipped by without a thought of home. Sometimes I thought about the Tyne near our Walker school; the allotments, pigeons and gasometer; the council houses, dim and sunny on a summer afternoon; the ferry and the ship-yards. But the things that had shocked me so bitterly three years before, when new to teaching — school like a barracks, children ill-fed, dirty and neglected in Low Walker and 'the Dwellings' — were far less constantly in my mind. We are not goaded to anything like the same extent by the evils we do not see.

In Arnistone everything was different. If there were unhygienic cottages, they were still picturesque, and the children from them were clean, sturdy and well-fed. It was not a case of teachers coming like migrant birds to perch for a few hours daily among the local sparrows, as in Walker. Here it was teachers, farmers and their families in one community. Miss Morton, the infant teacher, played the organ on Sundays, and the older boys and girls made up the choir. In Walker, our acquaintance with our pupils ended daily at four o'clock. On the clang of the school bell, 650 children were hustled out, with their balls and 'hitchies', leaving the playground grey and deserted, and ten minutes later at least half the teachers, with coats and handbags flying, raced down the road, as if life depended on catching the ten past four bus.

We were in Arnistone for tragic reasons, yet after the first two months of confusion, it was impossible to feel anything but happy there. I found myself singing constantly, and the walk to school was a never failing source of joy and surprise. Coming down from Hill Top on winter mornings, I could see across frosted pastures to the grey and purple Yorkshire moors, and watch the Tees winding through the meadows far below. The west wind, in gusts of exuberance, would lift my hat from my head and feet from the road, and I would go panting and laughing into school, ready to face fifty delinquent adolescents if need be — to find only twenty village juniors after all.

This life came suddenly and sadly to an end. It was announced in mid December that there would be a week's holiday for Christmas. With customary optimism — and what was soon seen as wild imprudence — we decided, Mother and I, to make a dash to Newcastle, to collect much needed clothes, small kitchen items for our make-shift life, and above all books.

The journey was by bus to Barnard Castle, then two trains, bus again from Newcastle Central and then walk. It took six hours.

> **A cold coming we had of it**
> **Just the worst time of the year...** *

---

* *Journey of the Magi*, T S Eliot

And when we got there the sunny, cheerful home of roseate memory was damp, dreary and cold. We could not switch on a light till I had improvised a black out. And, while that was in process, Mother had a stroke.

We had no telephone, no relatives at hand. Somehow, through the endless kindness of neighbours, we got her to bed and the doctor to come. It was clear that even if partial recovery was made, she could never go back to the hard, rough life.

Anxious, hurried visits to the Education Office brought, at last, a decree that I could be recalled 'on compassionate grounds' and that I must start, on January 2nd at Elgin Road, the first school to be re-opened in the town. So

> **We returned to our places, these kingdoms**
> **But no longer at ease here, in the old dispensation.** *

---

* Ibid

CHAPTER EIGHT

This disorder'd spring

Poignant experience of hate

It was agonisingly cold in Newcastle, with grey, heavy skies and bitter wind. There was no deep snow to give beauty and stillness, only stinging hail that turned to dirty slush. Our home, so long empty, felt damp all through, and the hastily improvised black-out had to be lifted down each morning before I left for school, so that Mother could have at least sight of cheerful curtains to frame the desolate garden while I was away.

Complete recovery from cerebral haemorrhage was rare in those days, and Mother, having nursed her sisters, knew what she might expect. But with fierce determination she forced herself to walk again, though shakily, and in course of time taught herself to write with her left hand.

Sometimes going quickly into the sitting room I would find her at the piano, gazing, silently, with the Beethoven Sonatas on the music rest. Opus 81A *Les Adieux* was one of her favourites. The alternating themes of grief and consolation of the first movement, the restrained sorrow of the second, had been in my mind, as I'm sure in hers, while at Arnistone. We had anticipated bombing and destruction of home and city, and so the third movement, *The Return* was thankful in the sense that till now devastation had not happened. But I had never prepared my mind for the particular personal sadness that was the cause of our return. The old Scout adage 'Be prepared' has been to me extraordinarily useless as a precept. For fifty years I have prepared for crises that never happened, while every shock and deep emotional disturbance caught me unawares.

While I was away all day at school, good neighbours dropped in to see Mother, with flowers, books or a bit of baking, but there was always the fear of her falling while alone, and distress at the loneliness of her life. Rarely did she complain, but distress at her infirmity was deeply felt. One morning I was dusting and singing to myself. 'It's very appropriate,' she said dryly. I had hit upon the old North Country air *Sair Fyel'd, Hinnie*, the plaint of an old man who resents his growing infirmities and complains against fate.

It is a beautiful and poignant melody, a subject rarely, if ever, heard in other collections of folk-song. The unusual, short phrases and strange jerkiness of the tune perhaps suggest the movements of old age. I changed my song hastily, but too late.

When domestic cares were heaviest and January weather at its worst, school was a vision of the underworld. In those days, outside of villages, one rarely found a local authority school with charm; but many of the gaunt, forbidding, city buildings had character, and were respected if not loved. Westgate Hill, Raby Street, Chillingham Road, Jubilee — I have done country dancing and other liberal-minded projects in all those Newcastle schools and think of them with affection. But Elgin Road School, built in the late Twenties, and now happily pulled down, was without redeeming feature. It was a uniform shade of mud, cheapest brick outside and colour-wash within.

I arrived early on that first January morning, but several hundred girls with attendant mothers were already crowded in the hall, where a large lady in a huge hat was pushing her way through the milling crowd shouting

'Sevens and eights to right; nines and tens to left — Not THERE stupid — HERE. Elevens and twelves over there...'

More than any normal school scene the chaos suggested a cattle mart with a sleek lady auctioneer in charge.

'Yon's the new Headmistress I shouldn't wonder,' whispered a mother to me. 'Name's Hardcastle.'

Brusquely Miss Hardcastle dismissed the gaping mothers, leaving four huge squads of pupils waiting, like penned calves. We teachers, trying to look competent, stood about like eager collie dogs.

'Split them into year-groups,' commanded Miss Hardcastle. 'Here are new registers. Write them up tonight, and now take, each of you, the group I shall allot, and instruct them till I come. At assembly tomorrow I shall Give Out My Rules.' She always spoke like this, in capitals.

We led our groups — mine being standard VI, the twelve year olds — to identical mudcoloured boxes labelled Room 1, Room 2, Room 3 ... Grey light filtered through small windows blast-protected by wire netting.

Forty-seven pupils, equally strange to one another and to me, pushed and shuffled into seats and for want of better occupation, turned their sad, almost sullen gaze on me. Never before had I met a new class looking less eager or responsive. Five or six of the biggest girls sat slumped in their desks like Dürer's engraving *Melancholia*. Years later I read Kenneth Clark's note on this picture.

In the Middle Ages, Melancholia meant a combination of sloth, boredom and despondency.

And was that not precisely what these pupils had experienced since war had been declared? Do any of us realise how much we depend on the affection, routine and security of school until it is gone for ever?

By 'Instruct them', Miss Hardcastle meant 'Admonish them on cleanliness; follow with rapid mental arithmetic; drill in 'mechanical' (sums from the blackboard, since we had no books) and time left over to spelling.' This she made all too clear later that first day. But such teacher authority, while it would, to her eyes, have looked efficient, could have done nothing to melt the shyness of our pupils, nor heal their feelings of rejection. I believe shared tasks and laughter bring reassurance more surely than any display of maniacal activity by a teacher. This co-operation we had had in Arnistone village school and, after the freedom and kindliness there, the contrast was almost physically painful.

Oh call back yesterday, bid Time return ...*

Throughout the time I knew Miss Hardcastle, she wore the same suit and large hat, looking, in her gay moods, like the Queen Mother on a shooting party, but when enraged, like the Minotaur in full charge. The hat accompanied her even to assembly, which seemed a trifle odd. Assembly itself was odder still; a brief sojourn in the land of the public school story, which had little meaning for our pupils.

'... The first school reopened in the town ... We are being tested and watched ...We are on trial ... We must strive, strive for the honour of the school ...There's a girl in the third row picking her *nose*.'

I do not imply that we did not *wish* our girls to reach (in course of time) a feeling for 'our school', and be proud to do so. But natural pride is not produced by royal proclamation.

Perhaps the worst thing to bear was that we were never left alone to get on with anything in our own way. We would be trying, using all our ingenuity and imagination, to change the prison-like aura of our classroom,

---

* *Richard II*, Act III Sc ii, William Shakespeare

when suddenly she would be among us, setting the clock back fifty years: 'Girl! What are you doing with a paint brush?' 'Who is this we have here working with her neighbour? Why aren't the English language books out on the desks?' and, after a brief walk round, 'I can't see much to impress me in any of this work.'

All joy and spontaneity would vanish for the next twenty minutes. Brusque, self-contradictory, always trying to make those who were physically smaller feel her power and size, she treated mothers as well as teachers like naughty girls in a penitentiary, with herself conferring a favour by enrolling pupils at all. She would pretend to the poorer mothers that the school was too full to take their offspring. Occasionally she overdid the condescension and met her match. One day, going up the narrow stairs to her private room, I met such a one, followed by her embarrassed child. The mother barred my way.

'Who runs this school I'd like to know?' she demanded. 'I'd allus heard tell this 'ere was a *public* elementary school. Why isn't *my* child good enough for it? Will you tell me that?' She pointed to the sallow, rather shabby girl shrinking behind. 'What's wrong with Maureen, anyway?'

It was easy to see why Miss Hardcastle, with her peculiar philosophy, had rejected her. She simply was not up to standard for the imaginary academy of which Miss Hardcastle fancied herself Head.

'I can't keep a child in silk and satin on a rating's pay,' went on the slighted one. 'My man's in the Navy and it's men like him as keeps this country safe for the likes of her up there. I telled her straight. But I wouldn't send More-reen to this school now, whatever. She can sit at home till they open Jubilee. Her at Jubilee's a lady. Her up there —' She tossed her head towards Miss Hardcastle's private room and words failed, for once.

In the second week, Miss Hardcastle asked me, without please or thank you, to prepare a history scheme for the *entire* school.

'Have it ready by Friday so that other teachers can start working from it straight away. An inspector may look in any day and we must show that we know how to get off the mark.'

Anxiety filled my heart. It takes thinking, searching, writing, over weeks or months, not days, to prepare a good scheme — especially for such deprived and untended pupils as ours were at that point in the war. How could I hope to do it in the few crowded evening hours at home? Yet a certain pitch of desperation can be as potent as happiness in producing results. I went at it like a terrier, 'ratching' as we say in the Borders, in source books, biographies, old files. To re-read original sources can act like an electric charge, and the teacher, no matter how depressed initially, feels a surge of ability and confidence which she cannot fail to communicate in class. I found a tiny note that I had mislaid for several years — copy of part of a letter from Erasmus to a friend, describing Sir Thomas More. In the particular Slough of Despond that engulfed us at that moment in school, the vivid little description seemed extraordinarily apposite.

His eyes are a bluish-grey with some sort of tinting upon them. This kind of eye is thought to be a sign of the happiest character, a friendly cheerfulness ... He likes to be dressed simply and does not wear silk or purple or gold chains ... He seems to be born and made for friendship ... In company, his extraordinary kindness and sweetness of temper are such as to cheer the dullest spirit ... From boyhood he was always pleased with a joke ...

Two days later I ventured to begin his story. Helped by little extracts from Roper's *Life of More* perhaps the girls were able to form at least a tentative picture of him and his family. After some talk together ('talk' being still questions from teacher and brief answers from the more reflective pupils), I read the extract from the rediscovered letter. There was a deep silence.

Any teacher breaks into such silence with trepidation. If the subject of the lesson has made an impact, anything the teacher adds may be bathetic; yet one must try to help each child to link the story to her own restricted experience. I asked if any of them knew a person — friend or family — who resembled More in spirit, and, after thinking for a little while, to write a few lines about him or her. The resulting half hour was one of real effort and absorption. All wrote something, and some of those badly written and spelt were among the most revealing. Uncles, grannies, fathers and especially mothers were clearly deeply loved, and ten or a dozen girls wrote with real perception. Those who wished to read out their work did so in turn, and for the first time they really *listened* to each other and commented upon each others' work. They actually dug up thoughts from their own experience and the 'digging-up' seemed to liberate them all, as if we had been allowed out from that dark, restricting classroom on an all-too-brief archaeological dig.

At the end of the day I went with my history syllabus to Miss Hardcastle. Irritable as always at interruption she snapped 'What now? ... Oh — the scheme I asked for ... I'll glance through it if I've time.'

Two days later she strode into our room, tapped me on the shoulder and said 'Your scheme. I've skimmed through it. Not bad.'

Luckily for everyone, the next lesson was physical training. We ran and jumped till thoughts of rancour were forgotten, and were returning to the classroom in almost buoyant mood, when, turning a corner we faced our Head again. Looking me up and down distastefully she paused, then spoke.

'Kindly have your plimsolls cleaned Miss Dunn. They are dirty. We must set an example to these girls.'

Her comments were infuriating because true — my shoes *did* need whitening, more urgent tasks having taken priority. But justice told me she was not to know that. The deeper reason for my rage was that I held her responsible for the soul-destroying atmosphere in Elgin Road. In that place, we were all to some degree neurotic, anxiously awaiting the next verbal onslaught, never sure how or on whom it would fall. Present mirth hath present laughter — but in Elgin Road there was tension every day.

By contrast, in that bleak building in Washington Road in Walker — still in my heart 'my' school — I had realised by my second year that despite our sober reputation in the neighbourhood for good work, we had a healthy tradition among ourselves of 'school laughs'. There was, for example, an occasion when a class, inadvertently left teacherless for fifteen minutes, became obstreperous. Miss Ivinson, ever alert to earth tremors in her bailiwick, appeared in majesty at the door, and, in the shocked and sorrowing tones we knew so well, uttered the immortal words

'Girls!! Girls!! What *can* be the meaning of all this belling and yellowing?'

I felt that what we needed in Elgin Road was a sustained blast of belling and yellowing by staff and pupils together against the whole ridiculous regime. In fantasy I set it all to music, a 'choral *Fantasia*' accompanied by trumpets, horns and drums.

But the long, wet journey home was always sobering. Tired, hungry and clutching a heavy bag of books, I felt about as fitted to the modern scene as Dürer's *Knight*, weighed down, not as he was with protective armour, but with ponderous intellectual equipment that it had taken precious years of health, energy and mental effort to acquire.

And the upshot of that prolonged endeavour? Not only was I doing no historical study myself: I was making only a token gesture towards teaching it. We lacked even the patched up collections of books and pictures that I had assembled at Washington Road; the BBC pamphlets; the encyclopaedias. How could I ever enable even my own huge class, never mind six other classes, to learn *by enquiry*? To investigate, ponder, and begin to understand the fragmentary records left, over the centuries, by cunning, ambitious or bewildered human beings? How useless and misguided had been almost all my efforts of the past eight years: all those errors and omissions that had made my own first teaching term horrific ... And it was the reverse of consoling to be back now four years later, still at the lowest point of the ebb-tide, no more decisive or confident than Lewis Carroll's White Knight. Even that one lesson I had deduced for myself by the term of teaching at the training college — that mistakes — are inevitable and that a large part of the teacher's role is learning to bear frustration — had been forgotten before it could be put to proper use. Each pellet of wisdom I fondly imagined life had taught, was no sooner recognised than it mysteriously vanished from sight.

That January of 1940 I was blown out of my academical ivory tower; not only blown out, but disorientated by the blast. A few days later, hunting for poetry to read to my class, I found Robert Graves's little poem, *Flying Crooked*, which exactly expressed my unproductive state of lost direction, for the rest of the time I was in that school.

> **The butterfly, a cabbage-white**
> **(His honest idiocy of flight)**
> **Will never now, it is too late**
> **Master the art of flying straight,**
> **Yet has — who knows so well as I? —**
> **A just sense of how not to fly:**
> **He lurches here and there by guess**
> **And God and hope and hopelessness;**
> **Even the Aerobatic swift**
> **Has not his flying-crooked gift.**

Of the years I spent in teaching, the time in Elgin Road remains in memory as a spell of hopelessness, punctuated, if the sun shone continuously two hours together, by mad bursts of unquenchable optimism. Daily, on exhausting journeys back and forth across the town, energy was wasted in futile self-laceration and unending inner debate.

For I felt towards Miss Hardcastle like Gladstone towards the mule he once rode when on holiday in Sicily. 'I could neither like nor love her,' he wrote in his diary — adding with insight and humility, 'What that mule was to me, I have been to the Queen, but the period of three weeks is represented by one of thirty years.'

All teachers have a stock of 'jokes' and howlers, many of them tragicomical indeed. I will end this brief maledictory chapter with one more of mine.

Question: Take five away from eighty-seven as many times as you
    can:
What is the result?
Answer: I get eighty-two every time.

How I feel for that child in her impasse. At Elgin Road, convinced of the rightness of my view that the best learning takes place in a cheerful, 'easy' classroom, I tangled with Miss Hardcastle's absurd pretensions daily.

It is so obvious that I was not All Virtue and our Head, All Sin. But, like that misguided child with her arithmetic, I just kept on as before, growing ever more frustrated, under Miss Hardcastle's baton, by the futility of our contradictory efforts.

**Oh what a dusty answer gets the soul
When hot for certainties in this our life!***

---

*Modern Love, George Meredith

CHAPTER NINE

Pots, pans and poetry

Learning to listen again; seeing for the first time

It was in those long winter evenings of my Mother's illness that I began listening all over again. In four years as a teacher I had almost lost the art.

Without excusing, it is easy to see how this had occurred. In those first anguished terms of teaching and trying to keep a roof over our heads, I gave up concerts, radio, even visits to friends, to prepare school work and do the coaching which helped our meagre budget. And even after the return from evacuation, the blackout altered all pre-war habits. Every evening I cleared away the tea, made up a bright fire in Mother's bedroom and sat in the rocking chair, reading aloud to her. She chose first *Richard II*, then *As You Like It*, then *King Lear*. Remembering the boredom and self-consciousness of 'acting' Shakespeare at school, I began with foreboding, but very soon the readings became one of our greatest pleasures. At school, we had thought ourselves lucky if we got the sense. Not once had I realised that each character had his own voice, unmistakable as the voice of a living friend. And is there, in all the plays, a voice more self-revealing than that of Richard — so moving as poet, so lacking in wisdom or justice as a man? What could it be that led my mother, one of nature's stoics, forgetful of herself, to make her first choice for reading this monumental study of egotism; of a king 'full of tears', of whom Salisbury could say

Thy sun sets weeping in the lowly west
Witnessing storms to come, woe and unrest.

Why did I never ask her reasons at the time? Do all sons and daughters put up such clumsy barricades against parents, neither asking nor giving information, lest someone of the older generation should find a chink in the armour and peep through? After my father's death we lived seven years in harmony, Mother and I. Yet of all we felt most deeply, we rarely, if ever, spoke. So I do not know if she cared about problems of power and politics; or whether, as I think, she listened to the play primarily as a sustained outpouring of poetic genius. She herself could genuinely say with wise old Gaunt

All places that the eye of heaven visits, Are to a wise man, ports and
happy havens; Teach they necessity to reason thus.... Look what thy soul
holds dear; imagine it To lie that way thou go'st; not whence thou com'st

While I, like Bolingbroke, nursed inward discontent, dreading present banishment from world affairs and a future of captivity in nursing.

Sometimes in a pause from reading we sat quietly in fire and lamp-light, Mother wrapped in shawls, spectacles on nose like the invalid Tailor of Gloucester; myself watchful by the bed, like Simpkin the cat. For perhaps the first time since childhood, I really looked attentively at the familiar, homely objects in the room, and saw beauty in them.

'Still-life' when pointed out to us at school, had meant nothing. 'Life' then was sound and movement. Weary hours of art at school spent copying a black pot and a stick of celery, or half an over-ripe melon beside a purple plumed hat had added nothing of beauty or meaning to existence, and when, for my sixteenth birthday, a friend gave me a small framed picture — Chardin 's *Girl Peeling Vegetables*, I was less than enchanted. I looked at the peasant girl, day-dreaming among her pots and pans, as I might have looked at any magazine advertisement. With an egotism almost as complete as Richard 's, I wondered why Edith had given it to me, what had it to do with me? Was it a slight personal rebuke? Nevertheless, as in duty bound, I put the picture up on the bedroom wall, where, for eight years, it hung, in one home or another, unnoticed, save on cleaning day, when I dusted it with a small stab of bafflement.

Then, like a meteor in that first dark, cold, war-time winter, Chardin's humble pots, pans and potatoes, the block of wood, the maiden's stillness, all spoke to our condition. A seed, lodged in poor soil so long ago, germinated, and in explosive fashion. I made elaborate arrangements, one Saturday, to get to the university library for books on Chardin, and when I found them, was stunned by the force of his pictures, even in reproduction. He painted simple kitchen objects, in a way to make one see everyday tools of cooking or eating for ever after with changed eyes. Not till the war was over did I see any of Chardin's originals. There are three in the Hunterian Museum in Glasgow. *The Cellar Boy* and *The Scullery Maid* are tiny, and the *Lady Drinking Tea* not much bigger, but they are unforgettable. Some day, I thought, I will get to the Louvre to see the self-portraits and the *Silver Goblet*.

Till this time, I had imagined that we must cram every worthwhile experience into the syllabus of the secondary school — literature, languages, mathematics, sciences, the arts; all must somehow be treated 'comprehensively' within the four or five secondary years, since what our pupils didn't know before leaving they might never hear of again!

In that long winter of 1940, I learnt how disastrously mistaken this view was, and is. The thrill of discovering Chardin for myself far out-did any pleasure I ever had in those years of 'art' lessons at high school. And then a strange thing happened. For perhaps the first time, I began to think about teaching from the opposite end: not — as had been my habit until then — from the teacher's angle, how can I help these children to share the joy I feel in literature — in history — or in mathematics, but the other way round: why should it be that a whole subject is disliked by a pupil? What makes a lesson boring, hated, even feared at school? Is it the room? Is it the teacher — the homework? What *can* make it possible for a boy or girl to say 'I hate geography?' As one might say, 'I hate bananas' or 'lumps in the mattress'.

One would think certain aspects of almost any subject would form some link with the pupil's interests in life? Why had I found no pleasure in any single art lesson that we ever had in school? Our art room, called 'The Studio', was a sunless attic, its green walls hung with dirty plaster casts. Every room into which children go says something to them and this room, presided over by Miss Meredith, tall, black haired, masculine, with a deep growling voice, said 'Danger: storms'. I do believe now that she cared quite passionately about something — though what, we shall never know. Perhaps she had dreamed of inspiring female Dürers, but had sunk in disillusion. All we knew as children — and we were only nine or ten when first under her sway — was that she was the most temperamental of teachers, given to swift, stupendous rages, and to such devastating criticism when in bad humour that anxiety and apprehension were added to all our initial diffidence. In class, I sat beside my good friend June. All we both wanted was to while away the afternoon as unobtrusively as possible, passing the odd whispered word of help or condolence to one another as we toiled. Once we were asked to make a design for the back of a playing card. Mine must have been so completely characterless that I can no longer even see it in memory! But June had painted an apple tree, with apples falling into a skep beneath. Then, finding that, in execution, her idea looked simply idiotic, she lost her head and added the back view of a rabbit to balance the skep.

Miss Meridith drew near. She towered over us in one of her awesome silences, and tension spread round the room. Red to the ears, June and I fiddled with our brushes, waiting and wondering on which of us the weight of her tongue would fall. At last she spoke: 'June! Hilda! When your minds are blank, please LEAVE A BLANK.'

I do not doubt this was intended to be bracing, but intended results in education are rarely instantaneous, and at the time, we took the easy way out, assumed we 'couldn't do it' and simply ceased to try.

I think this teacher could have found a better way to feed our genuine artistic interests for, in the long run, we did each start afresh, and June became skilled in several crafts. But all that was after years of stultifying diffidence.

There was a time, once, when I thought 'diffidence' a pleasing trait, in adults or in children. Now I am not so sure. Was Bunyan right when he said

Giant Despair had a wife, and her name was Diffidence?*

It strikes me now, all these years later, that, secretly, I had thought always of Miss Meredith as Medea, and Medea killed her children. Can this explain my fear? Perhaps not: yet pupils — perhaps most pupils — do have irrational fears. Neither pupils nor teachers leave their emotional problems locked up in their desks, even through the most humdrum of lessons.

So, here we are back in the Elgin Road war-time classroom; bare walls; blast screens over windows dimming the already cheerless light; a class of thin, saddened rabbits, half fretfully smothering coughs, half rubbing reddened paws; a teacher vainly trying to conjure up Aladdin's cave so that hungry pupils would believe in 'Learning through Joy'.

And the sad truth was, a teacher could not do it — not in the charged atmosphere of Elgin Road. I have had to look back on the month as well-nigh total failure, save perhaps for the last few days, and for the long evening hours of darkness at home when, domestic chores done, I read to my mother and enjoyed listening to *her* thoughts. Somehow, in all that pre-war 'busy-ness' I had made little time for that.

But I got home one night to find that Kathleen, a friend from student days and a piano pupil of Mother's, had sent us a little volume of modern verse. What a treasure it became. From it, Auden's *Musée des Beaux Arts* written in 1938, spoke exactly for us at that moment in the war.

> About suffering they were never wrong,
> The old Masters: how well they understood
> Its human position; how it takes place
> While someone else is eating or opening a window or
> just walking dully along;

* *Pilgrim's Progress*

How, when the aged are reverently, passionately waiting
For the miraculous birth, there always must be
Children who did not specially want it to happen, skating
On a pond at the edge of the wood:
In Brueghel's Icarus, for instance: how everything turns away
Quite leisurely from the disaster; the ploughman may
Have heard the splash, the forsaken cry,
But for him it was not an important failure; the sun shone
As it had to on the white legs disappearing into the green
Water; and the expensive delicate ship that must have seen
Something amazing, a boy falling out of the sky,
Had somewhere to get to and sailed calmly on.

Like the 'expensive delicate ship' in the picture, I 'sailed calmly on', doing the grate, dusting the ornaments, reading and talking, exchanging thoughts and platitudes. What else could we do?

My Mother's birthday came, and, remembering how once in childhood when I had asked her her favourite instrument, she had replied 'the string quartet', I bought for her birthday the records of Beethoven's second *Rasumovsky Quartet*. Night after night we played this blessed, healing music, and I began to understand what she meant.

I suppose, through those dark winter months, I cooked meals, though I cannot remember. We lived on a diet of letters for breakfast, Shakespeare after tea and Beethoven before going to bed.

Letters were necessary then. They were daily bread; without their reassurance, feasts of Shakespeare or Beethoven would not have been enjoyed. In that war-time correspondence, longing, as everyone did, for sight of absent friends, I listened to the intimate and unselfconscious voice of each speaker as I had never listened for the voice in the written word before.

There were letters from my two brothers, one in the Air Force, one Houseman in a hospital; from old school friends, June and others; from Dorothy, Kathleen and other teachers, evacuated to Yorkshire or Cumbria; from the friends we had made in Arnistone. All were lively, stimulating, affectionate. But in a class of their own were the letters of Janet Riley whom I had met while teaching in Walker, before war was declared.

Mother had taken a deep and immediate liking to her. She liked her direct gaze, her tender-heartedness, her humour. To Janet, people were, in the main, both lovable and comical — though sometimes, unfortunately, greedy and selfish too. This view Mother shared, though she did not express it with such force. When, some years later I was to see and hear Janet in adult education classes, she made me think of Rodin's comment on Bernard Shaw: when asked if Shaw spoke French well, Rodin replied
Mr Shaw does not speak French well; but he expresses himself with

such violence that he imposes himself.

Janet, like Shaw, suffered acute nervousness in speaking before any group, yet, like him, she could marshal her thoughts with speed, and invariably spoke with such sincerity, clarity and immediacy that, without being in the slightest degree domineering, in Rodin's phrase, she 'imposed herself'.

From the outbreak of war, Janet had been working in west Cumbria, but because of the incessant coming and going of evacuated children, early in January, she was moved from Maryport to Penrith. So, the wheel of fortune dropped her off, not only in the town where she was born, but actually into her old home, from the entanglements of which she had fled twelve years earlier, to live on her own in Newcastle. To sustain her beloved Mother she was glad, but war-time tensions were hardly likely to make the old feuds between others in the household less soul-destroying than before. Nonetheless, pushing such fears behind, she flung herself into the struggle to find a useful role once more in Penrith.

Since she wrote as she spoke, her letters conveyed most warmly and engagingly her new school-work and the life of this close and independent market town.

Janet taught juniors, and in the sense that her turbulent spirit provoked discussion in her class, she was not always reckoned 'a good teacher'. Yet she was rich in those qualities which make a lasting impression on pupils, young or old. If girls asked me difficult questions, the cause of the war, for instance, or something about politics, I always had to go back to first principles. By the time we reached the present, interest had waned! But Janet could give succinct answers in a way I both envied and admired. She had also a gift for presenting problems briefly and squarely so that girls and boys could give their own thoughts about them, not a stock response.

Early in February, Janet wrote

Sunday: At last I am settled, with twenty-two little girls in the school I went to as a child. My room is so small it might be the study in Haworth Parsonage. From the window I have that same sad view of leaning tombstones in the old churchyard. Mine is the sort of class-room where dying flowers may droop for ever in increasingly stagnant water. I am a Philistine in many ways. It does not perturb me to live in rooms like those I have always had in Newcastle lodgings, with hideous ornaments all over the mantel-piece and pictures of actresses on the walls. Yet I am aware of a nice room such as the one in your house where your mother played Chopin to us; or a green and white room in the vicarage at Newton Reigny where I went to a meeting last Saturday and the vicar showed us his eighteenth century mezzotints. It is cold here; snow covered, with heavy grey sky and a bitter wind that gets very mournful up on this hill. In school, the girls huddle against the radiator, and all envy one classroom which has a bright,

homely fire.

I have enrolled as a 'helper' at the Wesleyan canteen. I did this as a penance, ashamed of being in this safe place, but it turns out the reverse. After whole days in the company of virtuous teachers, I enjoy talking to soldiers! Hundreds of lads line up patiently for sausage and chips. Unfortunately I had a 'fratch' last night — after hours — with a non-conformist parson. He is a little, fat, bald man, always moralising and denouncing. One of the helpers said to him quite innocently, 'People will never go to Church again as they did in my young days.' He waited till she had gone and then attacked her, adding 'People should never speak unless they can prove what they say.'

I said, 'In that case, most of us would be dumb from the cradle to the grave.'

Removing his pipe and beaming amiably, he said, 'You're right.'

The devil entered into me and I added, 'And that applies particularly to the preachers.' I only said it in fun, but he was outraged, and thundered and bellowed at me for nearly half an hour. In the end, I said to him, 'I can't argue with you because you only talk me down. That's what comes of having a pulpit. You get used to saying what you like without fear of challenge.'

I would not have said that if he had not been so blown up with conceit. The other two helpers were dumb. What a temper he was in: And Oh the emptiness, the verbiage, the vanity of his 'arguments' about the danger from people like me and the harm I can do to the 'ignorant' by being a communist!'

Here in Penrith, we are in no physical danger, but there is that other danger which seems to terrify me more — of saying what I know to be true, and of being isolated, distrusted and disliked. I dread being isolated — and more, far more, I dread that my mother should be isolated and disliked because of me ... This morning, just as I woke, I heard a train hooting and saw a triangle of spring sunshine on the wall of the house opposite. I thought the train was a ship and that, along with the sunshine, brought the Tyne and Tyneside back to me with such a pang I almost cried. I felt as if, here in Penrith, I were now a ghost; a ghost that had caught a glimpse of the life I once lived.

Sounds, perhaps more than pictures or photographs, do bring back the Tyne. I understand this well, for I have lived away from Tyneside now for many years. But, on that February morning in 1940, trudging to school through the drenched, smoke-blackened streets of Shieldfield, I knew that Janet's 'glimpse of the life I once lived' did not mean that she pictured again in any corporeal sense those same squalid streets through which I now daily journeyed. It was rather a poignant farewell to her brief freedom from domestic bondage which her years in Newcastle had brought. There, her life had at last seemed meaningful. She could teach with good grace when, at night, she could go, unquestioned, about her own pursuits, writing, drawing and attending meetings. Once back in Penrith, there was, for her, none of the peace which I had at home with my invalid. Mother and I, though sorely missing all close friends, nevertheless still lived our quiet life in Heaton among kindly, non-interfering neighbours, the very obverse of the situation claiming Janet. I knew her home town well and could understand how the good, but inbred, inward-looking people of that small community were startled, even scandalised, by someone so attuned to the life of politics and the Riverside that she stuck out among them like a tall and battered drifter gone aground among market stalls.

...No longer at ease here ... with an alien people clutching their gods...*

Without crucifying at least half of her personality she would never-more live contentedly within the bounds of a country market town.

I would guess that many teachers, not rebels when first evacuated in 1939, but possessed of observation and a modicum of critical sense, felt the shock of conflicting school and life-styles to such an extent that they never, thereafter, looked complacently on the education system again. To Janet, a rebel already even in 1939, the overwhelming shock, from which she never recovered, was the loss of her independence. To me, after our brief enjoyment of the kindly country regime, the shock came when the catastrophe of Mother's illness was followed by the lash of an arrogant Headteacher, that worst kind of bully in the school system.

Miss Hardcastle's total blindness to the sensitivity and effort shown by pupils, or to the cares, anxieties and good sense of parents — her refusal, in short, to allow feelings to anyone but herself, left me like a cat that has walked on wet tar — helpless and enraged.

My 'thoughts' that Friday morning, journeying to school after reading Janet's letter, declined into a kind of lenten lamentation with, as refrain, a line of poetry that kept coming into my head, unidentified and unasked

Never glad confident morning again...**

It was not city schools as such that had brought on this profound depression. Elgin Road School itself was the cause of our 'Disorder'd Spring'. For, in the days when Dorothy and I had tramped together daily — she to Jubilee in Byker, and I to Washington Road, we had talked with animation every step of the way. Whatever setbacks and discouragement had marred the week behind us, we both looked forward daily to our cheery pupils and to the making of fresh starts. Somehow at Elgin Road that mutual trust and sharing of effort never came to pass.

Could we have sustained and developed the partial breakthrough made during the time we spent studying Sir Thomas More, there would have been some return of self-confidence among the girls, which would

---

* *Journey of the Magi*, T S Eliot
** *The Lost Leader*, Robert Browning

surely, in time, have resulted in a more responsive and homogeneous class. But girls cannot become young historians without books and materials, any more that they can become cooks by copying down recipes. We had no history books, no library and no books for literature other than a deplorable collection of jingles called 'Junior Poesy'.

One unfortunate day the monitors put out these shallow booklets unbeknownst to me, and I had to explain why we could do better without them — drawing for ourselves on all the vast store of poetry in our own language. We looked at a 'poem' from the booklet which began:

The world's a very happy place,
Where every child should dance and sing,
And always have a smiling face,
And never sulk for anything.

With a little prodding, a few agreed that the sentiment was wholly false. I said that ordinary men and women, children too, often said things that were direct and true and somehow more like poetry than this verse we had just read, and I told them about Dr Henry Stokes of a famous medical family in Dublin, who was too kind to charge the poor and too proud to charge his friends, so lived always in exceeding poverty himself. An old woman from the Dublin slums said, 'Ah, Mr Henry Stokes, the darlin' man. There's no rhyme nor reason in him. He's like the love of God.'

Yes, we had a good discussion about true and artificial feelings, and the deeper thinkers certainly saw the distinction. There is never a time, unhappily, when all the members of an enormous class are ready together for such a theme. Nevertheless, at some risk — for the tail end of the class might get bored and restive — I decided to spend our fourth Friday afternoon poetry lesson in reading to them, all sixty-two verses of *John Gilpin*. It might just be within the comprehension of most, and the direct straight-forward language might arouse true feelings.

This turned into our first unalloyed success. They followed every detail of the story, and I was delighted by the compassion shown for Mrs Gilpin as well as for her husband. She, good-natured, careful soul, gets little scope from the poet to air her feelings about the outing, but my girls vied with one another to remedy that. The chapter of disasters captured all their minds and loosened every tongue. As in the old days at Washington Road, they hung about my desk at the day's end asking 'Can we go on with this next week?' It seemed as if, after four weeks of sullen weather, slogging upward through hail, rain and continuous wind, we had suddenly caught sight of a hospice where we were assured of a square meal, even perhaps a celebratory dance.

For the first time on the homeward trudge from Elgin Road, happy prospects filled my mind, of other journeys the class and I could make together in the future. Ironically, all that day, a letter from the Office had been waiting on the mantelpiece at home. I was to report, on the ensuing Monday morning, to Elgin Road no longer, but to the first school to re-open in Walker, Cooper Street, a newish building, with class rooms surrounding an open courtyard.

From our home I could reach it in thirty minutes' walk — under the railway arch, past the Fever Hospital, and on by the side of flat, sad fields, dusty with soot and ringed with collapsing hedges. Yet from early February on, larks sang there as ecstatically as in our Cheviot hills.

On reading my official letter, my first thought was of this road on which I would journey, and the song of the larks heard there since childhood. Then came the realisation that to start at one place must mean finish at the other; and finish on the Office say-so with neither hail nor farewell: leave those forty-seven pupils with whom I had been bound for four long, stressful weeks, unable to speak a word of regret for our parting, nor encouragement for their future careers.

We know such partings come each year end, to almost every child and teacher, yet this yearly administrative arrangement is accepted as a stage in the maturing of young minds. To part, as we parted then, without preparation, was a savage rending of all that we mean by 'education', and could only intensify the sense of alienation already suffered by our Elgin Road girls.

Worse turmoil, I am well aware, was the lot of occupied Europe. Yet Britain was *not* occupied, and had any consultations taken place with ordinary practising teachers, many of the pains of those instant schools of 1940 could have been less than they were.

Throughout that Saturday and Sunday I thought often of those girls I would not see again. I would know neither how they fared nor if their fragile joy in living perished. The lines that came unsought to mind and still do, were from a little poem of Thomas Hardy's, *Shelley's Skylark*

Somewhere afield here something lies
In Earth's oblivious eyeless trust
That moved a poet to prophecies
A pinch of unseen, unguarded dust:

The dust of the lark that Shelley heard
And made immortal in times to be;
Though it only lived like another bird,
And knew not its immortality:

Lived its meek life; then one day fell —
A little ball of feather and bone;
And how it perished, when piped farewell,
And where it wastes are alike unknown...

CHAPTER TEN

The best of times, the worst of times

Walker revisited

It was the best of times, it was the worst of times, it was the age of wisdom, it was the age of foolishness... it was the season of light, it was the season of darkness, it was the spring of hope, it was the winter of despair, we had everything before us, we had nothing before us... *

and of those words of Dickens every one was true at some point in 1940.

During the long hours while I was away at school, my mother re-read all of Dickens' later books, and she opened my eyes to Dickens' profoundly serious and searching view of life. I began to re-read him myself, and was amazed at all I had missed before. During the next few months, immured as I was in such bizarre school life, it struck me how memorably Dickens could have recorded life in a Walker school if only he had lived another eighty years.

Our old school, Washington Road, was not re-opened until 1941. The

---

* *Tale of Two Cities,* Charles Dickens

school used for Walker children till 1941 was the recently built Cooper Street. It was only thirty minutes walk from home, and the walk itself cheered up the start of every day. At Elgin Road we could have been sitting in any town in the land; at Cooper Street we were back in the heart of those industries which had made the Tyne what it once was.

Our new Headmistress, Miss Tait, was small and tetchy, very different in manner from the Elgin Road Head. She was in a perpetual state of nervous exhaustion, never seen without an anxious frown, harassed to distraction by the scarcity of teachers, the backwardness of children, and at having seniors to deal with when previously she had only experienced infants. The infants were, in fact, always her first, and chief concern.

I was given fifty-eight sadly dishevelled pupils, with only one thing in common: a chronological age of ten or eleven years.

'You've got a large class,' said Miss Tait, 'a very large class... I don't know how you'll manage...You'd better take the art room. It's the furthest off — up the stairs.'

How startling the memory's tricks! Although I had recalled so recently my loathing of 'drawing lessons' as a pupil, on that morning in Walker, that picture of the hated 'studio' never crossed my mind. Momentarily all was bliss and hope. Miss Tait's offer brought no recollection more alarming than the warmth and kindness of the art department of the Western High School wherein I had peeped while teaching there. And now, with all my new found joy in Chardin, a picture of an art room filled with practical, domestic 'busy-ness' sprang at once to mind. Off I set, my chattering flock at heel, all of us clattering up the stone stairs, eager to take possession of our promised Eldorado.

We found ourselves staring into what looked like an abandoned station waiting room, narrow, dusty, very, very long, with windows (grey netted) only on the northern side. There were forty-five desks and chairs, and not another stick or stone, not so much as an old calendar hanging on the wall. Extra desks and chairs were presently flung in upon us by a muttering, embittered caretaker, and we were left to make ourselves at home. Perhaps this challenge released some of the stultifying frustration of that long month at Elgin Road. With not a pot of paint or stick of chalk to bless us, I vowed we would produce a joyful, humming classroom, dedicated, if not to painting, then to the other arts.

We plunged right in with singing rounds, and Northumbrian songs, and presently Miss Tait appeared, breathless, at the door.

'Some paper — bring own pencils and pens — no books — try to get some — just keep them busy... stick to the three R's,' and she was gone.

I was given this challenging directive by every Head I served under from March 1940 to the early spring of 1942. Since I would have thought it physically impossible to 'Stick to the three R's' for five-and-a-half hours a day, I behaved like Squirrel Nutkin and, if asked what I was doing, 'answered him as I thought good...'

For some weeks, until additional teachers could be brought back from evacuated areas, we worked long shifts, Saturdays included, from 8.30 to 12.30 and then 1.00 to 4.00.

One day I was asked to take an infants' class for an absent teacher in the morning, before my own class in the afternoon.

I went to the classroom praying for guidance and was presented with what is technically known as 'fifty-six mixed infants', (which is to say fifty-six boys and girls of five-and-a-half to six-and-a-half years old). It was the longest morning I have ever put in, not forgetting school practice days. Never before have I been confronted with such self-righteous children.

Between every lesson, and at every pause, they queued up to tell me what someone else was doing wrong. Singing games or reading, plasticine modelling or number cards, there was always a procession of dribbling-nosed infants at my skirt, each holding up a hand, not in a self-reliant, straightforward way, stretched out in confidence, but cocked up to the level of one ear, as if to ward off a blow if I decided to retaliate.

'Miss, 'wer sum books is in the cupboard, and Alan Smedley's sitting' agin' the door,' one would whine plaintively. ('Wer, 'ower' in Tyneside, meaning 'our'.) 'Miss, I done a picture and Aileen Wilson's scribbled on it'. 'Miss, Ronnie Newman's taken me cheair'. 'Miss, our teacher learnt me and Tommy Craggs where to put the plasticine and Cameron Wilson's put it away wrong.'

Are they old enough to 'try a thing on' just because they knew I was strange? Or do they go on all day like that with a proper teacher? I kept saying 'Well, why come and tell me? Tell him to move,' or 'Keep out of his way,' or 'Then get another pencil if someone's taken yours,' but they seemed to have no idea of settling their own disputes. I felt like a hen wife trying to get rid of a lot of persistent, clacking fowls.

I know individual children at five and six can be really intelligent — in fact, I have always liked them at that age. But oh Heaven defend me from ever having to teach them, fifty-six together, before the age of eight — or preferably ten!

Very soon I realised it was not guidance I needed but the hands of six people and the tongues of twelve. I prayed simply that the ceiling would fall down, as it did on one auspicious occasion at Arnistone, in the infant room: not that I was so far gone in misanthropy as to wish the fifty-six class II infants bodily harm, but I thought I could do nicely with the remainder if thirty or forty were evacuated into the next room or sent home. Never have I been so thankful to hear the buzzer announcing the morning's end. I got everything nicely tidied away and said

'That's splendid, now all stand.' They did so and I said

'Well — er — goodbye — I expect your own teacher will be back tomorrow.'

Not a sign, not a movement. I began to wonder if I was in some Lewis Carroll nightmare — if I had drunk the wrong bottle and was going to be tied to these impossibly demanding infants for life.

I said faintly,

'Doesn't anybody *want* to go home?'

Still no move. Then Cameron advanced (hand, of course, raised to the level of his ear) and in his great gruff bellow said

'Miss, we nivver said wer prayers.'

I hadn't a notion what prayer they said at dinner time, but the years of training, night and morning, at Washington Road had not been in vain. I said the magic formula 'Hands together, eyes closed,' and watched it work like a charm. A great muttering wave swept round the room, ending triumphantly

'Feast in Paradise with Thee,' whereupon they all made for the door with 'Good morning, Miss,' and satisfied smiles.

I came away glowing. We had got through the four long hours without mishap or tantrums. They were pleased with themselves and school, and I had not failed them. Oh yes, it was the best of times ...

But there were harder and more tormenting days. More than half the children who attended Cooper Street School in those early weeks had not been evacuated at all. They had run wild for seven months. The rough speech and bad manners were superficial, but the backwardness in reading and all written subjects took months to repair. Skills that are not among a child's native interests decay rapidly away from school, unless there is encouragement from home.

On admission, I should think half of my class would have been credited with a reading age of seven. It had taken years to learn what had been forgotten in those seven untended months. No one who taught in 1940 could ever doubt the importance of all continuation classes and day release schemes.

In the frenzy to 'get them into school', children were simply grouped by age, and the span of intelligence in each class was immense. The problem of trying to give adequate individual attention to all was complicated by the fact that many children, as well as being dull, showed marked signs of emotional difficulty, and were, in addition, dirty, under-nourished and ill-clad.

There was Betty Beight, for instance, who looked so frightened if addressed, and so listless if ignored, that I wondered if she was bullied by someone at home.

One day I caught a furtive wraith of a child called Monica passing a note. It read:

'Betty Bate is scaby.'

The description, though unkind, was correct. Betty had psoriasis.

Monica herself was pitiful enough. Pale, pinched, with thin, lifeless brown hair, she looked like a starving sparrow, her skinny arms and legs protruding from a torn cotton frock. She had been absent one half day, and when asked why, sniffed and wriggled. Her excuses were multifarious. She had a bad head and a bad 'stumick'; the baby was bad and she had had to go for the doctor; her Mam was out and she had to mind the house. But others had seen her getting on to a city bound bus and she was forced to admit it at last. With a toss of her head, defying contradiction on this point she said,

'Aa went to Westgate Road to put me Granda's 'memory' in the paper'.

Her tiny sharp chin was level with the top of my desk, and she looked at me with the hard eyes of an embittered woman.

The following week she took another morning off. Next day she made her preliminary excuses half-heartedly. 'Me head' and 'me stummick' had only a mention, and without further prompting out came the triumphant news

'Aa went wi' me mam to git a pair silver slippers.'

There was a ring of pleasure in her voice for the first time. I looked down and saw the toe-less gym shoes she had worn for the past three weeks. Was the child romancing, or the mother mad? Who knows? Yet, true or false, was the child not emulating that Chinese sage who said

'If you have two loaves, sell one and buy a lily?'

Then there was Ellen, who looked a slattern if ever anyone did, slouched over her desk, her face nearly hidden by frowsty hair and one bare inky arm. If you called her, she shuffled out, dirty bare toes protruding from the holes in her gym shoes. The shoes had no laces and were split at the heels. We got some laces and stitched up the shoes, but it seemed as if these improvements did more harm to her feelings than good to her feet.

She was a big, well-developed girl with a thicket of dark curly hair, and cheeks like rosy berries, but a hunted look in her eyes. She walked with her shoulders hunched forward, always trying to hide herself, and reminded me of Jo in *Bleak House* — the shuffling nods, the arm across the face — 'always to be hustled, and jostled and moved on.'

She was often late, coming in after everyone else had started work to stand by the desk twisting the dirty rag that was her handkerchief. Unless one spoke gently to her she simply went dumb.

'What happened to make you late this morning?'

She would open her mouth, shut it again and then speak in hurried, gasping whispers, so that the other children could not hear.

'Me mam was out. I had te mind the little uns till she come back.'

Where would her mother be at 8.30 in the morning? Cleaning offices perhaps? I had seen the 'little uns', smaller editions of Ellen, playing with a bogey and an old shovel in a dirty, common yard behind the tenement flat where they lived. What sort of home life went on behind those tattered lace curtains?

I watched Ellen one playtime, standing alone by the window, gently touching some snowdrops and crocuses that we had put among ferns on the window sill. She was smiling to herself. Would contacting health visitor, district nurse or parish priest have helped? Perhaps. But there was no liaison between school and the other social services in those chaotic months. Besides, there were at least a dozen others almost as dirty and sickly as Betty and Monica, while Ellen was one of the comparatively few who did not look ill-fed. I could not send in reports on half the class — even if there was anyone to whom to send them.

After the first week, we had a timetable on which I was down to teach every subject, from needlework and arithmetic to music, geography, science and art. While it is obvious that I neither was, nor am, fit for this, the choice was between amateur teaching or none at all. To fit the bed of Procrustes, stretching the teacher seemed preferable to lopping the child. Intelligent children wanted a glimpse of the range of knowledge which the good 'reorganised schools' gave them before the war, while the retarded had to be helped to recover their basic skills. All, whatever their mental level, needed the solace and stimulus of creative subjects not less but more than before.

We had a timetable — but no syllabuses for work. Every young teacher derides and rails against her syllabus. But to have one, however bad, means that at least you have something to kick: Something that is not *your* responsibility when things go wrong. To have *no* syllabuses of any kind makes one feel remarkably like the March Hare

> **They drew all manner of things — everything that begins with an M.**
> **'Why with an M?' said Alice.**
> **'Why not?' said the March Hare.**

In English I could fumble along, since almost everything I introduced was new to them. But history? We had to *begin* somewhere. Ought I try to explain industrial Tyneside? Or the rise of nation states? And so come to the origins of World Wars I and II, in the hope that they could understand *something* of the turmoil we were in? But at their age?...

'Just go back to the Romans,' said Miss Tait sourly, adding with a strange logic of her own 'they need to begin at the beginning.'

But I decided against all these things. I went back to the time which, because of its fascination for me, I knew I could bring alive for them — to Bede in his monastery at Jarrow, less than two miles from us as the crow flies; and to his friend Eadfirth, working away at the first great surviving masterpiece of Celtic design — the *Lindisfarne Gospels*. I mounted my treasured pictures of the Lindisfarne Book, together with woodcuts of monks, perched on hard stools, working at painting and lettering. All these I hung on the wall.

The intricacy and fascination of these old Celtic paintings, done in that first amazing flowering of Northumbrian scholarship and art, had, since childhood, absorbed me. Now, with fifty eager adherents, together we pored over delicate flowers, heard birds sing, felt the sun. I tried to make vivid for them the reality of monastic life — cold hands, hard beds, dull food and the rough seas around the mouth of the Tyne and Lindisfarne. We discussed the reasons that would lead men to endure daily discipline, and long silent hours working in house or garden, or in the scriptorium. They made books of their own in which they could copy poetry, 'illuminating' their work. I think this welded us into one 'class' more than any other single subject, though of course, the impromptu drama and dancing played a part. Nevertheless, there were shocking gaps, and I thought often of Dr Johnson

Their learning is like bread in a besieged town, every man gets a little, but no man gets a full meal.

He was speaking, perhaps unfairly, of the Scots in his own time; but how truly his taunt foretold our own learning years later. Since we had no materials for 'art', no text books for science, history or geography, we were always adapting and making do. One thing I *could* do was to increase their mental stamina, and hope that the meagre fare I gave them would so fire their spirit that no obstructions would prevent them for learning for themselves in time.

Miss Tait had ordered practice in writing several times a week, to restore their care and competence. I had at home a beautifully illuminated little book of Indian sayings, and some of these seemed apt for inclusion in their own manuscript books.

A small minded man weighs what can hinder him;

Fearful, does not set to work.
Difficulties cause the average man to leave off;
A truly great man does not slacken until he has
succeeded, though obstacles tower a thousand fold.

and

God respects me when I work;
He loves me when I sing.

and

If you do not worry about a misfortune for three years,
it becomes a blessing.

Perhaps improvement in Mother's health made us both able to take pleasure, at last, in the return to our own home. Our bungalow was small but sunny, with a bay window in the sitting room and one also in my north-facing bedroom which, therefore, caught all the evening sun. The house was simply furnished, with curtains in textures and colours that we loved, and books in every room.

Long before I saw or heard it, we had taken the advice of Sir Winston Churchill

If you cannot read all your books, at any rate handle, or as it were
fondle them. Set them on shelves yourself so that if you do not
know what is in them, at least you know where they are.

Save for the history shelves, with some of which she did not bother, Mother knew better far than I what was in many of the volumes — especially the poetry and music sections, and novelists of the nineteenth century. It gave her never failing pleasure to help find poetry that my pupils would enjoy for some special project. She found Christopher Smart's *My Cat Jeoffry*, when we were thinking and writing about Bede, for clearly Jeoffry's ancestors were monastery cats.

Mother found me Katherine Mansfield's short story, *The Voyage*, too, and this touched our pupils deeply. Even in happier times the story would have found its way to their hearts, but coming when so many of them had recent experience of leaving home, it opened the way for discussion of what evacuation had meant, emotionally to them. To be able to talk about this searing experience in the neutral context of some other person's story was almost certainly enlightening. Voyages and journeys are always fascinating to young people — especially to ours, with their close connection with shipping and the sea. We tried, sometimes to link history and geography with our literature through stories of Marco Polo, Hakluyt, Raleigh and Drake.

Yet the lack of all books and apparatus for geography made this attempt at project teaching very sketchy and inadequate. I had to tell them too much, and often, especially after nights when they had been up for sirens, I felt that they were learning little. All they wanted was to settle undisturbed upon their hard chairs, allowing a sweet flow of distilled knowledge to drift over and lap round them.

In the months from February onward we built up a flourishing and stimulating class library, almost every pupil and myself bringing books from home. But we had still that great bugbear of state elementary schools, the weekly composition to face. This ritual was rigid and ceremonious at best: but sometimes, (because teachers found it tiring, and to many pupils it was incomprehensible) it was as traumatic as registering a death.

The subject for the week was written on the blackboard, and teacher had to ask pupils for ideas. These, too, were written up, higgledy-piggledy as offered. These disparate items had then to be sorted into topics, with paragraphs allotted to principle ideas. All this took so long that volatile young persons grew bored, and interest, excitement even, that an eager teacher had struggled to body forth were smothered. All too often, sanctimonious cliches took the place of thought.

We all need practice in organising thought. But where Headteachers demanded that this restricting scheme be used each week, (as many did in those days) the writing became 'thin', as if emanating from a single reed. The short writings of Mona McHafferty had flaws in syntax and spelling, but they were unmistakably her own, and her needs and longings could never be forgotten. 'Good' writing carries overtones and even young writers — perhaps especially young writers — can achieve this impression of a reflective mind if they are able to let all parts of their personality come into play.

In normal times one tackled problems of good writing daily, throughout the year, alone with each child. But with these fifty-eight, more than half of them so sorely backward, emergency measures were essential.

I thought that if I read to them for perhaps five or ten minutes for several days on end, from a book of limpid and elegant simplicity, perhaps a few girls might notice that prose, like poetry, can have a melodious sound: they might even begin to abhor the bumbling jumble made by their own loose sentences. I tried out this imitation theory by reading extracts from *The Vicar of Wakefield* which I had greatly enjoyed myself one spring-cleaning time some twelve years previously. I was supposed to be dusting the books in my parents' bedroom. In fact, I sat on the floor and read for nearly half the day. Perhaps my Walker girls would enjoy *The Vicar* too?

And they did. I read the first chapter in full, and then, through the next week, for the last fifteen minutes of each day, extracts from those parts most likely to appeal. They smiled over Dr Primroses's moralising habits and laughed at the way he always got the better of his wife and daughters. The hanging, over the chimney piece, of an admiring epitaph to his wife, while she was yet living, greatly appealed to our budding sociologists.

I sat on a desk to read, the girls drawing up their chairs as close as possible to try and achieve some sense of a theatre in the round, and this emphasised Goldsmith's drama.

The quiet evenings at home gave time to think constantly about aspects of learning that these city children would find arresting. Looking back at what had been most enjoyable, both to myself and brothers, when we were at the twelve-year age, the contrast between our life then (even in so-called 'depressed' Tyneside!) and the school life of my pupils hit me very hard.

All through life we need to feel, as my brothers and I had done most strongly, that our learning horizons are limitless. The interests of our parents reached out to the life of the whole parish, the music at home embraced every century. Family outings took us to Hadrian's Wall, to the castles of the days of Border warfare, and all over Northumberland and Durham to village churches and the Cathedral, and to the manuscripts of the medieval church. The vastness of our inheritance in time and space was felt again some eight years later in the university library, its great store of volumes linking us directly to the scholars of the past.

The contrast between our own rich experiences of youthful learning, and this war-time learning and teaching on Tyneside was stark. It was continually impressed upon us in 1940 that supplies were limited; that books were not available; that excursions must not be made. As a teacher, I began to feel that what was expected of me was no longer to help children to develop at their own pace, free from anxiety and interference, but to make up tiny parcels of 'information', to be fed to all the war-time Olivers, who were not to ask for more.

Regression is a necessary part of learning. Sometimes we must go back in imagination over old ground reliving old discoveries before we realise what rich opportunities still lie ahead. It struck me forcibly one night in bed, that all the sobering, and frightening appurtenances of war — air raids, black out, windows net-covered against blast, rationing of food as well as books, must have given our pupils an impression of life — especially school life, as a burden. They were not to know that only a few years before chance had brought us together in West Walker, our own hearts as teachers 'were young and gay' too. Shyness may-and in my case often did prohibit any reference to my own young life. How rarely we admit to feelings or experience we could share with them.

Is this not an effort we must make as we grow older? If we hope ever to make nation speak peace unto nation, surely teachers and pupils must speak freely to each other in school?

So, remembering how much I had always loved to get Mother talking about her school, on a day when we had no books for English literature, I decided to tell my class something of how girls' schools had changed over the past one hundred years. Brought up as all my pupils had been in mixed infant and junior schools, it had never entered their heads that anyone had had to fight for girls to have higher education at all. So, VA had to be introduced to those two dedicated persons who made possible a slow but steady revolution in girls' education

Miss Buss and Miss Beale
Cupid's darts do not feel:
How different from us
Miss Beale and Miss Buss.

This jingle, not quite fair, but always memorable, brought the founding of the Girls Public Day School Trust to their notice. I could link the efforts of the Misses Buss and Beale in the south of England to true stories of the pioneer Girls' High School in the North, in Gateshead, where, fifty years before our time my mother was herself a pupil. This made the whole tale vivid and believable to them.

School days at such a school were more arduous than our own. Mother and her companions from Heaton had a shattering journey to get there at all: by train to Newcastle Central, then on foot in all weathers over the Redheugh Bridge and up the long, steep streets to the very top of Windmill Hill. Once there, they had a gruelling course. There was no 'play way' in lessons, but lectures, reading, note-taking and learning by heart — and such learning: none of that rubbish we had been offered in the dreadful *Junior Poesie*, in Elgin Road, but Shakespeare, Milton, Keats, Coleridge, Browning, Tennyson — and they learned poetry not by the grudging inch but by the nautical mile.

Life in that high school was not work only — the girls had lectures on Italian painters, music recitals from the organist of Durham Cathedral; even a pilgrimage to the Roman Wall. They produced plays, and on one memorable occasion, there was a week's holiday near the Northumberland tarns, staying at Hot Bank Farm. During the celebrations for Queen Victoria's Diamond Jubilee, eight staff and eight senior pupils went to Keswick where they climbed Skiddaw and watched the lighting of the first bonfire. By 2.00am they could see, in the light of more than fifty other beacons, the outline of that great roll call of mountain tops —

Blencathra, Knott Rigg, Fleetwith, Helvellyn, Pike O' Stickle, Scafell...

My girls, with memories of perhaps a Sunday School picnic to Tynemouth Sands, and no school outings at any time to look back upon, found this little bit of authentic local history a revelation.

'It's like a story in a book,' they said, and for a while all were of the opinion that this high school (long before their time transferred from Gateshead to Newcastle) was the Mecca where they should all be. Then it occurred to one of the more reflective, that such schools would serve at best only a tiny fraction of all girl pupils on Tyneside. We tried to work it out, and thought perhaps one pupil from a school like ours every five or ten years. How could that be fair? What ought to be done?

It was fascinating to watch how, little by little, it dawned upon them that parents and pupils themselves could work to bring what was good about the Gateshead High School regime into the life of *all* schools. Until that day they had thought of school — any school — as something other people did to them. Slowly, they began to realise that in a democracy, people had choices; that they themselves were people, their parents, too, and that if they wanted to improve life, they had to make up their minds to work for changes that could ameliorate life for all.

Each girl went home that day with questions to ask mothers, grannies, aunts, about their schooling: where, how long, what was taught, and how. We had a splendid response, and all the information gathered led to more questioning and thought. For several years I kept all the replies, meaning to write about our discussions, but in the chaotic circumstances of that time, it was never done. I felt bothered that the matter had not been brought to a conclusion, but in time realised that it did not matter to *them* that it should be written up — only my own pride wanted a record. Important to them was the opening of their minds to new ideas about school and what schools might be in future. We had done some growing and learning together that we were unlikely to forget.

Many years later, when my own children were at school, I found a poem by Seamus Heaney suggesting better than any writing of my own, what had been achieved. It is called *Scaffolding*

> **Masons, when they start upon a building,**
> **Are careful to test out the scaffolding;**
>
> **Make sure the planks won't slip at busy points,**
> **Secure all ladders, tighten bolted joints.**
>
> **And yet all this comes down when the job's done**
> **Showing off walls of sure and solid stone.**
>
> **So if, my dear, there sometimes seem to be**

Old bridges breaking between you and me
Never fear. We may let the scaffolds fall
Confident that we have built our wall.

On that occasion, if no other, we had built our wall.

So with many setbacks we scraped ourselves together some sort of education for body, mind and spirit. If we fell short in painting (through my inadequacy) we made up for it in drama, dancing and music. We sang many rounds, old familiars and some rewardingly fresh, including Beethoven's joyful *Scale of D flat*, Mozart's *All is silent, nightingales only call with their voices, making sweet music* and Schuberts' *All the wold gleams like gold*. These last three rounds in particular opened the way for stories about the lives and work of these composers. It was astonishing how much music the girls managed to hear at home on the radio, once they had become alive to composers as individuals.

All that early summer of 1940 our large room was bright with flowers brought from their gardens. Often we had to spend a few hours in the shelters and it was cold, but we really pursued our way very much more usefully than in that fantastic summer term of list-making in 1939. We divided the huge class into nine groups, each of six or seven. They arranged themselves, close friends and those who lived nearest, so that they could do work together in the early evening, before the sirens went. Every child had a turn at being 'linkman' for her group, from which a few more permanent leaders emerged for certain activities. At least we avoided the electing of form captains, so often a school's only gesture to the democratic process, which, not infrequently, serves only to push feelings underground.

I had read of a Dutch school at Bilthoven, where a form of self-government which was part of the learning experience of the school was evolved. This is what we were groping towards in those six months at Cooper Street. I have thought since of many ways in which what we were doing then could have been extended and improved. We needed time, time to assess and record what had been done *in* school, time to go out together, in groups, in the locality; needed even the old-style half-term holiday to review and plan the rest of the journey we were taking. But at that stage in the war, time, half-term — or indeed any other holiday — was what we had not got. I did greatly lack, also, the companionship and stimulation of my long lasting friends, who were all evacuated still.

I believed in what I was doing; knowing that the borrowed time was paid back a hundred fold in the girls' eagerness to read, and talk and write; in their increased sense of responsibility and interest in the world.

Yet, confronted by the doubts of our two oldest teachers — expressed in sniffs or barbed comments like 'Do you have a games period or singing *every* day on your timetable?' dejection set in. These two older colleagues, with our Headmistress, boasted of one hundred teaching years between them. They *knew* that salvation depended upon a silent class, drill in the three Rs and no nonsense about drama or dancing. Could I arrogantly suppose they were all out of step?

To Miss Hepple, for instance (whom I liked) every project in our classroom was anathema. She had but one year till retirement and now taught the top class, standard VII, girls. She had been hitherto a junior teacher and took her responsibilities with these school leavers so earnestly that she made life a misery for them and for herself. It appalled her to think that they might leave school not knowing how to do a bill, and unable to put three simple sentences together. She worked herself into a frenzy trying to improve their work and some days could be heard two classrooms away screaming, 'Idle, insolent girls.'

They, poor things, were giggly, inattentive and generally shabby, through months of street wandering. They were living under conditions of unparalleled strain, many of them already shouldering responsibilities that would have horrified thirteen-year olds of the middle or upper class. Not of malice, therefore, but because they were young, they laughed at little Miss Hepple, who seemed to them dated and pathetic in her determination to make no concession to appearances. She looked thin and weary, like a half fed child, her face tiny, brown and shrivelled, her small hands never still. She never varied her black woollen dress, almost as if in love with dreariness. 'Mutton decked as lamb,' she would mutter wrathfully at the back view of Miss Rasmussen, who, though very little younger, had her hair styled and wore expensive clothes.

Miss Hepple had been, until evacuation, pupil, pupil-teacher and teacher at one school for upwards of fifty years. It was a record I have rarely seen approached elsewhere, and though for teaching purposes one would have thought a fatal one, yet she herself took pride in it, seeming to draw strength for her new ordeal from the recollection of those years of unswerving, if misguided loyalty. Maybe she was pathetic, but there was courage in her too. She never gave an inch in front of her tormentors.

In her own way she was a lovable, dogged little woman, nor did she lack her own unpredictable sense of fun. She spoke very fast with a south Durham accent. Protests had been voiced one morning in the staffroom about shoddy goods.

'Huh,' snorted Miss Hepple, 'You lot talk, but you don't *act*. I bought a pair of suspenders two years ago. One and fourpence halfpenny they cost. Trash, plain trash — and made in Germany at that. I put them in a parcel and sent them to Chamberlain. Why should we be paying good money for foreign fakes, I asked?'

How long, I wonder, did Miss Hepple's suspenders hang over our Prime Minister's 'In' tray, in 1938?

The juxtaposition of this tired but indomitable woman and our neglected and unruly oldest girls was one of the minor tragedies of war. In her own way, a cross, pernickety, old-fashioned way, she cared for those girls more than they ever realised. In this, as in much else, she was the antithesis of Miss Purdy, the teacher of standard VB, pretty but affected; good natured in a lazy way, but very casual about her teaching. Miss Purdy got on best with Miss Rasmussen, whose elegance and sophistication she much admired, and the two shared secret laughs, which made Miss Hepple moody and suspicious.

The Office, as if playing some macabre game of Happy Families, had given us, as a counterblast to Miss Rasmussen, Sallie Laughton, a Tynesider to her last eyelash: shrewd, warmhearted, the soul of generosity. Short, broad, 'graceful in a substantial way', she might, if she could have been induced to enter politics, have become in due course another of the distinguished 'ladies of the Left'. She did not mince her words, and, for a staffroom in those days, her choice of words was very free.

Against this backcloth, Miss Rasmussen played her role: fragile, unconquerable femininity against the raised voices of those others whom she considered 'not quite out of the top drawer'.

'She goes on and on, like an anaemic version of the bloody siren,' said Miss Laughton glumly, as we went to our classrooms one day. Indeed after nights of sick nursing, I found her unresting vivacity a strain.

When men of such diverse temperaments meet on a school staff perhaps they do not create the atmosphere of tension that ill-assorted women do. At Cooper Street School, our timid, anxious Miss Tait had to make a team of ten heterogeneous women with strangely varied temperaments and tastes. She did not make a team. In fact, all her staff together never appeared to belong to one school. Nevertheless, I believed then, and think now, that in our art room we were fumbling in the right direction.

I was brought up in the high school tradition of 'Train the Mind'. Senior schools, from the time of the Hadow Report, set themselves the same ideal. But emotions can grow rank if neglected, and they can rot just as readily as untended brains. To train the mind while ignoring emotions does not make sense, much less bring harmony.

A young friend of mine wrote in an intelligence test, 'The opposite of vacant is engaged' and I am sure she had no credit for it. But for the teacher, is this not profoundly true? Those fifty-eight standard VA girls at Cooper Street were not sitting vacant, despite the lack of textbooks, piano, atlases and paints. They were committed, mind and spirit, to everything we did.

I only know that I watched each girl develop; saw her sharing responsibility with her companions, and contributing to our joint happiness. This was what made it, without a doubt 'the best of times'. But there was that other side, the side we really did forget in school, but which was never lost in adult life: the war.

Janet wrote from Penrith in April

I feel as if my life here were very petty and restricted. My battles are with petty bureaucrats and certain tyrants in the educational world. But since, undoubtedly, that is just my weight and scale and scope, I should be content. A teacher here told me she longed to sacrifice her whole existence to some great ideal — to immolate herself. When I suggested she might help a little with the evacuees, she went red with fury. If I groan at my fate, I see I am being just as silly and puffed up with presumptuousness! How grand it would be just to be living in a homely, personal world, not in this incredible melodrama.

In Newcastle, through March and April, save for our daily following of 'the News', we *were* living in a 'homely, personal world'.

Frances came from Arnistone to stay for a few days, an unforgettably happy time. She was — and *is* — one of those who bring warmth and sunshine with them wherever they may be. She was like an adopted daughter to my mother — more patient than her own daughter, more domestic in all her skills and far less head-strong and impetuous. She sang to us both in the evenings *Auf dem Wasser zu singen*, *Du bist die Ruh*, *Das lied im Grunen*, songs from *Die Winterreise*, from *Die Schoner Mullerin* and Wolf's *Verborgenheit*

Lass, o Welt, o lass mich sein
Locket nicht mit liebesgabin...

The haunting phrase was like a dirge for all those in concentration camps to whom life with all its richness of opportunity had been shown, only to be snatched away. I had no illusions of glory about war. If, even in childhood, I ever had any, reading *Goodbye to all That* shattered them for good. But though war itself seemed always and everywhere evil, it must surely be wrong to do nothing positive to resist all that done in the name of Nazism? The 'teaching' we were doing at that time was so safe and, in some senses, easy, because there was so little interference, that it seemed as if we were simply standing aside from the war while others faced danger and death. The more we tried to make school secure and happy, the more it felt as if we were hiding in the children's nursery.

And the sunny days crept relentlessly on, seeming to mock our profound awareness of the horror we were in. 'The worst of times...' with the certain knowledge that they could only become more desperate as hostilities became world-wide.

Janet wrote again, quite quickly; letters were at this time an outlet for the desperation which she bottled up at home

> For the past week, we have had glorious summer sunshine, a snare and delusion for through it all blows that blasted Helm, (Penrith folk say 'Hellum') a most wicked, vicious wind that makes you believe in devils. It is so strange to see the smiling fields and the larch spraying against a sky of Italian blue and to feel the cruel bitterness of that wind, a wind which doesn't brace people, but pierces them and nips them and gets on their nerves. For days and days it has blown, making a mockery of the sunshine. The long white bar of cloud rests implacably on Cross Fell. As I go shivering along with freezing ears I swear at it. I feel like a fiddle having a bad tune played on it by unpleasant fingers.
>
> I don't think far ahead because I am not courageous enough to do so. After a few years, I hope things will be on the right road, but it will be a very rough road to begin with, and they will be years of great upheaval. I long to escape it, or to be only a spectator at a safe distance. Yet I know that is useless. Day by day I crawl forward, like someone in a dangerous tunnel hoping it won't fall in...

That last paragraph echoed in my mind like a premonition of disaster; 'a very rough road to begin with' and 'years of great upheaval'. Oslo, Bergen, Trondheim, Narvik — listening nightly to the news was like listening to some saga of the Dark Ages. Then came the fall of Holland, of Belgium, of Luxembourg

> ...news fitting to the night,*
> Black, fearful, comfortless and horrible.

For ordinary people there seemed nothing left to say. The one ray of hope that I recall in May of 1940 was the departure of Chamberlain.

I will not give my views on Chamberlain, not wishing this to become a political polemic. But Churchill wrote of his predecessor's ministries

> They are adamant for drift, all-powerful for impotence.

King John, William Shakespeare

And elsewhere, his advice in caring for a Prime Minister was

If he trips he must be sustained, if he makes mistakes they must be covered, if he sleeps he must not be wantonly disturbed, and if he is no good he must be pole-axed.

This was done on May 13th, 1940 and Churchill became Prime Minister.

CHAPTER ELEVEN

Through the desert
Teachers and pupils: pawns for people in power

From day to day and from week to week, through those momentous months of May, June and July of 1940, we lived in an almost unbearable tension of suspended animation. Yet that time means nothing at all to people only ten or twelve years younger than myself. For them, the war in Britain itself only began in August 1940, and it means the Battle of Britain, the dogged resistance of 1941, 1942 and 1943, the final triumph, and above all Churchill's tenacity. They know nothing of the era of mediocrity which preceded 1940.

All through the first half of 1940 the threat of a second evacuation hung over us, but nothing definite was said. We waited, waited for instructions from the Office that never came. We did not know where we were to go, nor whether we were to take our own children or not. Rumours of all kinds circulated. We were going to Hexham; to Morpeth; to Berwick; to Cumberland. We were not going to be evacuated at all. Evacuation would be compulsory and we were going to Canada. Early in the year, I had written to the Director suggesting that, if a second evacuation should occur, we might overcome the more obvious defects of the first by an evacuation camp school, taking a group of children, thirty or forty together, to a large country house, where they could live as in boarding school. I found a house that would be suitable for one such group, worked out practical details, and sent them to the Office (in duplicate). Six weeks later I was called to the Office to discuss the plans and hear the official reply.

After waiting twenty minutes in a draughty corridor, an office clerk appeared and said that the Director was engaged. He would not be able to see me that day after all.

'But,' the clerk added hastily, 'he is *most* interested in your idea. He suggests that you work it out a bit more fully, making lists of, say — well, er — making *lists*. Making it *CONCRETE*, if you know what I mean?'

'But I've done that already! Short of writing out the grocery order, I don't see what more I can do till we're told whether we're to go or not. I was asked to come here today to settle that.'

'Yes, yes, I know. It's all most unfortunate. Most unfortunate. If the Director himself had only been available ... However, I'm sure he'll be able to arrange a meeting at a later stage. And meanwhile, if you'd let us have your views in writing — just as and when convenient, of course you understand? Thank you, yes. Good-day.'

Two days later a three line note arrived from the Director, to say that the house we found was not, after all, suitable.

No explanation ever followed.

Every job had its own frustrations in those months. Janet wrote

I was at the canteen again last night, washing up solidly from 7.00 to 10.30, with sweat pouring down my nose and neck from the tropical heat of the crowded room and the cooking stove at my elbow. There is one helper who reduces me to quivering rage. I may be washing up single-handed and at great speed owing to constant demands, with not a moment to struggle through the crowd for more hot water, and in she pops, little, hard, self-contained and efficient, and begins remarking about the filthy water, and we really can't have this, and who on earth has put tea leaves into the sink, and surely there is a clean dish cloth. She has a solemn, plain face like an excessively virtuous child. Last night one of the soldiers stole her bicycle lamp and dynamo and she had to walk home. I felt really sorry for her for once. The minister (not the one I had the fight with) came in later and said 'The swine, the swine' but remembered his cloth and added hastily 'only a black sheep after all.

Last Saturday, I went to an NUT Committee meeting in Carlisle. There was a stout and exceedingly self-important Headteacher from Maryport present . She had arrived by car, and was sitting there in lonely state when the rest of us arrived. She was terribly sour, and when she went away early we all felt relieved.

'I am only a visitor, of course. But my knowledge tells me an amendment is *not* in order. The minute must be rescinded,' — uttered with

an expression of out-raged virtue. We all sighed when she'd gone, and
we felt our secret sins were safe.

It is against my grain to bother with committees but it has to be done
— so I say 'To Hell with my grain'. There are so many things to be
fought for and against. The one that gives me the worst shudders is
anti-semitism. It is rising — it is being whipped up. I am going to write
to Victor Gollancz and ask him to bring out a pamphlet. It isn't enough
to appeal to people's humanity and sympathy. These are sadly
overstrained and numbed by the war as it is. I think we should show
how anti-semitism is used to attack democracy.

I read all this to Mother, and she said 'Poor Janet...Life is a struggle
for her indeed. I read something last night that made me think of her.' And
she hunted in James' *Varieties of Religious Experience* and found this
paragraph

Some men and women indeed there are who can live on smiles and
the word 'yes' for ever. But for others this is too tepid and relaxed a
moral climate. Passive happiness is slack and insipid, and soon grows
mawkish and intolerable. Some austerity and wintry negativity, some
roughness, danger, stringency and effort, some 'no! no!' must be
mixed in , to produce the sense of an existence with character and
texture and power.

How true and just the attribution of this description to Janet.

Mother's life was dominated by music and domesticity; she was
without political education of any kind; she voted Conservative (though
more truly in the line of the young Charles James Fox), yet she welcomed
and loved the only Communist she ever met. Though, alas, they were to
know one another for less than two years, I heard no other person fix so
unerringly on what made Janet unique: the texture, power and austerity
of her character.

From Janet's letter, I was provoked, among other things to thoughts
on Headmistresses. Are those keepers of the public conscience, the
Headmistress from Maryport or Miss Hardcastle of Elgin Road, produced
by the teaching situation in itself, by years of unchallenged power over
pupils and underpaid staff? Or do such personages exist only in girls'
schools? It seemed unthinkable that the men I knew would submit to such
poseurs. But it happened in Germany. Could it conceivably, happen here?
Perhaps so, if people were not resolute in their challenge to all forms of
prejudice and abuse of power. But what brave stand had I ever made
myself? I had not openly challenged Miss Hardcastle's discrimination
between child and child, her denigration of those she deemed unfit. All I
had done was to skate round her with a deprecating glare. Was that the sin
of 'consent by silence'?

Through operation of that same sin, was the rise of Hitler something for which people of our own generation were, at least in part, responsible? We had looked on, with varying degrees of alarm, despondency and lamb-like bleatings, for at least five years, while Hitler intensified his despotism in Germany. Where was the line of progression between silence at the bullying of defenceless pupils and silence in the face of brutality to helpless Jews?

Can such problems be discussed with pupils even in their first year in secondary schools? Young people, even quite young children, quickly see injustice in, for example, Bible stories and fairy tales. Most of my class had read *The Water Babies* and knew full well Mrs Do-As-You-Would-Be-Done-By and Mrs Be-Done-By-As-You-Did. Could not their understanding of meaning here, help them to apply their concepts of justice to the social and political battles of modern times?

At Cooper Street, (as at Elgin Road School) the Headmistress had adjured me 'Be sure and teach them about democracy. They ought to know what it means.' But the hapless teacher can no more 'teach the meaning of democracy' than she can 'teach them to be good'. It is futile impertinence to think either possible.

Two things may indeed be tried. First, through general class life, to help pupils to become sensitive to other's feelings, giving each one scope for increased maturity and responsibility. Secondly, we must put 'facts' before them honestly, not confining the history we teach to the parts that we are proud of.

What I had to do, surely, was to press on with the history books that I had been trying to bring to birth before the outbreak of war. The first volume was well advanced already, quite thick and long, for it included extracts from original sources, letters, diaries, chronicles as well as contemporary poems and records from statesmen. I wanted pupils to realise there were copies, still in existence, of family letters written centuries ago. Even in the fifteenth century, the Paston family were writing letters to one another in stormy times not unlike our own; times of war, insurrection, sudden illness, death.

When evenings grew lighter, and a neighbour called sometimes to sit with Mother, I hoped at long last to make progress with my daunting task. But it seemed these books were destined never to be finished. Continuity was impossible. Evacuation I in fact. Evacuation II already imminent. In May all those stumbling, drunken steps began again.

Whit Monday 1940. From dawn the sun shone from a cloudless sky, but we spent ten hours in school. Another last minute medical inspection, in fear of an outcry against dirty evacuees as in 1939. Office instructions were to keep children quiet with games throughout the weekend 'holiday'.

Games and tempers were alike exhausted. It was mid afternoon before our girls went to the nurse, and after 8.00 at night when I got home.

In my room, sunlight still fell on a blue bowl of narcissi, the smell of sweet arabis and new mown grass blew in through the open window, and a little boy played in the garden opposite. It seemed an ordinary Whit holiday in any sunny suburb, save that the sky was littered with great grey balloons.

Mother was listening to the wireless in the sitting-room, and Chopin's *Study in E* from opus 10 came to me down the passage. It might have been herself playing in other years. For a moment the room was full of the sense of the past, as if all the happiness of our childhood was gathered into that bungalow which, in a matters of days, we expected to leave for the second time. I realised how much I was beginning to be tied by possessions: the books, china, my father's piano, even cushions and curtains that I had made with such impetuous pleasure for the new home — it was almost a physical wrench to think of leaving them all again, perhaps this time for good. Yet only six years earlier, possessions had meant nothing. Was the change wholly due to wartime narrowing of our horizon? Even in peacetime, many, many girls are in the position I was then. Anyone engaged in full-time work and also caring for an invalid finds the daily tasks so pressing that all sense of proportion can be lost. The world is seen dimly, through a haze of washing, dusting, shopping. Men seem able to forget home troubles in their 'proper' work, but women, never. At last I understood how harassed mothers, often worried about money, have neither time nor energy to keep up informed and intelligent criticism of current affairs. Only a week before I had been bemoaning our negligence about happenings in Germany throughout the Thirties — and almost in the next breath, here I was asking querulously how women could ever come to take their true democratic part? This was a question woefully unanswerable in those days. I only knew that all through 1940 and 1941, though I did isolated bits of 'work', I let organised, and continuous study slip very much.

I have known girls who lived alone with mothers who were cantankerous and self-pitying. My mother was never that. Though very frail, she did not lose memory, sight or hearing, and she was patient and gentle always. Yet, even though I realised, both at the time and after, how good she was to live with, there were moments when I grew exasperated almost beyond endurance with the paraphernalia of filling flasks with hot drinks, carrying trays, arranging necessities on the bedside table, and planning everything from meals to laundry for days ahead. We could not afford domestic help, and the slow daily routine of washing and dressing a partially paralysed person becomes in itself a strain when it continues for many months.

The very brilliance of those summer days of 1940 intensified the sense of frustration — youth slipping away like the bright summer, with all that we had planned of adventure and experiment, and no prospect of being able to direct our own future once more for years to come.

Were all teachers depressed then? The teacher's role is, of its essence, unspectacular. Was depression at this time in part a re-emergence of childish fantasies of 'doing something great'? But permanence is also basic to good teaching. A teacher must continue, unsung, not only through the weeks but through the years. And the one common factor in all war-time town teaching was its transience.

This was unsettling, yet not in itself enough to cause despair. For the first time in my life I was isolated. The friends with whom I had formed so close a community were all away. The only thing that had ever been individual or personal about my life had been amputated. I could almost feel where it had gone, as though it ached and bled. At school, I still looked cheerful — or hoped I did. In the staffroom I talked, quite amiably and indeed politely, and felt like a smiling image. I cannot now read the word 'frustration' without recalling the dust, heat and loneliness of those long walks home from school alone, throughout those anxious months.

At some point, every teacher must attempt to assess feelings about her job, and no doubt such feelings are always ambivalent. 'Anyone can be a teacher' we feel at one moment — for, by the stimulating wisdom of Providence, the things we *can* do always appear commonplace. Other jobs look more valuable, more learned and decidedly more glamorous. Yet at the very moment when we are doubting the worth of one job, we are capable of feeling that we are really cut out for something better — to be an explorer in Peru perhaps, or a foreign correspondent in Iran. For there is a sense in which teaching, *school* teaching, does not employ the whole of one's mind, indeed even prevents one employing it.

1940 seems in retrospect to have been a blazingly hot summer. I remember that through those hot nights I had begun to dream — not once but often, of struggling through sandy deserts: trying to escape ... or to reach? What? I could not tell.

Thinking about this recurring image of the desert (and perhaps also of our own nomadic experiences in evacuation) I began to ponder about the Jews, which, though it is a shame to say, I had never done before. Somehow the Jews made history out of their forty years' trek through the desert: *made* history — they did not just sit down and rail, though certainly they did that too. And they wrote down their history, not as tedious accounts of battles: they turned a wilderness of daily 'happening' into a continuous story of human lives.

Among those lost and bewildered thousands, struggling through the desert even as we were now doing in the war, some had grasped that events, like rocks and sands all round, are indifferent to men; that it is people themselves who must impress their vision of the future on the unpromising materials and circumstances of their lives. Those old Jews had come to see, however fitfully and complainingly, that they must get through the desert if they wished to reach a home, and, if they were not to die on the journey, the desert itself must be forced to yield fruit of a kind. However exacting and exhausting the times, I had to learn how to teach old things in new ways. Creative imagination was all I needed — exactly what I had not got.

It was the first time I had ever had to teach the same huge class all day, every day, in every subject for much more than a month. It had been comparatively easy to start with a flourish, but after perilous and bumpy journeys on uncharted terrain for four months, the engine had run into sand. New sustenance, new skills were urgently required.

Where to turn to make our waiting weeks yield nourishment? Ordinary books, plays, novels, poetry even, had lost their appeal. In hot summer evenings we could not sit reading Shakespeare as we had done in early spring. To share an occupation, Mother and I turned to a study of Beethoven's last Piano *Sonatas*, as played by Schnabel on records which my brother Denis had given us.

In our own time of trial, I heard this late piano music with wonder and amazement, as if with new ears. In earlier sonatas there are movements of pathos and mystery, but in opus 106, the *Hammerclavier*, Beethoven seems to have entered a new, and even more exalted region. He was writing this in the year 1818 when hope of marriage had been finally abandoned, and total deafness loomed ahead. His loneliness at that time must have been shattering, yet he wrote music of a sublimity rarely, if ever, attained before.

Mother asked often for the *Adagio Sostenuto* of this opus 106 Sonata, which Edwin Fischer called 'a passionate argument with God which ends in submission and humility'. What I learnt, on my layman's level, was that the old Guide and Scout law, inseparable from our adolescence —

a Guide smiles and sings under all difficulties

— was a child's way of looking at the world. There are tragedies which demand a response from deeper levels — the response we get when listening to *Hamlet* or *King Lear*. How does any ordinary teacher set out to learn what Beethoven had taught himself by 1820? By what miracle did he so impose himself on the desert that, from loneliness, deafness and disappointment, he could create music that generates courage still?

I had this notion, no doubt ludicrous to strangers, that by reading and re-reading every book we had on Beethoven and playing what little I could play myself on the piano, and chamber music on records, I would, in time, attain greater knowledge of his life and of his music, and from this, some secret might emerge: a secret bringing new insight into our classroom to propel us through the sand.

So, first. I tried thinking about his childhood and early life. But this led nowhere. At every step his experience had been the reverse of 'good educational practice': shut up alone from the age of four, to practise violin or harpsichord; put to play in the theatre orchestra from the age of eleven; neglected, so that he endured continual ill health; and burdened with responsibility far beyond his years. His schooling, too, seems to have been scanty and unsettled until he came under the care of the organist at the Court of Bonn. There seemed nothing to suggest that education in the formal sense had any part in making him the pioneer that he became. Yet, in spite of this upbringing, he extended almost every musical form far beyond the understanding of audiences and critics of his time, and succeeded in expressing his innermost feelings in a vast output of uniquely personal and memorable music.

In one of the biographies that I had read when still, myself, at school, three of Beethoven's thoughts on music, had lodged firmly in my mind

Music ought to create and fan the fire of the spirit of man ... Liberty and progress are the goals of art just as of our life in general.

And

According to my usual manner of composing, even in my instrumental music, I always have the whole in mind.*

As to the third 'thought' I did, in fact, almost always 'have the whole in mind'. I would lie in bed thinking about the lesson — the syllabus — the new history books, and, as if blowing bubbles in the garden, a chain of colourful, perfectly formed spheres would spread from my mouth to infinity. Alas, it was never so in practice. I began to fear that my search had been too grandiose. In the context of my elementary classroom, to embark on a special study of one of the world's greatest geniuses, even in the sacred cause of new vision for teaching, was perhaps seen as Hubris by the Gods?

Yet still I had this disturbed and uncomfortable feeling — almost like the onset of a fearsome head-cold that some insight was hovering just over, but beyond me. My first probings, though fascinating in and for themselves had led only to dead ends. But some way forward there must be and it would only be found by patient thought.

I went back to the other half of my problem: our Walker classroom. What could I learn from the study of Beethoven's life, his music and his way of working that could in any way help me to lift our work from the 'earnest and worthy' — which it often was — to a level where pupils, as well as

---

*Beethoven and Handel, Romain Rolland

teacher, could put into it five, or even ten times more effort of imagination than currently they did?

To do this would surely change the dolorous, occasionally even apathetic attitude to life of nearly half of my fifty-eight girls.

It had, for example, puzzled and distressed me throughout 1940 (and still does) that in the month at Elgin Road on our first return from Arnistone, and thereafter in Walker for at least the first four weeks, I had pupils whose lives showed evidence of neglect and savage usage, not unlike the childhood of Beethoven himself. Of those girls I taught in Elgin Road, forty-seven of them went I know not where. They were the 'unseen, unguarded dust': 'backward' pupils perhaps, who in their written skills had forgotten many of the scraps they had once known. But this did not make them incapable of sympathy to friends, nor of feeling for others, both in joy and sorrow and a wish to begin learning once more. Again, in Walker, the twenty odd who were moved after four weeks from my class to make room for other girls returned from evacuation, were picked entirely without consultation, by the Headmistress, I suspect because outwardly, each resembled her mental picture of a 'B class' girl, slouching, uncared-for, dirty.

I pleaded for all my originals to stay, as a 'mixed standard V'. When that was refused, I begged her to leave five who were making (as I thought) perceptible progress. Of these, grudgingly and crossly, she eventually suffered three to stay. But not Ellen *(see page 121)*. Ellen, with the other nineteen, went to Miss Purdy in VB. Miss Purdy would not be deliberately unkind, but her classroom method was so different from our own that Ellen, who had just begun to enjoy one schedule, popping her head up timidly with a shy smile to take note of other people, would retreat into her shell like a terrified tortoise. In her new lodgement she would chant spellings and tables and practise daily what (to me) seems the most soul-destroying of English exercises — reading out loud round the class. Her new teacher believed firmly in 'no nonsense', remarking often in the staffroom of the labour-saving satisfaction of her method — 'Least written, least to mark.'

Even as long ago as 1940 we had found ways of educating blind, deaf and otherwise disabled children to be responsive and responsible. Yet, strangely, how little care was taken to enrich imagination and sensitivity in those thousands deprived in other ways. I am not suggesting that in Walker we had hosts of children of hidden genius. What we had abundantly, like all other schools, were those whose talents were neither discovered nor deployed.

I could not speak, in that staffroom, of trying to help children in the use of imagination. Our teachers, (whatever their innermost feelings) talked more of discipline than of affection, and would have laughed and exclaimed in horror at a piece of work done by Ellen just before she left us for VB. It looked like the work of a six-year-old. There had been little time while she was with us to give her the individual daily help in writing which she had so sorely lacked. In the short time she was with us I gave her many short spells of spontaneous writing instead of the set, formalised 'composition', and one day asked if she would like to write about any picture in *A Child's Introduction to Geography*, an illustrated book which I had brought from home. From the chapter on the great rivers of Europe she chose a scene headed *Rivers provide pleasant picnic spots in the country*. 'The country', a place where she had never been. But she could at least imagine what 'pesflness' there would be. (Sound each letter to see how carefully she was spelling out the sounds that matter — and how much she had enjoyed the ten minutes when I read aloud to them at the end of each school day!) No-one could fail to be aware of her silent growth of spirit as she began to find a corner for herself in school. I missed her and the others very much when they were taken away.

One night, there was a BBC radio programme about Paganini, which several girls had listened to, and wanted to tell us about next day. They were puzzled by the use of a phrase 'He became one with his instrument'. Luckily in a book at home I had a small (black and white) photograph of Chagall's *The Musician*, which not only showed the Russian village background of Chagall's childhood memories, but also the happy peasant who had 'become one with his instrument' — in this case the 'cello, not the violin. It is a delightfully spontaneous and appealing picture, and I mounted it to take to school. Then, for my own interest, I hunted out Liszt's *Paganini Studies* — (to *look* at, not to play!) and was bowled over by the lovely designs the notes made on the page. Thinking about the enchanting Chagall picture, the visual design that Liszt's music made, and Ellen's mental picture of

Rest and
A pssfl
Rest

I began to wonder why we kept talking about 'making a plan' for every composition, instead of explaining that every communication, by word, by music, pen or paint, is more persuasive and more memorable if it is well designed.

Why, on that first grim evacuation, had I carried our token book, the massive and unwieldy Beethoven *Sonatas*, knowing that we had no prospect of being lodged with even an old harmonium in our billet, still less with a Bluthner piano? Surely because that music symbolised part of the structure of our lives. We needed the music with us, if only visually on the page, for in our family music had been one of our chief sources of communication always. And now, with evacuation II in immediate prospect, with all its problems still unknown, we needed to make lines of contact between friends, between families, as never before. In the short time before our parting, we talked about how over the centuries, feelings, thoughts and aspirations had been revealed through music, poetry and songs of many nations. Many pupils suggested lines from the Bible, others thought of old English folk songs including our own Tyneside or Northumbrian ones and I read them some of the amazing Paston family letters, preserved for over five hundred years, all written in a time of turmoil not unlike our own.

We became so busily involved with all this new work about 'communication' that suddenly I realised that I was through the desert and out of it, without having noticed the moment of change!

That great teacher Donald Tovey, said about Beethoven:

His music is a supremely masterly and hopeful criticism of life.

Like many thousands of others, I felt the truth of this then, and still do. In 1940 trouble was banging against our wall, but it was no good taking a stick and simply knocking back, in spite. Evacuation II would assuredly come, must be endured, and if possible put to use.

I set to work on arrangements for Mother to be taken to friends in the country when the moment came, packed for her books and clothes, and tried, with sober method, if not gladness, to plan useful school work for yet another three weeks to come.

It was, in fact, more than six weeks after that unforgettable Whit Monday before we had to leave home again. In the second half of May and during June, no notices about evacuation arrived. Perhaps, like the rest of us, the Office waited upon the news. All our anxiety was concentrated upon events in France, then the tragic but magnificent evacuation of Dunkirk. Life was the oddest mixture of dullness and melodrama, of the sublime and the ridiculous, of Beethoven and the BBC. We patronised the *Up in the Morning* exercises, with Colman Smith. Mother did her best at these, in bed. In the evening, she sat in the garden, which was gay with coreopsis, potentilla and phlox. Neighbours busy with their watering-cans, chatted over the fence. It was suburban life at its friendliest — till the sirens shattered our peace at nine o' clock.

How could I alter the 'waiting and noting' pattern of home and school life? Domestic work night and morning; decent, cheerful order to maintain in garden and home; the 'News', an invalid and sirens to listen for; necessities to lay out nightly lest instant departure should be decreed. Circumstances ruled.

At school, too, we could only go on living with props beside us, as if standing in the wings for the second act of the tragedy, not knowing who would be called, nor how or when. Even the children dwelt on an artificial plane of self-forgetful virtue, constrained by the times. They were less boisterous than usual, attentive to others' needs, pathetically grateful for even the dullest of routine school tasks. The regularity of school work was the most stable part of their tottering world. I remember a very ordinary morning that started in the time-honoured way with scripture and arithmetic, and ended with country dancing in the yard. After collecting their books from our classroom, they all set off down the passage for home. Mavis, a shy, mousey child, whose chief aim till then had seemed not to be noticed, turned back. She came across the empty room, put her elbows on the desk and gazed at me.

'Eh, Miss,' she said, 'at school, we do have the fun.'

Do we not occasionally exhaust ourselves in getting pupils through scholastic hoops to the extent of forgetting that they might be happier, kindlier, people if they enjoyed more simple, communal good-fellowship? I know that excellence matters; but it ought not to matter to the exclusion of joy, love and generosity.

I went home that day and heard of the collapse of France.

We left home for the second evacuation in July, my mother going twenty miles into the country to Riding Mill, to stay with old, dear friends.

CHAPTER TWELVE

A poet's second sight

Evacuation II: clutter, staff squabbles and waste

In the third class seat sat the journeying boy
And the roof lamps oily flame
Played down on his listless form and face
Bewrapt past knowing to what he was going
or whence he came.

What past can be yours, o journeying boy
Towards a world unknown
Who calmly, as if incurious quite
on all at stake can undertake
This plunge alone?

This moving poem of Thomas Hardy's played in my mind throughout the night before we left home again for evacuation II. Dead himself long before widespread apprehension of Hitler's intentions had been felt, how could he have foreseen with such insight the almost phobic withdrawal symptoms shown by so many of our pupils, boys as well as girls?

This second evacuation was, at the beginning, strongly reminiscent of the first: a desolating nine hour journey, ending in a slow march through staring crowds; a stand in the slave market while children were picked over cleanest taken, poorest left.

Three big boys who looked sensible and useful were quickly chosen and led away. There was then an awkward pause as if all the adult actors had forgotten their next lines. It seemed as if they could see nothing to attract them in any of those remaining.

Small girls quietly wept, and the two youngest boys, both five, howled. I felt angry at the time, but now years later, I can at least understand that it was doubt and apprehension, not criticism of our city children that filled the hearts of our prospective guardians. Even Zacharias was struck dumb by the unlooked for announcement that he was to have a son. Our assembled adults, mostly well on in middle-age, or older, had instant parenthood visited upon them for no other reason than they chanced to have a vacant room.

At last the matching of bodies to bedrooms was achieved and the new foster parents departed with their wilting travellers just after nine at night. I too was led away to my new billet, and a long way it seemed, uphill to the edge of town, quite out of sight of harbour and sea. My hostess, a widow, invited me to sit while she brought a cup of tea. Everything was spotless but the room had an air of opulence beyond anything I had ever known: thick carpets, polished little tables, each top-heavy with photographs in silver frames, vases of plastic flowers, and ornamental birds in rainbow colours on the walls. There was an escritoire and glossy magazines but no books.

After tea and a chat with my kindly hostess, to bed, to sing myself to sleep silently with that grand marching hymn-tune of Martin Shaw's to

Through the night of doubt and sorrow
Onward goes the pilgrim band
Singing songs of expectation
Marching to the Promised Land.*

As instructed by the Billetting Officer, evacuees met, bright and early the next morning in the entrance lobby of a very old church school. By some freak of light — or imagination — our pupils seemed to have shrunk: they looked shorter, curiously bundled, almost squat. With horror, I realised that, radiant July morning as it was, they were every one wearing their entire winter outfit: jerseys, top coats, woolly hats! After the humiliation they had suffered the night before, waiting to be chosen for a billet, how *could* I tell them that they looked idiotic in all their winter clothes?

I hustled five little ones across to 'Infants', the six boys who were eight years or older into 'Boys', and the remaining nineteen were pushed unceremoniously through the open door of 'Girls'. Luckily there were spare pegs in the cloakroom; what relief they must have felt to discard their burdensome winter clothes. But how could such an extraordinary message have got round to all those children in so short a time? Was it some maniacle

---

* Danish translation by S Baring Gould

idea of a joke? But we were not left to ponder this silly business. Miss Eversleigh, our new Headmistress, emerged from an inner room and silence fell.

In her long, dark dress and pince-nez, with grey hair pulled tightly back into a wispy bun, she looked like a a prison warder, especially as she carried with her the school hand-bell, her mark of office. She spoke no word of welcome, not even 'Good morning to you all.'

She said 'If there is any girl here now thirteen or turning thirteen in August, that girl must go to standard VII. Is there such a girl?'

I do believe she knew quite well that there was only Agnes — an asset to any top class: a steady, quiet, lasting help, who had assisted us all on the long train journey almost as intuitively as a young trained nurse. How I wanted to keep her with us. But if she met with an encouraging teacher, for her own sake it would be better for her to go. Nevertheless we felt bereft. For her the separation was yet another blow.

As she went, trying not to cry, I felt that we were *less*, all of us, both privately and publicly: Agnes, no longer mother's eldest daughter, her right hand; no longer 'monitor VIA'; centre first school netball team. She, like the rest of us, was now a non-person: just an evacuee.

Years later I discovered that Samuel Beckett had written a brief novel called *Lessness*, and I thought how on our travels we had exemplified that seldom-spoken-of condition.

But now there had arrived upon the scene someone the very opposite of a non-person, Miss Olivia Best, a stout middle-aged lady, destined to become a kind aunt or older sister to us all.

'You will share this room with Miss Best,' ordered our new Headmistress, waving us into an immensely high nineteenth century school hall, where twenty-five or more eight year olds were already scrambling about choosing who to sit with in the double desks, laughing and arguing.

Without further word Miss Eversleigh left, her duty done by graciously allocating some twenty seconds to introduce Miss Best to nineteen new pupils and the new colleague. Miss Best had smiled at us all with warm sympathy, but she had also looked sideways, with fear? with apprehension? at her Head.

We settled in: three rows of five double desks for them; two rows of five for us; two large blackboards stood out front, with a high chair for each teacher; bare walls, not a flower, though mid-July.

Miss Best said her class would follow their timetable: arithmetic, spelling, English exercise, and I prepared mine for immediate letters home. Hoping to cajole them into some 'ease', if scarcely fluency, I had written two imaginary letters, one from Dreary Dora and one from Sunny Sal, which did at least raise smiles. Providentially, squashed into my case had been coloured pencils — less common then than now. These were greeted with chirrups of pleasure when laid on their desks by our youngest good fairy. I asked them to draw pictures of their new guardians, so that parents might imagine the room where, for the time being, they were eating meals and making new friends. They set to work with a will.

But soon the little standard II's (aged eight and nine) weary of arithmetic and spelling, had become a chorus of dervishes, skirmishing behind their teacher's ample back whenever she was writing on the board.

Like a kindly middle-aged dog with a too large litter, indignation frequently boiled over, and she made ineffective swipes at the aggravators — which bothered them not at all.

For the time being, my girls merely looked on, mildly shocked. But we could not expect their restraint to last for ever: some method of teaching — really teaching — our forty-four young souls must be devised if any 'true learning' in this unknown environment were to be achieved.

At noon, the girls went home for dinner, Miss Best and I slipped out for sandwiches to eat on a sunny park-bench while we talked.

Time seemed so short: remembering as I did so vividly, the fatuity and frustration of sharing a room with standards I and II in Arnistone, for four whole months, I burst out like a demented soap-box orator — 'Can't we act as if we were two teachers to one class? In that way, we could combine history, geography and literature on a topic... My girls must make maps, in any case, to show where they now are in the North, and how they got here from Newcastle... Yours will already know the lie of Maryport, Workington and Whitehaven, and perhaps they will help to interest ours in that... and we can all start afresh on the Scottish Solway shore, the important industrial history of West Cumbria and its deepening decline — and we could also go much further back in history, to the coming of Christianity — St Bega fleeing from the Vikings and founding a monastery at St Bees...' I was in full flight ready to launch on the poets, — but horror! It was no discussion we were having. I had wholly monopolised the park bench pulpit. In shame, I tried to apologise, but in agitation she broke in

'Please don't stop. I am so glad to hear it all... I only became a teacher after my mother's death six years ago — she was an invalid. I imagined I would be able to work with a group. But this is the strangest school. Our Head thinks only of the Catechism — the colour of vestments for special Holy Days — all the finer points of church ceremonial. I feel as if I were here on sufferance. I would *love* to work on a plan like yours. You would have to do the history and geography but I could help with the literature. And my family were close friends of Jack Adams...we talked much with him on West Cumberland's declining industries...'

I was twenty-seven, she was thirty years older, but it did not seem to matter. We could, and did, work in harmony.

By mid-afternoon, the older girls looked heavy-eyed, while the little ones had turned increasingly fidgety. I wondered if I dared say 'Shall we have singing together?' when up spoke Miss Best

'Would you like a story? I'll tell you about the giant who had pink fits.' Attentive silence in seconds.

This story, intended to quieten the younger children, proved the solace all were needing after their past exhausting days. Miss Best told it so well, ending with a fine apocalyptic flourish when the 'fortieth fit' came on, so that, led by our older girls, there was a spontaneous outburst of applause. At four o'clock, all departed, locals and 'oncomers' chattering together unselfconsciously.

Alas, my acquaintance with West Cumbria on this occasion was destined to be shorter than we had thought. I had gone through to Riding Mill by train one Saturday, as usual, to spend time with Mother, but she had a second stroke. This was distressing not only for her, but for the two elderly friends with whom she was lodging as they wanted to go on caring for her. Yet it was unthinkable to ask them to take on any additional care or nursing. My brother and I must do that ourselves. Scarcity of telephones in those days made it extraordinarily difficult to make future arrangements. Ultimately the Newcastle Education Office gave me three days and I had to abandon 'my' share of care for our evacuees. My brother's young wife, a nurse in the Midlands, offered to make her home with mother and me in the bungalow in Newcastle, and there, after frenzied cleaning and arranging we managed to settle mother in some comfort.

The Office sent me to teach temporarily at Heaton High School, to which I could walk from home in half an hour. At school, the atmosphere was quiet, and happy, something between the concentration of an adult college and the domesticity of a village school. With a handful of teachers, we shared all subjects, helping each other out in a way too seldom possible in the hurly-burly of normal secondary school days.

For the last two weeks of February, the immediate problem for everyone in Newcastle was not the war but the snow. It was the heaviest and most prolonged snowfall I ever saw on Tyneside. It fell with silent, grey foreboding, and we awoke one morning to a stillness that brought home the meaning of Scott's 'eternal silence of the great white desert'.

It took me nearly an hour that first morning to wade three quarters of a mile from our house to the main road. The road itself was an astounding sight. On the un-built side, rolling whiteness stretched for miles. Down the centre of the highway, usually thronged with cars and buses, was a trail of matchstick figures, heads down, attaché cases in hand, plodding, a single file of weary pack horses, into the city.

For ten days the snow lay feet high at roadsides. Air-raid wardens marshalled street groups to clear narrow lanes, and there was much neighbourly kindliness. At night, when I got home, we settled in the kitchen, the warmest room. The bench scrubbed white, pans sparkling on the shelf, the white sink gleaming, there we sat with shawls around our shoulders, our feet half way up the chimney, reading Shakespeare*. 'The cloud capp'd towers', 'the gorgeous palaces', there, wedged between the oven and the sink we had them all

I went down to the river on the Saturday of that great snow, and stood beside the Walker ferry. Gulls darted and screamed around, regardless of human presences. Common gulls, Herring gulls, Kittiwakes, Black-headed gulls, they wheeled above my head, sometimes poised wild-eyed above the churning water, sometimes fighting to snatch a crust from my hand.

When at last the thaw came, it made a blue and golden pond in the middle of our snow-bound garden. Sparrows bathed there, chirping merrily, and the jasmine was in bloom. But in a few hours the sun had gone and dirty slush lay everywhere.

Splashing through the slush next morning I met the postman, with a three line Education Office whip. My old school, Washington Road, was reopening in March and I was to report back there. The old dilemma: to take the high road or the low? The high school Head had already asked me to go on her permanent staff. With Mother so ill, the quiet, friendly high school life was a boon.

Yet in the midst of a war, growing daily more disastrous, it seemed no time to desert the secondary modern school, so I returned to that tramp to Walker, wondering whether I was an ass, or a high-minded, self-deceiving humbug.

Washington Road, Walker. March 1941. In the same green tiled room, with the same antique double desks where I had begun my teaching life five and a half years before, we made what we could of 'activity methods' and 'sound learning' in the few square feet of space thoughtfully left vacant for the teacher's desk, the teacher and the blackboard.

Looked at objectively the room was harsh in colour, cold, crowded and shockingly lit. Yet I remember the life, not the room, with affection, and at first enjoyed being back with my 'scholarship class'. For a few weeks, teaching was, in many ways, easier than before the war. I was just enough older to have gained detachment yet not too old to have lost the sense of 'new every morning ...' that comes to learners in all jobs.

Outside our classroom, however, everything was changed. Our old Head, Miss Ivinson had retired, and almost all the old staff were evacuated

---

The Tempest, Act IV

still. On first acquaintance, the new Head, Miss Peterson, seemed pleasant and friendly, but she did not demand the former high standard of work. She reminded me often of A C Bradley's comment on Hamlet's mother

> **She loved to be happy like a sheep in the sun, and to do her justice it pleased her to see others happy like more sheep in the sun.**

That easy going attitude will not hold any staff together. Some of the new teachers, finding they were left to their own devices, made up for bad nights of raids by taking their ease in the day, popping up to the staff room for a quick smoke. This set the more righteous by the ears and a bad spirit developed, with petty feuds and jealousy.

It was a strange summer: happiness within the classroom, interspersed with distress at staff bickering, and despair at neglect of scholarship. Unlike Beethoven I never got my emotions 'fused'.

I had a splendid class, but our new Headmistress soon returned us to every last inch of the old dead routine and red tape. There was no freedom, as at Cooper Street, to make our own timetable and re-arrange our restricting desks. So we decided to make a magazine — if it did not sound too grand, I might say a co operative collage, with stories, poems, and paintings — these last mostly done at home. Every person in the class contributed. In three issues our production trebled in size, and there was a marked improvement in quality of work. My friend Kathleen's husband bound each copy for us, so that the volumes could be passed round and read at home at leisure. When, at the end of term, the girls moved up, the volumes were left with me. I have carried them with me throughout all removals of the past half century and have them still — sole tangible evidence of all those many young friends, some perhaps even now still in Walker, though middle-aged and no doubt thinking of the education of their grandchildren.

There were days of glorious sunshine that summer, reminiscent of the first weeks of evacuation in 1939. But beautiful days had their price. The sky was so clear all night that raids were intensified. After one particularly bad night, water supplies all over the east end of the city were cut off. We were without water for only twenty-four hours at home, but at school we had none for a week, which affected tempers sorely. This showed in all kinds of childish squabbles in the staffroom. No one was really well, and the back-biting never ceased, a horrible spider's web in which everyone, sooner or later, became entangled. It was all an object lesson in how complex a school is, as a social unit, and how relations between teachers, and between teachers and Head-mistress, can cause thunder, which reverberates through every class.

Our new Headmistress lost her dignity by quarrelling regularly with Miss Olroyd, the senior mistress. Puffy, querulous Miss Olroyd wandered about school in her little black boots, looking for anyone who would listen to her wrongs. It was fatal to meet her sad eyes, however briefly, for on the merest flicker of awareness of her presence she would snatch one's arm with 'Have you heard the latest?' I never could decide which was worse — to throw her off, rudely and abruptly, or mournfully to endure her denouciation of 'that woman' while she rubbed herself upon one's arm like a discontented pussy deprived of her favourite chair.

'That woman' our new Headmistress Miss Peterson, big, stout, and ponderous as she was, had the heart of a rabbit instead of a bull-dog. Unable to tolerate the thought that anyone might find her less than pleasant, she immured herself in her private room whence notes of instruction dropped upon us like heavenly rain.

The four of us left over from the era of Miss Ivinson now saw what we had lost in her: a law-giver certainly, yet one who was decisive, generous and just. Above all, one who could make things hum. Under her, we might have a love duet in the top corridor and 'Representation of Chaos' below, but under Miss Peterson, the school trudged daily through its time-table as if forever seeking its lost chord. If a teacher was ill, Miss Ivinson was in her room throughout her absence, giving every thing and every person in it a thorough overhaul. In the new regime, when teachers were absent, which was often, a note would come 'Miss Blank is absent, please take the top half of her class with yours.' With fifty in each class to start with this meant struggling for a whole day, perhaps longer, with seventy-five pupils, forty-five of whom had to sit three each to a double desk! The room became stuffy, children fidgety and teacher hoarse. All those defects and weaknesses normally kept hidden were revealed. Selfish, petty behaviour which one would have thought oneself incapable of, became possible beneath the unremitting pressure.

When I now read those Old Testament stories of deceit, rivalry and self-aggrandisement, I have greater sympathy with the ill-doers than I had when we read them at school in self-righteous adolescence. I recall all too vividly how teachers behaved themselves, when torn by nervous discord and the prolonged uncertainty of war.

Meanwhile on the road to school the open spaces multiplied — spaces littered with rubble, charred furniture and broken glass.

Physically, Tyneside suffered far less than London, but perhaps proportionately, more children were at home in the worst months of those years. The tension of recurrent night raids went on sufficiently long for us to know the meaning of total war. We had a clear picture of the horror heaped upon individuals. Neighbours and friends disappeared overnight. We saw the pitiful loss and bewilderment of those 'bombed out'; the pallor and fear on the faces of children at the obscene wailing of sirens. That time was like a prolonged Psalm of the Captivity, sung throughout in a minor key.

Since there could be no holiday that year, like Saul when in mental anguish, we turned again to music to assuage our grief. We bought another Beethoven Quartet. Mother asked for the A minor, opus 132, of which the slow movement is the 'Song of Thanksgiving to the Deity on recovery from an illness, in the Lydian Mode'. There are parts of this chorale-like, modal tune, particularly at its second appearance, which sound like the organ of a country church. I love this quartet, not only for its atmosphere of profound peace, but because it recalls our family life in Newcastle before the war, and all that the organ has signified to us, as a family, both then and since.

In August, I was urged by Professor Morison, as many times previously, to apply for a Leverhulme Research Fellowship offered by the London School of Economics, at that time evacuated to Cambridge. Since my sister-in-law, Vera was at home with Mother it was an opportunity to go, and she herself wanted it. To set out clearly, for others to criticise, that work which had been in my mind for several years, required a degree of concentration which I had seldom attempted since the start of war.

But a plan was at last despatched.

I had word to go to Cambridge for an interview, but five days before the date arranged Mother died.

It rained all the way to Cambridge. I had not given a thought to booking a room, and every hotel was full. Unable to find even a place to leave my case, I wandered wearily for two hours. At last I was taken in at a house where two students lodged. I remember only a large woman in black who provided food, and sitting and bedrooms so dark and ugly that it seemed impossible for any sense of joy in life for students or anyone else to survive in them.

The next day it was still raining when, like a dispirited otter, I arrived at the place of interview. Unable to shake off the atmosphere of that wet and dreary journey, and the previous sad days, the next hour was the only interview that I have ever experienced without feeling a keen sense of mental stimulation and enjoyment. I suppose the curve of feeling at an interview in normal circumstances is akin to that during a race. From a diffident, perhaps even a poor start, the candidate is challenged by others until self-consciousness is forgotten in the excitement of effort. The men who questioned me that day in Cambridge were intellectually gifted and versatile, and they gave me every possible opportunity for forty-five minutes. But I was too flat and stale to respond. The work I had planned seemed of no significance. I did not care whether I got the Fellowship or not

— and I did not.

When I got back to Newcastle, there was a letter from Janet

Yesterday I took the bus to Plumpton and turned off from there into quiet, lovely country which gradually became moorland. Have you — of course you have — ever fallen in love with some spot of country as if it just tuned in with something in yourself? I did with that road. The fields swept up and dipped down, and in the dips were tree-sheltered farmhouses. You could see the blue flowing Pennines on one side, and on the other the definite shapes of the Cumbrian hills. It was very quiet, very peaceful and kind, like a dreamed of home-coming.

To my mother, I am sure death was a 'home-coming' in its true Christian sense. Yet death was not, as I had been led to expect, a peaceful resigning of the soul to God, a quiet sleeping away. It was 'hard and bitter agony', as if, in Dr Johnson's words 'mere existence' was 'so much better than nothing that one would rather exist in pain than not exist'.

After the interview in Cambridge, I gave notice to Newcastle Education Committee, as, with my mother's death, that chapter of teaching was finished, whatever came next. I understand very well the feelings of D H Lawrence when he wrote

To think of the amount of blood and spirit I sold the Croydon Education Committee for £100 a year makes me wild.

No one who loves teaching grudges an ounce of the effort freely given to each class. What made teachers bitter towards their employers in those old days was the casual, impersonal and mercenary attitude of some local education authorities.

It makes me laugh to write this about the Office after all these years. I remind myself of the man in Stevie Smith's poem

The agony through which I go,
He said, is something that you ought to know,
And something that you will know too
When I have finished telling you.

It was all a long time ago. Are teachers treated noticeably better now? As I once heard Sir Henry Wood say somewhat deflatingly to the strings at a rehearsal

A little better, gentlemen— but not much.

The main difference now seems to be that while local education authorities have tried to be of more practical help to schools, more understanding and sensitive to teachers, the Government itself has submitted teachers to thirteen years of abuse and criticism. It may well be argued in years to come that the sweeping changes, introduced so often without consultation, have been more demoralising, and have done more lasting damage to our schools than all the years of two world wars.

CHAPTER THIRTEEN

Songs of a wayfarer
Technical drawing: a boys' school through the keyhole

After Mother's death it was necessary for my sister-in-law, Vera, to go south to Rugby where my brother had taken up an orthopaedic appointment. By this time women were being appointed, albeit reluctantly, to boys' secondary schools so when a job was advertised for maths and history for the Ralph Gardner* Boys' School in Tynemouth, I applied. Though my degree was in history, I had in fact done, in addition, two years of pure maths. Moreover, my mother's brother, her father and grandfather had all been professional engineers on the Tyne, so I felt I could at least show reasons for applying.

I had to admit that though I had yet no qualifications in technical drawing, which would be essential for their boys, I had been going to night classes in Newcastle since the job was advertised ... in hope. The small interviewing committee, clearly desperate, offered me the job, and sent a kindly middle-aged man, Mr Jack Jones, to show me round.

And the school *was* nice, newly built round a sunny courtyard, where the pupils were playing after their lunch break. They looked lively, and what was more, greeted my companion with warm smiles. He, though

---

* See page 161

Deputy Head and senior mathematician, was as simple and unpretentious as his name. We ended our tour in his classroom, where, since I had told him my apprehensions about technical drawing, he suggested diffidently that if I liked, I could watch his lessons with the top class for a few days. Gratefully, I began watching that very afternoon, and also learned the names of the top class, for he made out a chart of their desk places while they worked. This was typical of his quiet, practical efficiency.

While waiting for the bus home, I puzzled in bewilderment: where had I read a description of this quiet man before? I knew it was not in any book on teaching.

Not until the middle of the night did an answer come — and then I had to hunt for the book to make sure. It was Daniel Doyce, the engineer and inventor in Dickens' *Little Dorrit*. Dickens, not himself a scientist, but a great creative artist, has written into that story a wonderful description of a gifted teacher.

It had taken me long to find the relevant quotation as, on first reading *Little Dorrit,* the significance of the conversations between Doyle and Clennam had quite passed me by. At last I saw that Doyce influenced others by an attitude of mind that I was beginning to understand. His words were true to the letter of what I knew of my own father — a man never 'trained' to be a teacher at all, but achieving the ability to instruct through his own work as a choirmaster.

Dickens wrote of Doyce

**He had the power often to be found in union with such characters, of explaining what he himself perceived, and meant, with the direct force and distinctness with which it struck his own mind ...
His manner of demonstration was so orderly and neat and simple, that it was not easy to mistake him.**

His dismissal of himself from his description was hardly less remarkable ... He never said, I discovered this ... or that ... but showed the whole thing as if the Divine artificer had made it and he had happened to find it. So modest was he.

There is so much of interest in these passages for all teachers — and for those who now profess to be 'in the arts', that by 8.00am the following morning I sat on the Tynemouth bus with many things churning in my mind besides how to teach 'technical drawing' to the top class!

Only ten of the former all-male staff remained, themselves middle-aged or elderly. Women, of whom I was the ninth, filled the gaps. Two of these I soon knew well since we ate our lunch together daily.

Miss Jobling was like an enormous cockatoo, with pale pouched cheeks, many chins and a crest of grey curls perpetually nodding while she plaintively recounted her many humiliations. Boys laughed at her and were rude. Staff did not back her up. It was useless trying to teach her class, some of whom could not even count.

'They should be sent down the pit, every man Jack of them. They should be *made* to work.'

If there was any boy she liked she kept it secret, but one tall lad, slow in every way, yet wholly without malice, she could not abide. We ate our lack-lustre sandwiches to the threnody of his misdeeds.

' "Boy," I said to him 'repeat the six times table or I will cane you myself with my own hand' — and I heard him say to that great rough Taylor who sits by him 'Let her bloody well try.' I'm going straight to the Headmaster after lunch, don't you think I should?'

Our companion, Mrs Jewel, like a perky robin, in brown tweeds and russet jersey, was perfectly named. She could have made her fortune on the stage, for she had taken note of teaching styles over many years, and told her tales in blunt, broad Northumbrian. I must have been shivering one lunch time.

'Cold?' said she. 'Now see here, aa'm tellin' ye — this is nothing to what it'll be in the middle of December. These classrooms are wicked. Aa've an auld Harris tweed suit an' aa wore that all last winter to teach in, *with* a wool coat — an then aa was that cauld, aa many a time wore me hat into the bargain.

'Scripture? Eh, aa've had many a laugh. Now look you, there was a girl aa knew. She was takin' a lesson about Palm Sunday. An' there she was with 'er cane in 'er hand, proddin' the lads an' dashin' up and down the aisles. 'WHAT was Jesus ridin' on? Yes, he was ridin' on a donkey. WHERE had he got the donkey? What were the children doing? Yes, they were shoutin' 'Hosannah'. What else did any of the children do? ... You there Straker, get yourself awake. What time did you get up aa'd like to know? What else did the children do? Be sharp.'

'Miss' (in a whisper) 'pulled the donkey's tail.'

'By, ye get some queer answers from lads like these. There was another woman I knew; had a class like Jean Black's there — fifth stream — dumb but devils. Some o' them were interested tho', mind you. She'd bin givin' a lesson on Abraham or Jacob — one of those fellows — which was it was a long time getting married? Well Jacob then — and she'd bin' makin' it varry dramatic — 'an' Jacob loved Rachel very dearly. So, when all the years had passed, at last she stood before him on their wedding day. Jacob lifted the veil — an' it wasn't Rachel at all, it was Leah'. An' they were all listenin' that silent — they thought it was grand. An' when she came to 'Leah', one lad in the front gave a great sigh. 'Eh Miss,' e' said

'Wharrer suck-in.' '

'Wharrer suck-in' — Tyneside for 'what a disappointment' sounds like an all-too frequent comment on lessons, history lessons in particular. Young people come to them with a natural interest in discovering 'what happened next', but so often gobbets of pulped and predigested information are fed to the young, like owl pellets. While they suck, the pupils fall asleep. Students need to chew. At least this helps to keep some of them awake.

At Ralph Gardner I had to take over the history in the 'A' classes from Miss Hislop, a business-like lady of indeterminate years. She said 'You'll want to know what I've been teaching them, so here's the book I wrote their examination questions in. Never give anything but one-word tests to boys like these, or you'll get terrible results.'

I was touched at her generosity in wanting to help, but dumbfounded at what I saw. With the second-formers, nice lads, very bright and responsive and eager to do well, she had been overhauling Roman Britain for an entire term. Her 'examination' had one word answers neatly printed in a column at the side. The test began

   1. Who built the Wall?

   2. When was the Wall built?

   3. How high was the Wall?

   4. How wide was the Wall?

   5. How long was the Wall?

   6. In what direction did the Wall run? ... etc. etc.

And the answer to the sixth was 'straight'.

Perhaps there is a place for tabulated information in history teaching, though I have seldom found it.

Once, in hospital, I came out of an anaesthetic to a most heavenly vision of music, hills and snow. Snow-capped peaks rose on massive chords, while, like mountain streams, wild arpeggios raced down between the frosty firs. Buried, as I thought, in the warmth of heavy snow, I did not know if I were hearing hills or seeing chords. Two nurses came in and out, but I could not move, nor tell them that I heard their conversation. When their mumbles had spoilt the dream they went away. I tried to think myself back into the mountains and music ... Schnabel playing the *Emperor* concerto? But I never found the road back there again.

I have often thought that youthful dream was a premonition of life-long confused attempts at history teaching — attempts to relate events to one another, to reveal movements both vast and vague; always the struggle to explain, to others, truths which themselves are only dimly understood.

Many an evening I wandered about in Shields — the neighbouring district — after school, getting to know the feel of the old town. There were streets and buildings and groups of people that might have come straight from Hogarth's engravings, and once I came upon some rickety steps, a pawnbroker's shop and a group of ragged dirty children that might have existed two hundred years ago.

One night I found a beautiful old square, built round a garden, where there was a cherry tree in bloom. Delight was followed by a moment of foreboding as if dark clouds had crept across the sun.

Now, of my three score years and ten, twenty will not come again...*

More than twenty years gone — close on seven years of teaching, and what had I learnt or done? I had learnt to put continuity and permanence high among pupils' requirements; had learnt that, for me, the sense of permanence came only through knowing the lie of the land. I had to tramp the streets where our pupils lived and played and ran their messages, to see and hear what they had heard all their lives; to discover what kinds of employment they knew, what patterns of buildings and spaces made up their world. Then only did I begin to feel I belonged.

Some of the old tenement houses near the river had been pulled down and the inmates moved to a huge new block of flats, perched high on a crag overlooking the old Priory at Tynemouth and the mouth of the river itself. One evening I stood there, watching the sun shining on the far bank, scarred and blackened. A trawler was coming in on the tide, with gulls circling and screaming overhead. They swept down on steady wings. A few feet from the water, they poised, white tails spread, wings lifted, black legs dropped. They skimmed the surface and soared again. There was a lovely rhythm in their movement, and I thought about my symphony of the Tyne and wondered who would write it. I seemed to hear it with a kind of racial memory, as if living again forgotten raids and shipwrecks, and the evanescent hopes of peace each time the old Priory church was stormed.

It was the first time I had ever been in a school called after a real and lovable person — Ralph Gardner, Brewer, of Chyrton in Shields. Well-nigh forgotten now, he was a famous fighter for freedom in his day. Born in 1625, he began his attack on the monopolists of the big city, Newcastle, when he was only twenty-five. The 'free Host-men' of Newcastle had

---

Loveliest of trees, the cherry now. A E Housman

usurped the right to bake and brew for Shields and all ships in the harbour. The Company of Bakers and Brewers of Newcastle ordered him to desist from brewing and he was flung into prison for refusing to obey. While in prison, he wrote his indictment of the 'tyrannical oppression' of Newcastle Corporation, *England's Grievance Discovered*. I persuaded the custodians of North Shields Public library to take out from lock and key their copy of this ancient outburst. It ought to be more widely known, if only for is majestic opening words

I appeal to God and the world ...

Boys enjoyed hearing this true story. Why the Director of Education, when I first met him, had called them 'rough' I never understood. They were all shapes and sizes, some hobbledehoys, but good nature and straightforwardness were characteristic.

It was the first school in which I had taught where Assembly was a genuine act of prayer, conducted with dignity. I found it strengthening to look at the assembled school, in quiet, and see what we were working for.

There was a little fellow in the second form, who, with his quiet, lilting voice and hesitating manner, reminded me of one of the Brahms variations on the Saint Anthony Chorale.

Sitting on the platform in the hall one morning, waiting for prayers, and looking at the sea of pale faces staring up at us, it struck me that the final variation, the splendid *passacaglia*, of that Brahms music, really spoke for the whole school. There is a solemn, majestic bass, reminding us of those sombre days of war, but above it tramps the continuous stream of boys, with trumpets, drums and banners flying.

We had enough of disaster and misery in those days, and music, and the thought of music, was to many people our greatest strengthener.

With both my brothers and their wives so far away, I was fortunate in having still one cousin and one dear friend living near Shields where I could visit them weekly after school. The big, old house, Ravensworth, which had been my aunties' school, had long been sold, and Aunt Lucy had died, but Miss Baldock and my cousin Joyce, now a worker in the first-aid post, still lived in Cullercoats together. It was pleasant to sit at tea with them, looking out upon the sunny garden, telling them stories of the boys. School was their world too. They wanted to hear about it and I enjoyed making them laugh.

On the wall of the sitting room was the old familiar portrait of Thomas Bewick which had hung in the hall at Ravensworth. Often, as in childhood, I looked at old books of my aunt's which contained engravings of his — pictures of old farms, of boys making a snowman, of boys playing on waste ground behind houses and a church — pictures that might have been inspired by people and places of Shields.

Looking at those old engravings and thinking about school, I realised that, for the first time, I could look at school without feeling overwhelmed by it. In the first few years, confused by class and staffroom problems, I was conscious always of growing further and further away from the secret world of childhood that perhaps one would never enter again. Now, suddenly, like the coming of spring, that secret life, with its doubts, hesitations, bursts of enthusiasm — and its tempers and mischief too was, at least in part, observable. At Ralph Gardner it really was possible to stand and stare. War tension was as it had been before, and raids went on, ever more fiercely, yet there was a blessed absence of niggling complaints and fault finding. Was this because it was a mixed staff? Men and women worked equally hard, and there was an easy companionship. I enjoyed it all and had constant surprises. It was like those long walks through the woods at Arnistone. Only now and again did I come across something unpleasant underneath a log — the discovery that I could still be seized by a mixture of panic, anger and exasperation and hit out in imaginary self-defence.

This happened once with the top class, in which was a huge fellow, Tom Balderstone, bigger than I, slouching, with red hair and a perpetual mocking grin. He was well-known for 'scenes' and had been several times in court. Once, after a fight with a master, he ran away and was dragged back. Yet something could have been made of him. He had a good brain, but had (so Jack Jones told me) a rough time at home.

I had this top class every day for maths, and on Fridays four times, double history and double maths. Normally I liked teaching them, they were so quick and alert. But on his bad days, one Tom Balderstone, is enough to turn a Saint and Senior Wrangler sour. An ordinary, unsaintly teacher is turned first sour, then nasty. One day I told him to rewrite a shocking piece of work. He replied with an insolent shrug and laid down his pen. Feeling tired and with a bad cold, I was in no mood to argue. I just walked down the aisle and gave one hearty cuff to the side of his head. It was the first time I had touched one of them. Enraged, he flung his book on the desk, his pen on the floor.

'Pick that up,' I said, knocking at the knees, not just with fright but with horror at my violent reaction.

He did so furiously, and went on with his work. After a few minutes, he ostentatiously put on his gloves.

'Take those off,' I said as quietly as I could, feeling a queer concentrated hatred. Sullenly he took off one, banging it on the desk like a spoilt child. He made no move to take off the other.

He sat. I stood, glowering. Neither of us spoke. In a few minutes he took off his other glove.

There was an unnatural stillness in the classroom for the remaining quarter of an hour. Had I won a momentary victory for authority at the cost of making his unhappy human relations worse — made an ugly incident out of something that could perhaps have been avoided by a laugh? And yet, the fact that, to some small extent, I understood his difficulties and *did* care for him, should surely not mean that he must be treated always with 'woolly permissiveness'?

At four o'clock, Tom went with the rest, morosely. I marked a pile of books, aware of damp cold feet and a confused miserableness of sore throat and hopelessness. Then I went for the bus. A few hundred yards from the school, I passed Tom, hands in pockets, alone. Suddenly I heard heavy feet behind me, running in time with my own. Dusk was falling. It was a perfect moment for his revenge.

I walked on wondering what to do, and then stopped and faced round. It was Lockwood, a simple, partly crippled boy in IIID, who was constantly asking 'Can I carry your books?' 'Can I take in the pens?' 'Can I do anything?' There he was, puffing behind me, with an amiable dog-like grin.

'Miss, I brought you this piece of chocolate. At home I've got a book ...'

'Can't stop — miss bus,' I wheezed, and fled.

I related this sorry episode to Janet who replied by return, enclosing her copy of *Road to Life* by Makarenko. This description of how he built up the Gorky Colony for young delinquents, waifs of the Revolution of 1917, is little known here. It breathes honesty and enthusiasm in every line. He must have had his heart broken over and over again by the follies and badness of both his boys and his girls. He had to find a way of breaking through, to reach each person as a human being. The young, he says, do not necessarily take to those who are demonstrative to them. What attracts them is assured and exact knowledge, intelligence and capable hands.

You could be as curt as you liked with them, and exacting to the point of captiousness ... indifferent to their likes and dislikes, but if you were successful in your work ... they were all on your side and would never let you down.

I am sure this ties up with what David Wills, writing a generation later, says in his *Story of an Experimental Approved School* — that it is fatal for any worker sincerely trying to give affection to a deprived child to gloss over and excuse bad behaviour. Reason tells me that this must be so: that it is *no* kindness to allow the boy (or girl) to believe that his bad work, his violence, or his lack of consideration for others 'are not really his fault'. Delinquent behaviour is wrong, and confrontation sometimes inevitable. The real problems are when and how? In public or in private? In anger, in the heat of a lesson, there is not time to debate calmly within oneself whether the right moment has come for the showdown. To answer 'now or never' at that point means that the confrontation will almost certainly *not* be made unemotionally.

I was well aware, within myself, that space and time away from the problem youths, to think out a policy, and guidance in how best to practise it, were what I required. And by the strangest of coincidences, while I pondered on Makarenko and his Gorky Colony, our own Board of Education was beginning to push the need for 'more youth clubs' here at home. Circular 1598 on *Emergency Training for Youth leadership* had been sent to all education authorities, early that year, closely followed by a notice to schools of a training course to be held in Cambridge in the summer of 1943. Our Headmaster, knowing my interest, asked if I would like to be nominated for the course. He applied for me to go: I was accepted, and so, by a strange route, did reach Cambridge as a student, adult though it might be, in the end.

I can truthfully say that when accepted, and for quite six weeks thereafter, I believed that what we were about to receive was insight into dealing with boys — or girls — like Tom Balderstone. In other words, I imagined that a 'a course' could give us the kind of wisdom that people like Makarenko, and all those who have come after him — Mr Lyward, Dr Winnicott, Richard Balbernie and many others — had spent a life-time in acquiring.

I never cease to be amazed at the way my isolated bits of knowledge fail to coalesce. Even at that age, I would have scorned a course called *Learn to Play the Piano in Ten Easy Lessons*. How could I *ever* have supposed it possible to learn *How to Deal with Problem Adolescents in Ten Easy Weeks*? And in an unknown setting, among total strangers? How my parents would have laughed at the woolly-minded idea.

When I was in the Education Department in the university, all students had to spend three weeks of their Easter vacation marking Eleven Plus scholarship papers, a tedious waste of study time, but the very small wage was vital. Asked to give the meaning of 'transparent' one child wrote 'Something you can see through, for instance a keyhole.'

The little I have written about this, my first boys' school, must surely be labelled 'through the keyhole'.

I saw it only for a year and a half, had much more to learn, and would have liked to stay several more years. It was a truly rewarding and happy place to be.

The staff gave me many promises of a warm welcome if I *did* return after the Cambridge course, or ever.

CHAPTER FOURTEEN

Transit camp
Alleys that are often blind

With trunk and battered bicycle I departed for Cambridge like every other student. I had been allocated not to the college, but to lodgings, for which I was grateful, picturing quiet hours of working there at night. But that fantasy soon went. I stayed with a widow and her devoted friend, both extremely talkative and inquiring. All meals were to be taken at Homerton, a women's college two miles off.

To a home-bred student from a northern industrial town Cambridge in early summer had all the mystery and charm that, from reading, I had expected to find only in the south of France. Narrow lanes twisted down to the river, where sunlight fell through overhanging trees. Beneath old arch ways were glimpses of lilac with roses tumbling over rough stone walls. And the *colour*. I have a little book picturing old Russian icons, and to look at those pictures with their old gold, soft greens and blues and rusty red, set in carved frames garlanded with silver, is to bring back instantly the vivid impression that Cambridge made on me, all those years ago. It is not that Tyneside is without colour — on the contrary. But there, one is conscious always of tones of grey, of sombre brooding distance, with touches of purple and heliotrope.

Twelve assembled to take the course with its imposing title 'Youth Leadership'. We were centred on a women's training college, where the other students were housed. Elizabeth and I were the odd ones, lodged in town, and drawn together by admiration for Jane Austen and Chekov and a wish for greater freedom in education.

On the first evening, our eyes grew ever wider as we listened to a brief run-through of the scope and intention of the course. Only bygone visions of imperial greatness could have led to the planning of so vast and nebulous a schedule — and in the middle of a ferocious war, at that. We were to have art, music and PE (including dance) with the training college students; special courses on the history and development of the Social Services; lectures on women's employment and Labour law, for which we would cycle to women's colleges of the university; lectures on club management given by our tutor, Miss Langley, in a wooden pavilion in the college grounds; and hygiene and psychology courses given by college staff. The wooden pavilion was to be our base and it was hoped that we should have many profitable discussions there on 'work in club'.

This was the strangest term of listening I ever sat through. Miss Langley, elegant, with drawling voice, had had no training in lecturing, and her remarks were strung together as tenuously as daisy-chains.

'The youth leader should have … um … ah … sense of …er… humour and … err … infinite patience and … um … tact … er … she must be … um … adult herself and um … a whole personality.'

Summarised, and leaving out the mannerisms, this became

A Club Leader Should Have:
Real love of humanity and faith in it.
Belief in her work and desire to do it (others must see this)
(How and Why? I muttered to Elizabeth)
Vitality, imagination and enthusiasm.
Sympathy, and desire to help.
A sense of humour and infinite patience.
Tolerance and tact.
Humility, to realise the size of the job.

A Club Leader Must Be:
Adult herself, a whole personality.
Progressive, alive.
Have her own life and have time and energy to continue her development.

This, transcribed from my note-book, is an hour long lecture on 'Qualities required for club leadership'. This Model Leader was dangled for the next ten weeks before us, like a pharmaceutical advertisement for 'Radiant Woman'.

We sat in a circle, scribbling conscientiously at intervals, and observing Miss Langley, who talked with one beautifully manicured hand twirling her dark glasses, her long legs gracefully crossed.

There we were, once more at the receiving end of 'education', and it had all changed very little from the boring exhortations we were conscious of, but did not listen to, at the age of eight in second form.

We had evening work in clubs, but the daytime programme was so light that I found it possible to fit in two courses of lectures at the London School of Economics (evacuated to Cambridge) and a few hours reading in the university library almost every day. All my life I shall remember those weeks in Cambridge because of that library and the happiness of working there. I went, in trepidation, imagining a rebuff, but when I said I was a graduate of Durham and might I work there, without demur or suspicion, the librarian agreed. I might have been a wandering scholar from Florence or Padua, so helpful and kind he was. There will be libraries like this in Heaven — unless indeed our libraries are the nearest we shall ever get to Heaven.

I did much history reading, as well as reading for the essays we were asked to write. Some of the topics set were so enormous that whole terms could have been spent in preparation.

'What do you understand by 'character'? How can it be trained, at home, at school and in the club?'

or

'What do you understand by 'discipline'? Discuss the question of discipline in clubs.'

Elizabeth, who was a painter, was another awkward student. Either we wrote fifty pages and had to give our work in, hopefully pencilling 'unfinished' at the end; or, as in the case of 'Describe the working class boy or girl against the background of home, school and club life', we wrote two introductory pages tearing the title to shreds. There was something very patronising towards the 'working class' in the attitudes of lecturers in club work at that time.

To a teacher, particularly one from state schools, accustomed to working at high pressure with large classes, the most striking thing about the clubs we visited was their pottering way of going on. Rarely was anything decided and done. A new project, say a drama class, was talked about aimlessly in groups, forgotten for three weeks, resurrected by the leader, and finally postponed till next session — it being, by then, too late to start. Nothing began on time. If the club opened at 7.00, the leader hung about in desultory conversation with stragglers until 8.30 and then with luck, the evening programme, if any might begin.

All those dreary nights we spent in clubs made me feel like a car being driven for two thousand miles in bottom gear, with the engine always on the point of seizing up.

I do not think I am a hustler by nature, but to waste a June evening in a barren, dusty hall, waiting two hours for six people to turn up, and the rest of the evening playing table tennis or exchanging badinage, is to me the summit of educational idiocy. If the role of the teacher is not precise, that of the youth club leader is so diffuse as to be well-nigh invisible.

I had gone to Cambridge not just — nor indeed primarily — because I passionately longed to study there; but because I hoped to find, in youth work, scope for teaching in a context of freedom. I hoped to escape from the atmosphere of stress and bossiness of the grammar schools, which secondary moderns, and later comprehensives, had set out to imitate. Do this; do that. Write here; run there. Sit up; sit down. Work faster; try harder. Get *on* and *be quick*.

As an adolescent, I had doubted the use of this. As a teacher, in my first term, I vowed I would never do it. Yet I acquired the knack, like everyone else, through daily listening.

And now here I was, in the 'freedom' of youth clubs — only to find it a thousand-fold worse. The things which, to me, mattered most in education — the happy, stable framework, the continuity and permanence — these did not exist.

To be able to wait is vital in education. Yet our nightly waiting in those Cambridge clubs was unconstructive. *We* waited; the young were not there. In our lectures, we had made lists of 'essential qualities' in a club leader; had been exhorted to be 'adult' and 'whole'. We were anxious to comply but no nearer achievement. The approach was concentrated on this mythical young person — 'the boy (or girl) in club'. Every aspect of the course was seen as something that could be lectured upon and filed. The course was a facade.

Should I go back to teaching? Apply for a job in Cambridge perhaps? But I couldn't forget the good sense of a former pupil's definition: '*Clumsy* — to fall into something you seen already'. I had seen something in school teaching I wanted to escape, if only for half a dozen years. There is something too soft, too cosy, too restrictive, in school life, if it continues too long without change. But the Ministry of Labour ruling prevented even a temporary break. Perhaps I should just return to Ralph Gardner School where I would be so warmly welcomed if I did return.

Through the days of this interior monologue, I was badgered by my landlady and her supporting friend with questions, 'What are you going to do? When? Isn't it time you decided?' The friend was a nursery school Head, large and warm, given to cuddling adults as if they were lonely beginners on their first day at school. Her heart surged with affection, like an overflowing pan of dough. She felt — 'felt very strongly' — that I must teach, and in Cambridge. She said 'Teaching satisfies every need in me — and it's so *secure.*'

There was no argument. We approached teaching on different roads, she the Earth Mother, providing 'my little people' with a cushion against the rigours of the world, until her pension would provide her with a cushion in her turn. I detested the prospect of 'the life-long teacher' with all its dreary associations in so many minds. I remembered that Kay Shuttleworth in 1846 had publicly proclaimed

> **There is little or nothing in the profession of schoolmaster to tempt a man .... to exchange the certainty of a respectable livelihood in a subordinate position in industry or commerce for the mean drudgery of instructing children in an elementary school.**

And, as if to bear witness to that embittered statement, the Bronte sisters had done their share to spread the vision of the teacher-drudge. Yet schools are, and should be, full of laughter, enthusiasm, fire and energy. I felt proud and glad to have *been* a teacher. I just did not want to go on being one for evermore. I wanted a more sharply articulated, much more team-minded role, a kind of 'teaching' that could merge with some harder, tougher occupation for a few years every now and then. My landlady and her friend sought to tame me by offering their wartime sweet coupons — a gesture equally generous and absurd.

In that last week of term, another letter came from Janet: this letter, as so often in the past three years, cut obliquely into my muddled thoughts. She told of a very fine man. A German refugee, imprisoned in Dachau, whom she had met in Penrith, to whom she had written in sympathy.

> **This is part of his reply,**

she wrote.

> **I shall keep it always, it shows such unflinching courage:**
> **'Why should I despair and lose faith in humanity when millions throughout the whole world are fighting and sacrificing their lives for our common ideal? The human race is still very young and we must be satisfied in seeing the dawn of a new and better society.'**
> **I wanted to tell you about seeing the sailor. I lost all pleasure in looking forward to it because after my intensive study of timetables, I *knew* he would not come by the only train that stopped at Penrith. However, martyr-like, I stood on the platform watching expresses whizz by and even waited for the one that did stop — just to have the melancholy satisfaction of knowing that he wasn't on it. And he was!! He was there, out of the train in a jiffy, standing with the baby in his arms and hailing me in the same old, cheerful fashion. The old sense**

overcame me that darkness and fear had slipped away. The baby was beautiful, with a handsome little face, rather like a young lion's: gentle, but formidable; crisp fair curls, big blue eyes that looked attentive in a mildly puzzled way, rosy cheeks and a chin that I recognised.

The sailor pushed the little lad's face towards me for a kiss and followed it up with one himself. The wife, pleasant and nice-looking, laughed, seized the baby and climbed back into the train; he followed, leaned on the window and spoke about the Russians. But he did what he always did — just went. I thought he'd lean out and wave but he didn't. The damned train went round the bend and stopped. So I stopped too, until all the back part had finished its quite irrelevant goings-on, and the front part, without a backward glance, snorted and set off, and the whole caboodle was gone.

I'm just telling you. I don't want you to feel sorry for me because there's no need. What was — and maybe is — between us, had nothing to do with being married. It meant the Tyne, and ships; the sea, strange ports. It meant Drake and Raleigh, Devon and Somerset. It meant 'The Grand' at Byker, and old pubs by the Quayside. In short, it meant practically everything.

Nothing passes. For days I ruminated on this letter, recalling others Janet had written in the previous four years. These letters had illuminated, with concise and specific detail, general arguments given us in lectures by Dr Cobban. Together they had exploded my fantasy-picture of political and economic life. Yet how could I hope to have practical views on history or politics when I had lived my entire life in home or school, sheltered from reality? I had virtually no experience of human relationships other than those of parent-child, and pupil-teacher, certainly none of working with other adults to achieve some common aim. I was living a prolonged adolescence, and it was time to change. 'Youth work' would not provide an answer, that was clear. I had gone down one of those

Shadowy entries, streets that wind,
Alleys that are often blind.

Tony Connor warned of this in his poem which describes so vividly the street games of the Tyne.

These thoughts recalled an idea first put to me by Dr Cobban in 1938 before the war began. After one of his 'International Affairs' classes he had said to me 'I think you would fit into adult education. Why not go down to the District Secretary of the Worker's Educational Association, and ask if he could give you a class. Say I sent you.'

So I set to work, entranced by the idea of studying history with those who, unlike school pupils, had some experience of life. I prepared a syllabus, and made an appointment with the Secretary of the Newcastle WEA.

After a long wait, I was shown into a small room where a dark man with a sharp nose looked me down, down to my square-toed walking shoes, and up. 'Too young,' he said.

I was almost out of the room when he half-relented.

'Is that your syllabus? Show me it.' I laid it on the desk between us, thin and pathetic, a premature child.

'Huh,' he said with faint animation. 'Not bad ... Come back in five years,' and there I was outside the door.

For quite two hours that night I raged inwardly. Not one whole sentence had I uttered! Only 'Good morning' (twice). Why had I never mentioned *someone* who, though young, had yet been trusted? Harry Hotspur? Mozart? Pitt? To glory such as theirs I did not aspire, but surely I could do something so insignificant as take a class? To and fro, with fretful repetition, went my recriminations, an inner stream of futile complaint, criticism and anger.

Superficially the episode was forgotten, amid all the preparation for evacuation, followed by war. Now, in 1943 it came upon me with a shock, that almost five years had already passed since my first ignominious effort to become a tutor. I would go back, and try again to find a minute place in the adult education movement.

So, the youth course ended, I sped to Newcastle, spent one night with a friend in edgy anticipation, and early next day made for the WEA office.

In five years, only a week had gone by there. The District Secretary looked me down as before, down — and up. 'Too late,' he said. 'We advertised five weeks ago. The university needs a Tutor-Organiser for the western area, Cumberland and south west Northumberland. We're interviewing a short list of six at the University this afternoon ...'

'But I was in Cambridge — never saw the advertisement,' I stammered.

'Too bad. You're just too late,' he reiterated, shuffling papers on his desk.

Perhaps it was his wintry negativity that did it. First 'too young' and now 'too late'. That little man with the nose jolted some mechanism that had been idling in my brain for thirteen years — in fact from my final day in high school as a pupil. 'Immature' I was called then. Was I going to waste my whole life being picked over and rejected like a damaged biscuit? That tutor-organiser's job in Cumberland was for me. The blood of all my Border ancestors, Redes, Halls, Charltons, Hawdons, thundered in my head, and a firm clear voice, unquestionably mine, said 'Can I not be interviewed as well?'

He was aghast; but recovering his best diplomatic, non-committal manner, he suggested perhaps ... all things considered ... since, in fact I had been interested in the past — and would have applied if I had not been in Cambridge — it might be arranged. Perhaps he would phone the Director of Extra-Mural Studies at the university …

I waited. My name was added to the list. I remember nothing of that long interview but the last two questions: Have you a car? Can you drive? I could get one. I could learn.

A week later I was in Cumbria, with a less than reliable second-hand Ford car, on which I had had five driving lessons. A new life began.

CHAPTER FIFTEEN

Variations on a theme
A commercial traveller in education

I had never dreamt of leaving school-teaching in Newcastle for good. Five or six years in Cumberland was the intention. I thought and hoped, that in learning the very different approach necessary for adult education I would at least begin to mature; and that the study and discussion of history, political thought and 'social problems' would be on a more detailed and worthwhile level than it could ever be in school. After five or six years of hard experience, I would go back to the Tyne.

But, having marrried, and since my husband's work was in Cumbria, there with our family, we remained, but that is another story.

A spell in adult education, however brief, has a bearing on what we try to do in school. My years as a tutor organiser were essentially a new attempt, let us hope with slightly more finesse, to link subjects and syllabuses so that knowledge might indeed be seen as a 'seemless web'.

In Cumbria, as in those Walker schools in the early years of war, I was 'on my own' — a commercial traveller in education.

It was autumn, start of the new year, when, in theory, adult students chose their new subject of study. At various Branch opening meetings I was given opportunity to suggest to students that in genuine history, rather than in the then popular 'social problems' or 'post-war Reconstruction', they would find long-lasting food. And in Carlisle I did get one group to undertake a three year tutorial class in history. The aim of such a class is to reach university level; but, given the very different circumstances of undergraduates and our students, at work all day, this is always difficult, sometimes impossible.

'Not further back than Queen Elizabeth,' one man insisted, so we agreed to make a start on the explorers of the sixteenth century, with a little study of the way Hakluyt wrote his *Voyages*.

This modest man, who signed his great works simply 'Richard Hakluyt, Preacher,' was not, so far as we know, endowed with the more brilliant creative gifts. Nevertheless, his works directed the thoughts of adventurous scholars, statesmen and merchants, outwards across the oceans of the world. And upwards of three hundred years later, in one small provincial town, he inspired us to follow and learn from him. Through industry, he had, as he said,

redeemed from obscurity and perishing, old records, patents, privileges, letters...

In that frozen winter of 1943, sitting in the cold Carlisle library, we held communion with him

What heat, what cold I have endured...how many famous libraries I have searched into...

We felt we understood him well.

Since the subject matter of history embraces all human endeavour, and achievement; all successes, inventions and artistic creativity; all disasters nobly or ignobly born; all devastations of war and famine, it would take a very poor teacher not to move or thrill some of her students at least some of the time, and in Carlisle, it did not take us long to develop a comradeship of ideas.

Yet I still *talked* with our women students only in their own homes, among their household goods and children. In class, they sat gravely silent.

The stage has to be peopled with recognisable human beings, and a constant source of these is to be found in the paintings and writings of the seventeenth and eighteenth centuries. This is a period of particular attraction to a new group of adult students, who all know, vaguely, of the changes taking place in farming, transport, literature, justice, between the time of Defoe to the coming of the Georges. They can feel 'at home' because so many names are known to them, though what the famous people actually did, or wrote or intended, may be hazy in their minds. The tutor must make a provocatively ingenious and questioning syllabus, so that each term's work helps in the building of a gigantic jigsaw, bringing town and country life, with its changes, into focus.

Hogarth led the way

My picture is my stage, and men and women my players...*

He was both storyteller, and moralist. All our students knew *of* him, but none had thought about him or about his work.

A stranger to almost all of them was Thomas Bewick, born fifty years after Hogarth close to the Tyne, at Ovingham, where his father was a miner and small farmer. Apprenticed at fourteen, Bewick became one of the greatest of engravers, in his day or any other. He served seven years in Newcastle, then, because of his success was drawn to London. He enjoyed seeing the excellent work

> **in every art and science — painting, statuary, engraving, carving... yet I did not like London... a world of extreme riches, extreme poverty, extreme grandeur and extreme wretchedness... The country of my old friends — the manners of the people of that day — the scenery of Tyneside — seemed altogether a paradise for me, and I longed to see it again...****

So, like many another before and since, he returned to the Tyne, never to leave it again.

I had never given a lesson on Bewick before, nor indeed ever talked about him, yet in quotation from that splendid man, in words and pictures, I was wholly carried away. Many of his tiny pictures brought back memories of our living, lively boys at Shields, for no one can have depicted boys and their impish pranks more amusingly and touchingly; nor country people at every task more exactly. Nor could he have described with less acrimony the constant 'whackings' that followed his own boyish escapades — 'the overflowings of an active, wild disposition.'

Here was a boy, by his own account, as often in trouble as any of our lads at the Ralph Gardner School, yet, aided only by his parents' commonsense, what a superb thing he made of life.

All our students had heard of, and a few had read, *The Vicar of Wakefield,* but although so near the Border, not one student knew John Galt, the long-suffering Scottish writer and 'man o' parts' whose *Annals of the Parish* is quite as enchanting as Goldsmith's 'Vicar', and probably even more valuable as a record of social life. It is an intimate portrait of Ayrshire during the rise of the cotton mills, not only one of the most vivid, enlightening and entertaining accounts of village life ever written, but certainly the most melodious to read.

One day, hunting in the Carlisle library for other books by John Galt for our students I found an ancient review of his *Tales of My Landlord* written by the Scottish Judge, Francis Jeffrey. In that review, written in the eighteen twenties, in a time of turmoil, shortages and hardship so like the one we ourselves were passing through in 1943 and '44, I came upon

---

**Hogarth*, (World's Masters New Series), Intro. Antony Bertram
** Memoir of Thomas Bewick (Frank Graham)

words of such good sense then that they have remained with me ever since.

The quiet undercurrent of life keeps its deep and steady course... long tracts in the history of every country seem to be darkened with an oppressive cloud of unbroken misery, yet most of those who lived through the whole acts of the tragedy will have enjoyed a fair average share of felicity...

We seem now in a new stage of continuously oppressive world misery, but at the time of writing, Galt's words surely contained a sober truth?

Of felicity, I for one felt that I was enjoying more than my fair share. I was lodged with a middle aged, semi-retired farmer and his wife, and all through the golden autumn of my first term in Cumbria with the River Eden before us, sparkling through the tawny trees, I felt translated to the Forest of Arden. The Editor of the Arden edition of *As You Like It* says: 'Life in Arden is naturally happy and wholesome, good men flourish there, free from human malice.' Yes... a great generalisation perhaps, though certainly true of the two I lived with, Mr and Mrs Fairish. Mr Fairish had Corin's homespun philosophy. One Sunday evening, taking a little walk together, we looked over a neighbour's wall at some rather weedy piglets. 'If them ever makes pigs, aa'll eat hay wid horse,' was his blunt dismissal of the little creatures. He was wrong in his judgment, (as we often are about our pupils), but he had the grace to admit it later.

I found endless delight in listening to him for his comments were always fresh and usually apt. One night, when I was off to a class in Carlisle, having promised to take Mrs Fairish with me to see a friend, I was fidgeting because she was not ready. 'Yu's nobbut good for a neet watchman. Aa nivver saw a body sae uneasy when she's barred oop — fizzling about, like cat on a griddle.'

Mrs F was her husband's equal in cheerful, unflustered moto perpetuum throughout the daylight hours. We all breakfasted together at 7.15, then he went out to his work while she continued her fifteen hour day: hens, chickens, baking, cleaning — wash (in the poss tub) iron, polish — '10 o'clocks' 3 o'clocks' and 'proper meals' in between. All she ever read was 'Births, Deaths and Marriages' on Friday night in the *Cumberland News*, and *The Peoples' Friend* for perhaps an hour on Sunday afternoon. She, like her husband, was quite ready to see improvement for the poor and needy, but the idea of taking *thought* about it, of actually trying to *do* anything to change the future, would have seemed as absurd as the idea of walking round to Buckingham Palace for a rubber of whist with royalty.

While Mrs F busied herself in her clogs, in and out the dairy, the back kitchen and the stack yard, I busied myself on the kitchen table writing letters to Branch Secretaries, to existing or prospective tutors, and endlessly studying and preparing for five different weekly classes, as well as Saturday and week-end 'schools'. Though too polite to say so, it was clear they both thought my job probably pointless, and certainly very, very odd.

'Can't you just preach them summat you've preached afore?' Mrs F said wistfully one day; and one wild winter afternoon, as I was setting off twenty-five miles over Hartside to a class at Nenthead, Mr F, looking forward to a night by the fire, announced 'Aa's ganna clip cloots if aa had a bit shave first. 'Tisn't ivverybody as can clip cloots.' (cut rags into little pieces, to make a 'proggy mat') and he was right, I never had time even for that.

Over the years, Mr and Mrs Fairish gave a welcome to me as if to the daughter they had never had. But how like a changeling I must have seemed at first, an 'Organising-Tutor' being as far from their experience as a shogun from Japan. They themselves had attended one-teacher village schools, and very occasionally went to church 'to hear the sermon'.

In my studying by day and ranging the countryside at night, I must have seemed to them a kind of itinerant nocturnal preacher crossed with a Hammer-Headed bat. I could not make them understand that I was not there to *preach* . The only form of schooling they recognised was drawn from their own experience: Teacher talks; pupils repeat, repeat, repeat; and if 'successful', learn by heart. I had found, from visiting a variety of classes, that most tutors *did* talk continuously, though what the students recollected of all they 'listened' to, no one ever knew. But surely that great flow of exposition can never be the most important teaching function? It is the give and take between individual minds which is the source of life and learning. A teacher (so I thought, and think) must consciously and continuously *listen* , while students must talk as well as listen if they are ever to make new ideas of their own. There must be reciprocity.

Perhaps it was while studying the Bewick engravings so assiduously for Carlisle class that I began to understand that *listening* may be to teachers what *looking* is to artists. In addition to Bewick's autobiography, I had with me in Cumberland a book of Rembrandt drawings (pen and bistre wash) found long before in a Newcastle bookshop. Having no music in Cumberland, every Sunday I used to look at these superb drawings — *Interior of a kitchen*, *Study of a tree trunk*, *Trees and a river at dusk*, *Women in a doorway* and the wonderful *Lion lying down*, from the Boymans Museum in Rotterdam, and they gave the same kind of comfort that Beethoven used to give in those years of Mother's illness.

I remembered that Chardin used to say to pupils 'Hand and palette are needed to paint; but a painting is not made with the hand or the palette.' Would it not be equally true to say 'voice and chalk are needed by teachers:

but a teacher is not made by the voice or the chalk'? How many times in the past, I had walked down that school corridor in Washington Road, seeing pupils in the back seats giggling and playing, while strident teacher-voices shrilled from every glass-framed cage; and not only were these hard-pressed teachers shouting, they waved their arms in frantic or despairing imprecation, ever and anon turning to write feverishly on the board.

...Not waving but drowning...

I know the temptation, and had, at times, succumbed. Probably this irrational behaviour sprang from fear of several kinds: memories of our own school days, when we, too, tormented nervous teachers, perhaps now feeling that we suffered just reward; fear that the gifts we were so anxious to offer — of knowledge, of understanding were not wanted; that the end of year, end of life itself would come and all that we tried to teach be wasted. Such fears, and others, can be felt, in every degree of exaggeration, if the teacher is tired, or despondent, and may produce that shouting at the class which is so destructive to teacher and demoralising to pupils.

When I first started the new job, it had seemed plain that such travesties of learning would be impossible in *adult* education! With twelve or fifteen in a class instead of forty, we would have genuine 'dialogue' each day. We would learn together. What a new-found opportunity to put all notions of 'good teaching' to the test!

So I imagined us, drawing up our chairs in a cosy circle, where, after an arresting introduction, we would launch into thoughtful and satisfying debate. What I found in practice, as a famous artist found in painting, was that 'there is no way to success in our art but to take off your coat, grind paint, and work like a digger on the railway all day and every day'. In every class, I was faced by a phalanx of silent women, all clearly intimidated by half-a-dozen men, mostly middle-aged.

Not that our men were a vintage year of former film stars either. Marianne Dashwood would not have given one of them a second glance, all but one being so obviously destined, before the course was over, for age, infirmity and flannel waistcoats. It could scarcely have been adoration which silenced our women — intelligent and strong-minded, managers of shops, schools, or homes with several children. No, it seemed an endemic female passivity in front of men; as if it was not seemly to speak except to one's consecrated husband and not always even then.

I saw this daily in my lodging, where Mrs Fairish behaved as if it were divinely ordained for her to work, and to suffer, if that were called for, in silence. If Mr Fairish had a cold he sat in the chair with his feet on the fender, murmuring in a wan voice, 'Aa's in sic a bad fettle — sic a bad fettle.' And if not enough sympathy ensued, he would grumble wistfully, 'Aa doan't think thou knaw's aa's as badly as aa is.' When Mrs Fairish was ill, on the contrary, she drooped about, martyr-like in her clogs, till I drove her to bed. All the women I knew then in rural Cumbria, however voluble to their own friends in their own kitchens, accepted their men's opinions on social or any other question with amazing docility.

I asked one farmer if his wife would come to the class I was running in the village. 'Nay, I doan't think it,' he said, shaking his head gloomily. 'I doan't like 'er to go t'Institute an' that. She gets wid a lot o' wimmin and gets gabby.' And the most macabre comment ever uttered in my hearing was made one morning when, on one of my journeys, I called, as asked, to leave a parcel at an isolated Pennine farm. I was shown into the kitchen only to be told that the farmer's wife had died the previous night. While trying to express sympathy to him, I found the sitting room door flung open, and myself staring at the corpse.

'Just luk at that' the farmer rasped. 'Luk at that, and sic a lot o' grand work in 'er yet.' Though perhaps sincerely sorry, he spoke in what sounded more like exasperation than remorse.

Oh yes, attitudes have changed in nearly fifty years; and among them attitudes to women. Yet not everywhere in rural Britain have attitudes to women (and women's thoughts about themselves) changed as much as people commonly suppose.

In our Carlisle class, when, by dint of carefully thought out questions, I did get nearly everyone to speak a little, the comments were more hesitant, more convoluted, more repetitive than those of our eleven or twelve-year-olds at Washington Road. The human mind tends to rotate, and its progress round a given subject often appears, during 'discussion', to be imperceptible. A new tutor (myself for instance) is *afraid* of this apparent stagnation: the anguished thoughts chase one another 'We are getting nowhere — everyone will be bored — the class will fold up,' and the temptation to interfere is fierce.

I did try to wait, patiently, as an artist must wait while concentrating on his subject; and, generally, someone would move the discussion forward an inch, and a comment of real illumination often followed.

In that wonderful extension of our adult classes, the Open University, I am delighted to see things that I was groping after in Cumbria in those war, and post-war years, now being done in a much more 'structured' way. What we strove for at varying levels in all our adult classes — through halting, unassertive exchange of opinion — was to reach individually and together — a wider view of learning and of life.

But I am letting the tutoring side of my new enterprise run far ahead of the organising half. That unwelcome aspect loomed over me, part of the 'contract' I had agreed to in Newcastle so innocently and eagerly.

There may be a place for organisers in production or distribution of commodities. But in education? And if we decide, on balance, we should try having them, what should be their special skills? If there is any book where this topic is debated I had not read it. Perhaps the simple truth was that, in my hasty application, I had wanted *half* the job, honestly believing I could do that part. To the rest, I had shut my eyes, half wishing, half dreaming that magic would spirit it away.

In those first few weeks in Cumbria, when I imagined myself dispassionately observing how others conducted adult education, it was interesting to see how quickly roots of my own infantile behaviour were revealed! And not only once. In a matter of days, I had said and done things in an innocent, simple minded manner that brought untold trouble later. With foresight and experience could I have managed relations with the Carlisle Branch Chairman so that they would have been tranquil? The trouble is that foresight and experience are just what the novice has not got. I was unwary. And it is hard for anyone unwary to become a diplomat.

After the Extra-Mural Board meeting at which I had been selected for the job, the Chairman of the Carlisle Branch of the Workers' Educational Association told me to call upon him in his office when I arrived in Cumbria. This I duly did, and the whole interview was so reminiscent of that chapter in *Our Mutual Friend* where Mr Podsnap questions the 'foreign gentleman' at Georgina's birthday party, that it was hard not to laugh.

'How do you like Cumbria? You'll find it very different from Newcastle: more trees; more mountains; more space. People are individuals here you know.'

He gave me no time for comment.

'What you *ought* to do is watch a few classes taken by Plunkett. He's been tutoring for years. Very good man. Very sound. I'll fix that for you. Now let's see — there's Balderstone. He's another pal of mine: starting *his* classes next week, too. I could get you in to watch him. Then you'd have a notion how things should go on...

'I've fixed you up with lodgings two doors away from me. You'll be all right there. Woman on her own; husband in the Army; just one child; about a year old. If you're there, I'll know what you're up to — see you're on right lines — sort out any difficulties.'

I murmured 'Very kind; but I think...' He waved me silent. Clearly it was not mine to reason why, anywhere on his battlefield. Like the original Mr Podsnap, he believed that what he put behind him was put out of his existence. What I thought did not signify.

From then on, every time we met, he went immediately into attack. I responded with deference first, but when he continually played authority, I took fright, as now.

Were even lodgings to be chosen for me? And by someone I hardly knew, and certainly did not respect. I evaded —

'I am thinking of living in the country.'

To this he gave snorting dismissal.

'You can't possibly do that.'

I had not, till that minute, made up my mind; but that decided me. He grew bitter and bullying: to be ten miles out of town, down rural lanes, would make night travelling that much worse. He *knew*. Oncomers should accept advice. Everything he said was sensible. I knew neither people in the district nor winter weather in mountainous terrain.

I had no reasoned answer, only intuition. I could not, and would not, live under his foot. To him, I was exploitable — as exploitable as Mozart's Susanna, though in a different way. While willing to be exploited for my own idea of education, *his* idea of education, so blatantly one of dominating authority, was not a cause for which I would die.

Should we have had a confrontation *then*? In the long run, perhaps that would have been wiser. But I pursued guerilla tactics, hoping that if I side-stepped often enough, he would finally tire of the pursuit. He never did.

When November drew on, with ceaseless rain and constant fog with nightly journeys in an aging Ford car with no heating and masked and minimal car head lights, few telephones and no sign posts anywhere, my allegiance to Arden almost failed. Then, without warning, would come once more a perfect day, with blue sky over gleaned harvest fields, and black-faced sheep higher up the fells. And beyond them the mountains, bronze and blue in sunset, with folds deeply marked in shadow, and white washed cottages at the foot of the slopes. Sometimes, journeying to see tutors or secretaries, I had to drive through the hills, to Cockermouth, or further, to Whitehaven and the sea. And alone in my car I would sing all the way, knowing I never wanted to live out of sight of the hills again. Getting to know that vast, mountainous and sparsely populated region — one quarter the size of Wales — provided problems that strained physique, as well as testing (and defeating) my small stock of car maintenance skill. But when the car broke down, I still had two good feet, and I learnt, in time, to know my district like a native. I do believe, moreover, that, living *like* a native in the country, I learnt more and belonged more quickly than I would ever have done if living even three times as long as a bourgeois 'oncomer' in a suburban 'semi' in Carlisle.

But let me not give any impression that I learnt to know this area *alone*. Only the quiet, unremitting kindness of students and Branch Secretaries, who gave me tea, or bed and breakfast, times without number, saved me from death by petrifraction long ago.

How often I have been asked 'What made you go into adult education? You could have stayed on in Newcastle and become a Head?' as if we were all expected to see the future in terms only of power and 'success'. In making any change in life the mind has conscious and unconscious motives. Consciously, as already noted, I wanted, for a time, to pursue the study of history with adults. But there was also a need — not identified until, in those years in Cumbria it was so richly satisfied, to strike off on my own; to do the unexpected; to venture up hills where every route was not marked by stone corridors and forty minute bells.

The contrast between the rich experiences of learning that my brothers and I shared in youth, and the years of war-time teaching on Tyneside was stark. In Cumbria too there was a rich store of local history dating back to prehistoric times.

I had been trying, over a period, to find a form of teaching in which pupils and staff could grow together. But neither the boys' school at Tynemouth, nor youth work in Cambridgeshire had offered scope for such experiment. War-time conditions forbade all out-of-school activities in the one, while benevolent dictatorship ossified all participants in the other. In adult education, however, restrictions and worries of the war proved an incentive to students. If there were rifts between officials, and occasional tiffs between the WEA organisation in Newcastle and the impetuous tutor 'in the field', at least our friction was fresh and productive, not a slow atrophy, as in my experience of the Cambridge youth world.

Above all this, Cumbria — if lacking in some of the cultural amenities thought necessary for salvation — offers always and everywhere, colour and space. Like drama, music, poetry, these free the imagination too. The Eden valley, the Pennine hills, trees by the old farmsteads, ferns in stone walls, all these brought back our years of walking holidays in Northumberland. Young and old, people sing when happy. And I sang as I had not sung for years. Certain things in life seem only obtainable obliquely — happiness certainly, and education at least in part. There are aspects of learning over which we can exert no direct control. That teacher at Ralph Gardner School, Miss Hislop who 'taught Roman Britain' by making her boys learn the dimensions of the wall (in feet and inches!) never knew what strange ships of fancy her class might embark upon while she talked.

Miss Hislop, most earnest of teachers, gave me her class 'examination paper', generously intending to help someone young and 'new'. Far from being a help, it was a horrifying glimpse of what any one of us might come to after twenty years of continuous school teaching, if we never paused long enough to enter dry dock for a refit.

Cumbria was my dock — though even so incurable an optimist as I could scarcely call it 'dry'.

As an 'Organiser' in adult education the demands were great: time and energy were spent in constant travel; in efforts to promote goodwill between rival part-time tutors often jealous of each other; in efforts to promote classes in starved soil. But the rewards, as a tutor, far outweighed the distracting demands. It is enriching to be part of an educational movement where people come to classes purely for the joy of learning; a movement which exists for no other reason but that knowledge has value of its own. This, too, linked with some of our best school work in Walker when, in our great adversity in those early months of 1940, we had experienced the sustaining power of seeking knowledge for ourselves.

Without doubt, the search for knowledge sustained us yet again in the dark days of 1943 and 1944 in our adult classes. Yet we were not sombre about it, not at all. Many a time I was asked to give 'A little talk about education,' Church and Chapel organisations being particularly fond of filling up a weekly meeting in this decent, earnest fashion. I went to one such gathering called 'Women's Bright Hour' at Aspatria. Some twenty women sat on hard chairs, in a cold, dark, room avoiding my eye, but gazing at one another with expressions of self-lacerating misery. I told them I had been invited, the week before, to high tea at a farmhouse, where the ten year old daughter was bidden to 'Ask a blessing' before we began. She closed her eyes and said, without pause for breath,

'Forwhatweareabouttoreceivemakeustrulythankful — Mother what a *little* kipper you've given me.'

I thought that was how many people (especially women) felt about education. They looked forward to it so much in the beginning, but by the end, were so often disappointed.

Students were, in general, a more cheerful bunch than tutors for there was very little to attract any one to part-time tutoring in those days. All of ours were middle-aged or elderly, mainly teachers from minor rural grammar schools who wanted to make a little extra money. They were amazingly cynical, and the few parsons included in our allotment, even more jaundiced.

To this there was one outstanding exception, an astronomer, T L MacDonald, who, after a distinguished academic career, because of his care for the deprived and the 'drop-outs', had become Youth Organiser for Carlisle and District. He was brilliant in science and unusually knowledgeable in literature and politics. He lived alone and had strange habits reminiscent of Dr Johnson. Officials like our Carlisle Branch Secretary, 'Mr Podsnap' used to laugh at him, but all his students were his devoted slaves, and would walk three miles in snow and tempest not to miss a class. I had listened to him in his office and talking informally at weekend schools, recalling always that splendid comment 'curiosity is, in great and generous minds, the first passion and the last,' for he had that capacity, which Sir Isaiah Berlin has to so marked a degree, to fire his students with his own enthusiasm. Could we not make Macdonald's gifts available to tutors?

For the previous two years at least, I had felt that the best way to meet our problems was to keep a mental list of assets and drawbacks, trying to use one to minimise the other. T L MacDonald was one undoubted asset; our lovely countryside another. A major drawback was isolation from any university and consequent staleness and lack of intellectual stimulus and vitality; there was a total lack of 'bookshops' in the real sense, though four or five of the larger towns had a stationer with a handful of recent paperback novels.

To revive our less than buoyant tutorial spirits, I had started a branch of the Tutors' Association, but evening meetings were impossible for people twenty to forty miles apart, so we relied on Saturday and weekend schools for corporate inspiration. Weekends were always enjoyable, and tutors went away in a mildly more co-operative temper. We met several times in the Newlands Valley at the foot of Causey Pike, in a Holiday Fellowship guest house. At other times, we met at Dalston Hall, a Border pele tower with later additions, including mullioned turrets and pleasant grounds.

One of the best schools was at Maryport, a once-elegant little west coast town which had fallen on hard times by the nineteen forties, We stayed at the Golden Lion Hotel overlooking the tiny harbour, at a charge of 12/6d a day, dinner, bed and breakfast. (Can that 12/6d, 62p today — really have included *Bed* as well as Board?) We had some splendid speakers: Thomas Hodgkin of the Oxford Extra-Mural Delegacy; an HMI for Adult Education; Thomas Balogh (later Lord Balogh) then Director of the Oxford Institute of Statistics; Dennis Chapman who had been Director of the War Time Social Survey.

In arranging these Schools I was supported always by my 'boss', Herbert Highton, Director of Extra-Mural Studies at Newcastle upon Tyne,a gruff but fatherly Glaswegian. At the Maryport school, T L MacDonald spoke on 'The Lost years: bridging the gap between the youth service and adult education'. Since he was peculiarly fitted for this subject, and we had all experienced the problem, both talk and discussion were unwontedly successful, stirring even our reserved members to applause.

Speaking about this afterward with Mr Highton, I learned that he and Mr MacDonald had been students in Glasgow University together and that he had known and admired him then. He added casually, in one of the dry asides in which he always made his useful comments 'He gave the Ford lectures once, you know.'

This put a match to a small fire I had been unobtrusively preparing in the background, intending it to be lighted perhaps several months ahead. It seemed as if the only way to build up something lasting and productive between tutors — a constant mental stimulas rather than the agreeable but evanescent exchanges at weekends — would be to run a weekly class for tutors. At the same time, I was disturbed by the lack, in Cumbria, of classes in science subjects, by lack of teachers trained to take such classes, and by what seemed a general lack of interest in the matter. Would it be possible to tackle both these drawbacks together? I had at that time a predilection for trying to do two things at once. Experience has shown this to be a short cut only to disaster, but *then* in roseate youth, a science class for tutors seemed a happy thought. We had no idea of converting arts graduates into scientists through a ten-week course; but hoped that tutors might stir the interest of students in the natural sciences if their own curiosity were aroused.

But if we *had* such a class, who could be the lecturer?

Would our tutors be willing, even flattered, to be taught by a Ford lecturer? Especially when they had just heard him speak with such success?

Mr Highton thought they might. Soundings were taken: most were mildly warm, a few were enthusiastic: Mr MacDonald was invited, and agreed. It was roses all the way. In a matter of weeks, T L MacDonald sent his title and syllabus, and I felt my first qualms:

'Scientific Method: with an outline of the history of science and the development of the scientific outlook; some discussion of how science works and its application and relationship to other subjects; with a sketch of the present position of important branches of science today.'

It all sounded strangely like 'The World and Its Workings in Ten Easy Lessons'. But who was I to argue? Besides, the bureaucratic work was almost complete, firm promises of attendance had been given, and when, where and how had been arranged. A hundred other matters claimed attention, and I left this tutors' class to be picked up at New Year.

How I would love to say the course was the triumph of the season. Alas, it was not so. In the County Hotel, at Carlisle station, we met at 2.30 for ten Sundays, starting the first bleak Sunday of the year. To my perturbation (for as instigator, I felt myself to blame,) I knew from the first meeting that the class would never flourish.

Why did it fail? The place was wrong. Windows looked out on a drab, dusty, station forecourt, with no relief from gloom — no flowers, no grass, only rubbish blowing in the January wind. The time was wrong. The men missed their snooze, smoke, and Sunday papers. For me, Sunday afternoons had been, from childhood, looked forward to, denoting freedom from household chores, school work, or other peoples' demands. We had all *agreed* to sacrifice our Sundays, there being no other way to meet, yet, in practice perhaps we resented it?

All this being admitted, the uncongeniality of time and place were really incidental scapegoats for something deeper. Our lecturer, in eagerness to give his best, treated us weekly to ninety or one hundred minutes of close-packed discourse on scientific matters as if we were an audience of learned dons. Theoretically, everyone attending that class *wanted* to learn: but we were all students of the humanities. It was too much, too late, too abstract, and too remote from anything we had ever done before. The more we struggled to hide our yawns of incomprehension and exhaustion, the more he strove to give a complete history of the known universe. With true Scots' fairness, he wanted to give value for our fees.

Could we not have told him simply that we needed to be *taught,* not lectured at? But that would have been a criticism of his whole technique. There was he, clearly striving to give the most impressive course of lectures on scientific principles ever delivered north of Watford; and there were we, trying to glean a mite here, a mite there amid the alien corn. We could not meet.

We continued to the end of term but it was through iron determination and respect for our lecturer rather than involvement or delight. We learnt — at least negatively — that teachers must listen themselves as well as spout, and that if pupils don't discuss, they seldom learn. It was a brave try, but an object lesson in how to take the horse to water without enabling it to drink.

Twenty five years later, what I had had in mind for that tutors' class was done with superb success by Dr Bronowski in his television series *The Ascent of Man*. Bronowski had for his lectures everything that T L MacDonald lacked: sound, colour, continuous illustration, opportunity to involve his audience through their ears as well as eyes, and so in imagination, through every other sense. Had we, too, been able to *read* Macdonald's lectures afterwards, as later we could read Bronowski's, our undersanding would have been so much enhanced.

So, back to the Carlisle Branch of the Workers' Educational Association, some hundred and thirty souls, a more diverse and individualistic lot altogether than our thirty tutors. With all their idiosyncrasies and varied tones of voice, they often reminded me, (especially when we held socials or Christmas parties,) of the characters in Brueghel's *Battle between Carnival and Lent*— some plump, smiling, buxom as if still nourished with the hearty fare of Carnival, while the more sober — in the main, those who attended history and economics classes — preferring the quiet life of Lent.

Among these contemplative persons was a young, silent, Yorkshire man, a member of our history class for three years. Courteous in attention to other members when they spoke, he himself was heard only when he murmured an occasional dry joke. Quite suddenly it appeared that this dedicated listener intended to marry that other dedicated listener, myself. And if he specialised in practice and I in theory, that might assist domestic harmony.

So, in a summer of phenomenal rain even for the north country, just two days after the Tyne had washed away a bridge that had stood for four hundred years, we were married. We had a perfect day, and were attended by a host of well-wishers from adult education, as well as friends from earlier times. We found a small flat in Carlisle in which to live.

I continued as a tutor, but was glad to give up all the organising side. Co-opted on to Carlisle Education Committee it was enlightening to serve there nearly twenty years, so remaining closely in touch with schools, pupils and teachers, both then and since.

I cannot be sufficiently grateful to have had the chance to stay at home and watch our children grow. No amount of enlightened teacher training can fully take the place of daily care of babies and young children, and observation of how they learn for themselves, and among themselves. Not that it should become obligatory for all intending teachers to work some time in a creche — that might at times invite infanticide. I am saying only that, for some, experience of parenthood makes it one hundred per cent easier and more rewarding to be a teacher, and to be understanding and constant as a friend of the young.

Until our children were at, or near, secondary school age, I did only adult classes, at night. Annan, and Langholm, both over the Border, were regular haunts for years, as from each there was a late bus back home to Carlisle. Class members were knowledgeable and endearing in both towns, and our discussions there sent me home each week wishing we could have a 'follow-up' session at least three or four times a year. The long rackety bus journeys home, cold, draughty and often in snow or rain, induced a kind of brooding, akin to mournful Scottish pipe-music.

One night our study had been about nineteenth century industrial development, and we were taking special note of the novelists and other writers in whose work social changes are so vividly and horrifyingly revealed. Comments made by Charles Darwin in his autobiography also struck me many times. After the death of his mother, when he was eight, Charles was taught by Caroline, one of his sisters, then herself only sixteen. It had not been a success. Perhaps Caroline, herself so young, had 'been very zealous' for her father's good name, and upbraided her young pupil too much? Years later Charles wrote

> **After this long interval of years I remember saying to myself when about to enter a room where she was 'What will she blame me for now?' and I made myself dogged, so as not to care what she might say.**

'Made myself dogged.' Is there a teacher anywhere who has not met this in boy or girl — and felt her own incompetence?

But, much later in his autobiography, there was a page which gave me hope — encouragement even, for some things I have tried to do with every class whether with children or adults. Finding that he no longer read any poetry, Darwin admitted that something had withered in him.

> **My mind seems to have become a kind of machine for grinding general laws out of collections of facts...If I had to live my life again, I would have made a rule to read some poetry and listen to some music at least once every week...The loss of these tastes is a loss of happiness...**

There were sayings of William Blake's, too, that I mulled over on those dark homeward journeys, in particular

> **The tigers of wrath are wiser than the horses of instruction.** *

Why horses? I associated horses with 'plodding on', a trait I personally much admire. What of all those horses in fairy tales — especially Grimm's? They seemed most often to fill a guarding function and usually showed themselves wise? No adequate explanation offered itself to me then. Now, I wonder if Macdonald, giving his fantastically comprehensive'lectures' was a 'horse of instruction'?

Throughout these years my newcomer's share of work for a local education authority gave enormous pleasure. Plans for much needed new schools in Carlisle were resurrected and in 1958 a number of new schools were opened in this one small northern city. By the mid-Sixties many of the things I had longed to see in Walker in the Thirties were coming to pass: good science teaching, with laboratory experience for every pupil; preparation, through technical knowledge for the changing world of our time; school visits to new industries. The town was proud of its schools, its pupils and its teachers.

These new schools, bright, happy, busy places, provided the needed spur for revival in all our local schools. I knew many of the teachers well, and we hoped that pupils, with such fine opportunities would grow up sensitive to beauty, thoughtful to their neighbours, friendly to the whole world. And I am sure many of them did. We felt that we really were catching up with the 'New Era in Education', written and talked about in other places for upwards of forty years. We had splendid play productions, and a memorable performance of Britten's opera *Noyes Flude* in the Cathedral.

* *Proverbs of Hell*

Over a period of at least fifteen years, Carlisle seemed alive with enthusiasm for education.

But what happened? How or why did all that dedication vanish?

Some time during the Seventies and early Eighties, Cabinet Ministers and those who make headlines, turned sour, becoming fiercely critical of schools, of pupils who can neither write nor spell, and above all, of teachers — for whom no generalised sneers of condemnation seemed too absurd.

Some at least of these depressing times appear to have passed me by in the (temporary) domestic haze that had engulfed us. We had, as a family, accepted a wholly unexpected offer to buy a small plot overlooking the river on a hillside in Armathwaite. There, over the next three years, we built a home and moved to this idyllic valley. It seemed like a return to that dream world of childhood holidays, and for a time, my 'work' seemed largely manual. When at last we moved in, there was still a garden to make, a golden retriever puppy to train and our children to set forth on training for their careers — the girl to be a music teacher, the boy, an astronomer. Since Armathwaite is outside the Carlisle boundary, I resigned from the Education Committee. It was saddening to lose touch with Carlisle schools known well for so many years, but worse, much worse was to find that the 'great war' versus teachers was growing almost daily worse — as if it had become the Educational Minister's way of life. No doubt it was a good idea to renew our old educational planks, but to demolish half the structure at once, replacing it with untried, untested prefabricated tactics invited opprobrium. Before schools could implement one set of rules, the ever-changing Education Ministers had thought up another. Result — as expected — confusion and rage.

The schools I knew so well on Tyneside almost half a century ago were formal and deficient in many ways. But in the best of them there was genuine respect between teachers and pupils, and a belief that what we were doing was worthwhile. How many teachers would subscribe to those words today?

In the consumer and competitive society which has been created, in the divisive drive to restore selection and to create a managerial elite, are we not already sacrificing much of the understanding and feeling of respect for work of every variety which good teachers have always aimed to create?

Would those who died for 'freedom' in our generation be happy about our present stratified society? About the contrasting poverty and affluence of our modern world? What has become of 'Freedom from Want' since that time?

Deploring dictatorship and bureaucracy, as we theoretically do, how are we to help pupils to be anything but cynical and rebellious about the society in which we live? How are teachers, harried and enraged at having to spend ever more time on testing and paperwork, and less on each child, ever to grow to maturity themselves in the climate created by the proud man's contumely?

Northumbria and Tyneside are renowned for their local songs, songs of work, sorrow, struggle and disaster. Many of these songs, especially the sad minor melodies, reflect the underlying insecurity that life has always had in these parts. Many end on a rising phrase, a form which is unusual, for it gives no air of finality, only a sense of wandering on into the future.

Many of these are work songs: *Gan to the kye wi' me ma luv*, *Buy broom buzzems*, *The oak and the ash*, *The collier laddie*, *The wife who sells the barley*, *The bonnie fisher lad*.

What I have written is a little work song too, an attempt to put into words what I have learnt at home and school. It, too, is unfinished.

If my vision of celestial learning was, and is, romantic, I hope that my factual descriptions of schools as I have found them are realistic in detail. Any true description of school should convey, like the Luttrell Psalter of the fourteenth century, the plodding rhythm of the seasons, but should not ignore the humours and grotesques. Teachers and pupils may, to outsiders, look morose, even violent on occasion. Nevertheless, within the classroom, fantasy, affection and exuberance do keep breaking in — and let us hope they always will.